Castle, Coast
and
Cottage

*The National Trust
in Northern Ireland*

CASTLE, COAST AND COTTAGE

The National Trust in Northern Ireland

Second edition

LYN GALLAGHER & DICK ROGERS

THE
BLACKSTAFF
PRESS

...aphs and illustrations courtesy of M. Armstrong, ...*elegraph*, Lord Erne, David McFarland, the National Trust, ...onal Trust Photographic Library, the Northern Ireland Tourist ...rd, the Patterson family, Ron H. Thompson, the Ulster Museum, and the *Ulster Tatler*.

First published in 1986 by
The Blackstaff Press
3 Galway Park, Dundonald, Belfast BT16 0AN, Northern Ireland
in association with the National Trust, Northern Ireland Region
and with the assistance of the Esmé Mitchell Trust

This fully revised and updated edition published in 1992

Typeset by The Brown Fox and Textflow Services Limited

Printed in Northern Ireland by
Nicholson & Bass Limited

British Library Cataloguing in Publication Data
Gallagher, Lyn
Castle, Coast and Cottage: National Trust
in Northern Ireland. – 2Rev.ed
I. Title II. Rogers, Dick
363.69060416

ISBN 0-85640-497-7

for
Kitty Rogers and Victor Kelly

CONTENTS

History of the National Trust in Northern Ireland
by Dick Rogers

FOREWORD

In 1986 the Northern Ireland Region of the National Trust celebrated its fiftieth anniversary with the publication of the first edition of this book on its work within the province. Six years on, that edition is now out of print, and the authors, Lyn Gallagher and Dick Rogers, have taken the opportunity to bring the record up to date.

This new edition's publication is timely, for much has happened during the past six years. We have some splendid new properties, including, for example, the woodlands of the Crom estate in Co. Fermanagh, beautiful in any season and of the greatest ecological interest; Patterson's Spade Mill at Templepatrick in Co. Antrim, the last working mill of its type in Ireland and a worthy complement to the beetling mill at Wellbrook in Co. Tyrone; and Slieve Donard, highest and most majestic of the Mountains of Mourne, loved by generations of hill walkers. These new acquisitions add to the quality and extent of the Trust's land holdings in Northern Ireland, and represent a range of properties of which we can be truly proud.

The story of these properties and their acquisition makes fascinating reading. Our first property, Rough Fort near Limavady, was an archaeological site amounting to one acre in size, donated by the region's first Chairman, Marcus McCausland; we now own more than 22,715 acres, and like the Trust at national level, have become one of the province's major landowners. This is a remarkable achievement, made possible by the dedication and hard work of chairmen such as Lord Antrim, Lord Clanwilliam and Lord O'Neill, and administrators of the calibre and imagination of John Lewis-Crosby and Anthony Lord. Dick Rogers himself played a notable part in this story, as a Committee member of some forty years' standing, and in his professional capacity as a civil servant: during the 1960s he was largely responsible for preparing and implementing Northern Ireland's first conservation legislation, the Amenity Lands Act of 1965, as well as establishing the government's first conservation administrative unit, of which he was head until his retirement in 1973.

The present guardians of this inheritance are largely a new team, appointed since the first publication of this book. Lord O'Neill completed his ten years as Chairman in the autumn of 1991, and earlier in the same year Anthony Lord was succeeded as Regional Director by Ian McQuiston, a former civil servant. By a strange coincidence, though one not uncommon in small communities like Northern Ireland, Ian began his civil service career in the Amenity Lands Branch of the former Ministry of Development, working as a field officer under none other than Dick Rogers.

Like its predecessors, the present Regional Committee and staff face many challenges. We have as fine a portfolio of properties as any of the Trust's regions, but our holdings are unevenly spread throughout the province – for example, we own little land in west Fermanagh, in the Sperrin Mountains, in south Armagh and in the Antrim hills west of Belfast. We do own outstanding properties in the Mournes, around the shores of Upper Lough Erne and its islands, and along the coasts of Antrim and Down; we need to consolidate and extend these holdings, and in some instances, provide better amenities for the public to enjoy them.

The basis for this strategy is simply to ensure the long-term conservation of Northern Ireland's finest landscapes and natural habitats, working alongside statutory agencies and other voluntary bodies. Our countryside is under less pressure and suffers less degradation than many parts of Britain, but we do have particular local problems, the results of unsympathetic and inappropriate housing development, of urban growth, quarrying and road schemes. Physical planning has been notably less effective in dealing with these problems than elsewhere in the United Kingdom, and the situation is not helped by the absence of the statutory protection afforded to outstanding landscapes by National Parks in England and Wales. Agencies such as the Countryside Commission likewise provide major assistance to public bodies and private landowners elsewhere in Britain, providing practical advice and grant aid for landscape protection and enhancement, for countryside recreation and the development of public awareness in the use of the countryside and its conservation. Unhappily its remit does not extend to Northern Ireland and hence the National Trust has a particularly important role to play, with its ability to own land inalienably and to manage it primarily for its conservation interest and value. For these reasons it is inevitable and proper that the Trust should be an active advocate for conservation in the region and pursue an energetic policy for land acquisition, as resources permit.

One other challenge should be mentioned: the continuing difficulties caused by civil unrest and political debate concerning Northern Ireland's future. The Trust's work in Northern Ireland is, of course, affected by these problems, but its conservation aims and values are not just for the present: they are for all time and for all people. The environment concerns us all, and provides a common inheritance which transcends political and sectarian differences.

Ronald Buchanan
Regional Chairman
Strangford, 1992

ACKNOWLEDGEMENTS

The authors gratefully acknowledge the help of the following people and organisations in the preparation of this book:

Ards Historical Society; Nigel Brady; Gordon Brand; Charles A. Brett; Sir Charles E.B. Brett for his sustained encouragement and critical comment; Austin Brown; Dr Bob Brown for his detailed assistance; Ronald Buchanan; Ian Burns; The Lady Mairi Bury; Carrickfergus and District Historical Society; Patrick and Ann Casement; John Cowdy; Walter Culbert; the Department of the Environment; David Dunlop; Jan Eccles; Richard Ellis; Una Farrington; Sandra Finlay for typing much of the text; Diane Forbes; George Forde; John Forth; Brian, Fergus, Laura and Michael Gallagher for their fieldwork; John Gaze; Margaret Gray for help throughout the project; Dr E.M. Griffith; Lord Anthony Hamilton; Sue Hanlon; Diane Harron; Ian Herbert; George Hutchison; Gordon Johnston; Marion Kelly; Mary Kelly; Victor Kelly for his diligence, patience and scholarship; Paul Kendrick; William Leitch, former Chief Parliamentary Draughtsman of the Northern Ireland Government; John Lewis-Crosby; Kathy Lindsay; the Linen Hall Library and its staff; Anthony Lord; Bertie Lyttle; Christine McCawl; Margaret MacCormick; Tom McErlean; Dan McLaughlin; Ian McQuiston; Brian McQuitty; Marian Machell; Peter Marlow; Eric Montgomery; Hubert Mullan; David Paterson-Morgan; the Patterson family; Peg Pollock; the Public Record Office of Northern Ireland and in particular Brian Trainor and Anthony Malcomson; Peter Rankin for his advice and critical comment; Harry Reid, former Secretary of Armagh County Council; Gerald Reside; Kitty and Richard Willis Rogers for their encouragement and critical comment; the Royal Society for the Protection of Birds; George Ryan; George Sheridan; Dorothy Smith; Mike Snowden; Jack Suckling; the Ulster Architectural Heritage Society; the Ulster Trust for Nature Conservation; Don Wadey; Philip Watson; and Jim Wells.

Thanks go to the National Trust for permitting the use of Lord Antrim's papers, given to the Trust by his widow, Angela, Countess of Antrim; and for access to Tom McErlean's unpublished 'Historical Development of the Park at Castle Coole'. The authors are also grateful to the staff of the Trust generally for all their help.

BELFAST
PROPERTIES

■ Collin Glen
▲ Crown Liquor Saloon
■ Minnowburn Beeches
■ Lisnabreeny

Giant's Causeway
White Park Bay
North Antrim Cliff Path
Larrybane
Carrick-a-Rede

Bar Mouth/
Portstewart Strand

Downhill
▲ Hezlett House
■ Rough Fort
Coleraine

Fair Head
Murlough Bay
Cushendun
Layde
■ Torr Head

DONEGAL

LONDONDERRY

• Ballymena

Glenarm
Glenoe ■

ANTRIM

• Strabane
▲ Gray's Printing Press

TYRONE

Springhill
▲

Wellbrook Beetling Mill ▲

• Omagh

Templetown Mausoleum
▲ Ballymacormick Point/
Orlock Point

Patterson's Spade Mill

Lough
Neagh

BELFAST •

Islandmagee

■ Lighthouse Island

Killynether

▲ Mount Stewart

■ Coney Island

The Argory ▲

■ Strangford Lough
Wildlife Scheme

Lower Lough Erne

▲ Ardress House

Rowallane ▲

■ Kearney and
Knockinelder

▲ Castle Ward

FERMANAGH

Enniskillen • ▲ Castle Coole

Clough Castle ▲

DOWN

Downpatrick

Florence Court ▲

Upper Lough Erne

ARMAGH

• Armagh

■ Murlough National Nature Reserve/
Dundrum Coastal Path

■ Tonregee Island
■ Crom

Derrymore House
Ballymoyer

Slieve Donard
• Newcastle
■ Mourne Coastal Path

THE REPUBLIC OF IRELAND

■ Blockhouse Island and Green Island

IRISH SEA

▲ Buildings and gardens
■ Coast and country

MAP OF NATIONAL TRUST PROPERTIES IN NORTHERN IRELAND

GAZETTEER

of

National Trust properties

in

Northern Ireland

The map references in this gazetteer which are shown in square brackets [ ], enable the property to be located on maps bearing the National Grid. The National Grid is shown on Ordnance Survey maps of every scale. The system is applied to different kinds of National Trust property as follows: for buildings, the map reference gives the position of the building itself, or (if it stands in large grounds) of the entrance; for open spaces, the map reference indicates approximately the centre of the property or the summit of a hill.

   To find out if properties are open, use the current local touring guide, available from the regional office at Rowallane, Saintfield, Co. Down, and all properties. Most properties are signposted and can be identified by signs carrying the oakleaf emblem of the National Trust.

ARDRESS HOUSE

On the Portadown–Moy road (B28), 7 miles from Portadown [H914559]

It is exactly right that the first impression of Ardress is through rows of old-fashioned, mature apple trees, as the house is set in the middle of Armagh, the orchard county of Ulster. Appropriate, too, because this is no grand stately home, but a gentleman farmer's house, which combines one of the most elegant drawing-rooms in Ireland with simple and modest comfort.

Once past the orchard, the approach crosses the old county road through an elegant but unpretentious gateway, and after a short curve under limes planted two centuries ago, there is the first sight of Ardress. It has a graceful, pink-washed front; a simple doorway has columns made from local limestone; and there are three urns at roof level. The impression is of a balanced sweep of windows in the fine proportion and just taste of the second half of the eighteenth century, but a closer look at the façade reveals more of the story of Ardress.

The two gables which can be seen are those of the simple seventeenth-century building, a typical 1660 farmhouse, of the double-pile construction which has twin rows of rooms; the fine array of orderly windows contains no fewer than five fakes, mere glass backed by plastered walls painted matt black. The story of the architecture of Ardress, in common with that of many country houses, lies in a marriage, in this case that of George Ensor, a Dublin architect, to Sarah Clarke, in 1760. A house belonging to the Clarke family stood here early in the seventeenth century, but was destroyed around 1641–2, and the 1660s' house was built in a style more common in England than in Ireland, with roof timbers designed for slates, tiles or shingles, not for thatch. We know little of the Clarkes apart from their early possession of Ardress soon after the plantation of Ulster, and their connections with many well known local families. The Ensors originally came from Warwickshire and had associations with Ireland as early as 1612. The George Ensor to whom Ardress owes its refinement came to Dublin with his brother John about 1730. Both were architects, and while John found a place with Richard Castle, the leading architect of the day, George Ensor became clerk of works to the Surveyor-General and worked from Dublin Castle.

Sarah and George did not come to live at Ardress, from the relative sophistication of late-eighteenth-century Dublin, until 1770, ten years after their marriage, but when they did so, they brought some of the capital's style and taste with them. The jigsaw of Ardress's architecture is a fascinating riddle for historians who debate the order and reason of the modifications, but the resulting house, which stitches together the old and the new in a rather haphazard fashion, has one superb feature – a drawing-room which glories in the plasterwork of one of Ireland's most celebrated stuccodores, Michael

The farmyard at Ardress

1

Stapleton. Geometric patterns, garlands, festoons, circular and oval plaques and classical figures abound, in decoration which, while very close to that of Robert Adam, has a more relaxed, natural feel, harking back to the free rococo work in which Irish stuccodores delighted earlier in the century. Today the room is painted in subtle Georgian shades, in faithful and meticulous work which was part of the National Trust restoration in the 1960s. However, Roger Weatherup, curator of Armagh Museum and a friend of the Ensors, remembers with some affection and regret 'the old plain ceiling (much off-white) and the apple green walls'. Two Ensors coming to see the house as National Trust visitors recently and recalling boyhood holidays spent at Ardress, while claiming familiarity with the woods and gardens, felt strange in the drawing-room, because the only time they had been there was on Christmas Day.

After the elegance of the drawing-room the rest of the house is homely by comparison, with rooms which are pleasant and well proportioned, rather than splendid. The front door, with its handsome lock, opens into a welcoming hall with a wide archway to the right leading to a former dining-room. The deep cream walls and plain, polished pine floor blend with simple furniture native to the house or to Co. Armagh. The modest parlour to the left has simple decoration, with a hand-blocked wallpaper based on an eighteenth-century chintz design, and a plain Italian marble fireplace. The airy bedroom has a charming country feel, with honey-coloured paper and matching hangings.

Curiosity is roused again when, after touring hall, parlour, drawing-room and bedroom, the guide begins an elaborate business with keys and then proceeds to escort visitors out of the back door and into the open air, through the inner yard to enter the dining-room. The hapless eighteenth-century dinner guests seemingly went from drawing-room to dining-room by a conservatory, and because of an extraordinarily casual architectural arrangement, were forced to brave the Armagh draughts after their preprandial sherry and again after their port. George Ensor has always been blamed for this awkward eccentricity, but more recent architectural examination has tended to suggest that it was his son who at a later date added the dining-room with library above. It seems he simply tacked the addition on, with extensions of façades and urns, and because of a natural wish to avoid intruding into the plasterwork of the drawing-room, he found no better way of linking the two parts of the house.

This theory at least makes sense in connecting George Ensor junior with the library, for as a prolific writer he was the best known of the Ensor family. He was educated at the Royal School, Armagh, and at Trinity College, Dublin, and was called to the Irish Bar in 1792. On his father's death he came back to Ardress to manage the estate and produced a series of titles which are almost guaranteed not to be read now, but which reveal his advanced views on religion and politics – *Radical Reform, the restoration of Usurped Rights, A Defense of the Irish and the Means of their Redemption, The Principles of Morality* and *Of Property and of its equal Distribution*. The one exception is *An Inquiry concerning the Population of Nations*, a refutation of Malthusian population theory which was reprinted in 1967 in an economic history series.

The façade, Ardress

Ardress boasts some of the finest furniture of any of the National Trust houses in Northern Ireland; these have often acquired a characteristic accumulation of furniture over several centuries, but at Ardress the furniture is of a high quality thanks to a series of generous loans in recent years. The four commodes in the drawing and dining-rooms are fascinating studies of that form, the two gilt settees and torchères, or lamp-holders, are excellent examples of neo-classical furniture. In the parlour there are pieces of great charm – the bureau bookcase is of fine provincial workmanship, while the William-and-Mary chest-on-stand is delightful. That distinctive form of furniture the Irish side table is represented in the dining-room. The pictures in the house are the result of another generous loan; of particular interest are landscapes by Theobald Michau and Paul Bril, an assembly of animals and birds by Pieter Boal and a portrait of a man with a spear by Bartolomme Passerotti.

Outside, the farmyard at Ardress is a place of unique atmosphere. In most big houses the farm offices are at a discreet distance or elaborately screened to keep the offending noises and smells from disturbing the grander occupants of the house. At Ardress the farmyard is right up beside the house and the farm buildings are in a very complete state of repair. The yard has the feel of a working farmyard: bantams, turkeys and silky hens pick their way over moss and cobbles; a saddleback sow, perhaps even with piglets, grunts in a sty; and carts stand ready under shelter. Craigavon Historical Society has helped to gather together a representative collection of implements likely to have been used at a Co. Armagh farm before the advent of the tractor revolutionised

3

The drawing-room, Ardress

agricultural life. Threshing barns, dairy, forge, milking parlour, and cart-house are filled with equipment which has been rescued, restored and set in place. Ploughs, harrows, grubbers, scarifiers, drills and distributors, stand ready, some brightly painted, others looking more workmanlike.

Ardress has a pleasant garden with a splendid, deep, old-fashioned herbaceous border and a little formal rose garden, recently created and filled with delicate shrub roses. The old woods come right up to the house, and beside the carpark they now accommodate a good adventure playground and a picnic site. 'The Ladies' Mile', which records show to have been laid out some 150 years ago, leads the walker in an arc to the east of the house, through old oak, beech, pine and chestnut with some elm, ash, wild cherry and plenty of sycamore. Traces of badgers can be seen, and grey squirrels are common, although the red squirrels have all but disappeared.

Lyn Gallagher

The Argory, west front

THE ARGORY

4 miles from Moy on the Derrycaw Road [H872580]

'The hill of the garden' is the evocative translation of the name 'The Argory', said to have been derived from the Irish *ard garraidhe*. The Argory has a fine setting on a slight rise overlooking a pleasant winding stretch of the Blackwater river, among rich meadowlands, woods and orchards. Indeed, the 'garden' may have been an orchard, because a plantation of fruit trees did stand at that place before Walter McGeough decided to build a house there in the early 1820s. When he moved into his new home in 1824 he assumed the additional surname of Bond as a mark of respect to his paternal grandmother, whose name it had been.

It was an extremely curious will which influenced his decision. The family lived originally in Drumsill House, just outside Armagh, now rebuilt as a hotel. Walter was the second son of Joshua McGeough, who, when he died in 1817, left his eldest son, William, only £400, while Drumsill House and the bulk of his fortune went to Walter and his three daughters. He also stipulated that Walter might not live there after his marriage as long as two of his sisters remained unmarried. Isabella died within the year, but Walter's assessment of his remaining sisters' matrimonial prospects did not encourage him to bide his time waiting for wedding bells, and so he decided to make the move. In fact the two women never did marry and they became known as eccentric spinsters. A Mr Maxwell, a house painter from Armagh, speaking at the beginning of this century, recalled the final outcome of the sisters' joint occupation of Drumsill House, and 'minded the day when the two halves of [the front] door were painted different colours', a demarcation of taste and ownership which was carried into the house with a broad line painted up the middle of the main staircase.

The architects Walter McGeough chose were the Williamson brothers who were relatively obscure and probably came on the recommendation of Armagh-born Francis Johnston, a distant relation of the family: as one of the leading architects in Ireland, he had worked on Drumsill. The Argory originally consisted of a single rectangular block in Caledon stone, with Navan limestone sills, quoins and foundations. The subsequent architectural evolution of the house was complicated by the addition of the octagonal block, a porch and corridors, and by the effects of a fire in 1898.

The main entrance is in the front or west portico facing the river. It has been described as 'charmingly naive' and is dominated by a rather amiable lion from whose mouth an acanthus sprouts. Inside the house the entrance hall gleams. The elegant brass banisters of the fine cantilevered staircase reflect the shining black and white tiled floor and the dominant 'marbled' walls repainted in the 1980s using traditional methods. There are two outstanding burnished bronze dogs, a mastiff and a greyhound crafted in 1832 by Charles Fratin, a renowned *animalier* sculptor. A huge cast-iron stove sits squarely in the centre. It was designed in the 1820s to heat the whole house, but a smaller, more efficient stove was added later. A recent attempt to light the latter resulted in inches of dust, so the attempt was not repeated.

Above the cast-iron stove hangs an early-nineteenth-century Colza oil lamp which has been modified for gas, an indication of one of the most attractive features of the Argory. The house was given to the National Trust in 1979 by Nevill MacGeough Bond, the great-grandson of the builder. Since the Second World War it had remained cared for and well maintained but largely unoccupied, with the result that it was given few modern conveniences, and electricity was never installed. In fact, the house still boasts its own working acetylene gas plant, housed in the stableyard, and installed by the Sunbeam

Part of the central corridor in the Argory

6

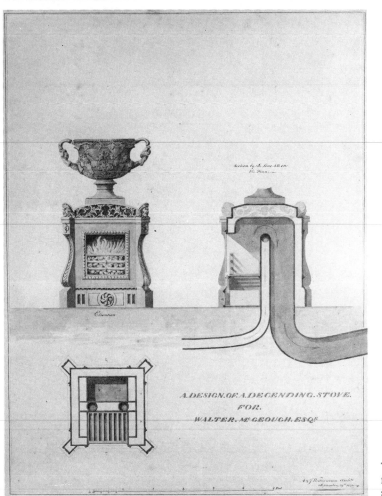

The Williamsons' design
for the original 'decending'
stove at the Argory

Acetylene Gas Company of Belfast in 1906 at an all-in cost of £250. All the
light fittings in the house are charming gas installations in a variety of styles.

Up the sweep of the staircase, the marbled walls enhance an imposing
display of gilt-framed early-nineteenth-century engravings and lead into the
organ gallery, with the most celebrated feature of the house, an early pianola
barrel organ. At about the same time as the house was built, Walter McGeough
commissioned from James Bishop of London a cabinet barrel organ, perhaps
the most important of its kind in existence and now in perfect working order.
This instrument has the appearance of a handsome manual organ with pipes,
but a small room behind the pipes houses the barrel mechanism, and three
barrels hold a rich variety of music chosen on the advice of Samuel Wesley,
nephew of John Wesley, the founder of Methodism. Samuel himself was a
hymn writer of repute, and his composition 'See the conquering hero comes'
is one of the tunes which resounds through the house with great gusto when
the barrels have been set in motion.

Equally distinctive is the billiard room, a splendidly adorned traditional
male retreat. The table itself is an early-nineteenth-century example by
Burroughs and Watts, with a fine set of accessories including cues, scoreboard,
level and rests. An impression of masculine comfort is created by the look of

warm wood, but in fact, as with the 'marbling' of the hall and stairs, the wood effect of the dado and shutters is created by the technique of painted graining, once so valued throughout Ulster, and here the *trompe-l'oeil* achieved is entirely satisfactory. The massive oak bookcase is real enough, with its heavy, intricate carving. It came from Church Hill, a neighbouring house formerly the home of the Verner family. Around the walls of the billiard room, as a foil to its masculinity, are six charming pastels of children of the family, which were commissioned in Paris from Hugues Fourau in the 1840s and 1850s.

Of all the rooms, it is the drawing-room which best evokes the full flavour of a nineteenth-century Irish country house, looking comfortable with rich curtains and upholstery, a generous supply of cushions and fur-draped chairs. It has an abundance of furniture, *objets* and pictures but avoids looking oppressively cluttered. Two large mirrors reflect the natural light afforded by four windows, and the room looks bright and inviting. A workbox stands ready for use, a book has been taken from the revolving bookcase, the 1898 Steinway rosewood grand piano is open and the nice touch of a humble wastepaper basket completes the sense of a room used and lived in. While the overall effect is of pleasing harmony, there are a few items which especially attract attention. Lady Bond's late-seventeenth-century Spanish chest (a *vargueño*) is striking, as are the *pietra dura* tables. One table displays a series of rare butterflies while the other shows the Bond family coat of arms which is repeated over the door in the later-nineteenth-century architrave and includes the family motto, *Nemo me impune lacessit* – 'No one provokes me with impunity'.

The dining-room is full of atmosphere: the table is set with the family silver and china as if awaiting guests for tea, the family's traditional time for entertaining. There are sets of amusing side tables and round tables – which, with the aid of a system of pulleys, transform themselves into dumbwaiters – and some of the necessary conveniences of country-house living: handsome brass-bound plate buckets, a tea caddy and a warming cabinet.

The bedrooms are full of family associations. The donor's grandmother, Mary Nichols, left her mark in a series of pretty watercolours hung throughout the bedrooms, while his mother, Lady Bond, and her love of inlaid continental furniture, are recalled in examples which are especially good in the bedroom named after her. The 'cedar room' offers an intriguing glimpse of Lady Bond's 1920s' Parisian *couture* – the finest of draped silk and satin, and tiny little shoes, slippers and boots handmade in exquisite leathers. Another bedroom is named after Captain Ralph Shelton, who chose to use his second Christian name as a surname in 1873. He is chiefly remembered for his fortunate survival of the sinking of the *Birkenhead*, an escape attributed in Burke's *Landed Gentry of Ireland* to his good sense in keeping his trousers on . . . 'the sharks having first attacked those without protection'.

The family's love of travel, of music and of art, in evidence everywhere in the Argory, survives into the 1980s through the interest of Nevill MacGeough Bond who gave the house to the National Trust. His study is still very much in use, furnished with his books and papers, and his additions of twentieth-century paintings and sculpture blend happily with the furnishings of 150 years ago.

There are no massive formal gardens at the Argory; a little rose garden was laid out in the 1830s and equipped with a sundial bearing the exhortation: 'Here Reader Mark the Silent Steps of Never Ending Time'. The Pleasure Grounds to the north of the house must have been a pleasant place of resort, enclosed on three sides by hornbeams, oaks and rhododendrons, open on the fourth to the river, shaded by cedars and tulip trees, flanked by pretty pavilions and centring on yew arbours.

For many people the best time to visit the Argory is late winter when a carpet of snowdrops is spread out under the splendid Lime Avenue beside the river.

Lyn Gallagher

BALLYMACORMICK POINT

1–3 miles NE of Bangor (A2) [J525837]

Ballymacormick Point lies to the west and Orlock Point to the south east of the little village of Groomsport, Co. Down. These points are not the manicured marine walks now common around Belfast Lough, but rocky outcrops covered in gorse, good for rough walking and for spotting birds, flowers and foxes. Because they are in a relatively natural state and close to large centres of population, they are vulnerable areas in need of constant care.

The best approach to Ballymacormick Point is by Groomsport, although at low tide it is possible to reach it from the east end of Ballyholme beach. Groomsport is still a pretty harbour, full of boats, with a pier said to date from the Vikings and two low, whitewashed cottages, one of them thatched, the remnants of a cluster of fishermen's dwellings, known as Cockle Row, which once stood around the bay. Orlock Point which can be reached from the Groomsport–Donaghadee road, has remnants of an ancient road cut through up-tilted ridges of rock.

A little way out to sea from Groomsport is the protective shoal of Cockle Island, one of the smallest individual National Trust properties anywhere, half an acre of rock and grass, but a valuable area for birds, favoured by a small colony of arctic and common terns as well as several pairs of ringed plover and some black-headed gulls.

Ballymacormick is just on the edge of Belfast Lough, so there are interesting views north and west. It is impossible to avoid seeing the dominant profile of Kilroot power station, but sharp eyes on a clear day can identify other landmarks on the Co. Antrim escarpment of strong black basalt –Carrickfergus, the Knockagh monument, and the coast curving towards Whitehead. There is nearly always a ship using the busy channel to Belfast. Out to sea, the coast of Galloway can be seen surprisingly sharply on a clear day.

There is something for birdwatchers at all times of the year. The combination of rough grass, gorse and rocks forms an inviting breeding ground for oystercatchers, skylarks, meadow and rock pipits, stonechats, reed buntings, willow warblers and linnets. In winter waders such as dunlin, redshank, curlew, purple sandpiper and ringed plover can be seen on the shore or among the rocks, while out to sea there is a likelihood of seeing redbreasted merganser, eider and shelduck, and almost a certainty of spotting cormorant and shag. Summer brings the sandwich terns – to join the nearby breeding arctic and common terns – with their eyecatching flights, loops and dives in search of fish.

The promontory of Ballymacormick has claimed its share of wrecks. On the night of the 'Big Wind' on 22 December 1894 the three-masted schooner *Doctor* went ashore and is said to have been reduced to matchwood in five minutes, with the loss of most of her crew. Four other vessels foundered on that shoreline on the same night. At that time the lifeboat was based at Groomsport and horses had to pull the boat to Bangor: on at least one occasion a team of horses from Ballymacormick Farm was called into service to carry rocket apparatus to fire a lifeline to be attached to the rigging.

Lyn Gallagher

Arctic tern

BALLYMOYER

4 miles NE of Newtownhamilton (A29) [H969305]

Ballymoyer is a pleasant, remote, wooded glen in south Armagh, eight miles from Newry and four miles from Newtownhamilton. The glen is leased to the Forest Service of the Department of Agriculture, which has planted hardwoods to blend with the long-established oaks and beeches and the more recent larch and spruce; some very fine Douglas firs dominate the skyline. A cobbled salmon weir spans a stream, one of three which meet on what used to be the lawn of Ballymoyer House. Beside the stream is an early sweathouse, the forerunner of the modern sauna.

Ballymoyer was given to the National Trust in 1937 by the Hart-Synnot family. Nineteenth-century guides and gazetteers enthuse about a locality where the roads were good, improvements had altered the face of the country and 'neither poverty nor riches have been allotted to the people of this parish, a few are in a comparative state of opulence, a large proportion possess all the comforts of life, and none are without its necessaries'. The curate of the parish who wrote about these satisfactory circumstances in 1816, Revd Joseph Ferguson, also remarked that 'some remnants of Pagan superstitions still exist, as also the belief in fairies, and in lucky and unlucky days'. Ballymoyer has all the atmosphere of a fairy glen, with deep, mossy, ferned banks, clothed in spring with primroses, celandines and bluebells. It is surrounded by the wild and dramatic scenery of the Fews mountains, once the haunt of robbers and highwaymen, remembered perhaps in the local name 'Deadman's Hill'.

The area has associations with the MacMoyre family, who for generations held the magnificent ninth-century illuminated manuscript Book of Armagh in their hereditary custody. In 1680 Florence MacMoyre pledged the book for £5 to enable him to go to England where he gave evidence against Archbishop Oliver Plunkett, who was put to death in 1681; the pledge for the book was never redeemed. The grave of MacMoyre is marked in the local ruined churchyard.

Lyn Gallagher

13

BAR MOUTH

2 miles, by road, E of Castlerock [C792355]

The river Bann is wide and slow as it winds around its last broad curve into the sea between Castlerock and Portstewart. Viewed from the higher ground to the south, this is a landscape of blue and green, a wide flat expanse, threaded by the river, and skirted by buff-edged dunes.

The National Trust land at Bar Mouth and Grangemore dunes lies on the west bank of the river, where saltmarsh, freshwater marsh and ancient dunes form a combination of habitats unique in Northern Ireland.

The archaeological importance of Bar Mouth is well known, dating from Ireland's earliest settlements of around 7000 BC. This is a fragile site of botanical and ornithological importance. Much of the land has been undisturbed by ploughing or reseeding, and the importance of Bar Mouth for birds means that disturbance should be kept to a minimum. Access to this sensitive area is therefore restricted.

Bar Mouth is a stopping place for migratory birds, so there is the opportunity for seeing a great variety of species, as well as the chance of spotting one of the rarities which have been sighted here. Winter brings geese and swans passing through, as well as teal, wigeon and goldeneye. The estuary is famous for sanderling, and up to 1,000 golden plover cross its waters. The north wind sometimes brings in gannets from the mouth of the river, as well as skuas, gulls and the occasional American visitor.

Cormorants are sometimes joined by shags and grey heron come in to feed. Mute swans, moorhen and coot are nearly always to be seen, while birds nesting on the property, or nearby, include shelduck, mallard, eider, red-breasted merganser and redshank. This is naturally a favourite spot for ornithologists, and a hide, which was converted to be accessible to wheelchairs, has been well used.

The wooden pier once carried a tramway and played its part in the navigation and transport controversies which surrounded this part of the river and concerned the people of Coleraine for centuries. Small ships can still travel up the river to Coleraine through the cantilevered railway bridge which allows them to pass, but the sandbar and ford always constituted a dangerous deterrent to navigation, making Derry and Portrush the preferred ports. As early as 1622 there were arguments that something should be done about the sandbank, but no action was taken, partly because the Irish Society jealously guarded the fisheries in what Spenser had called 'the fishy, fruitfull Bann'. Shipwrecks, privateers and treacherous pilots are steadily recorded throughout the eighteenth and nineteenth centuries. Eventually, in the 1860s, the town commissioners seriously addressed the problem, employing John Coode who began the work of dredging and scouring the entrance, and constructed training walls at the river mouth. The nineteenth-century work was prolonged and provided many opportunities for tours of inspection on the river by the notables of the town and the Irish Society, followed by lavish tented banquets and wines of rare vintage.

On one occasion the contractor, faced with bankruptcy and the confiscation of his equipment, took the steamer to sea in a dreadful storm, with dredger, tug and barges in tow, eventually bringing the dredger at least safely to Derry. The first scheme was finished in 1883, and a second scheme undertaken in the 1930s. The remnants of pier and tramline which carried material for the construction are all that can be seen now, but a dredger, the *Bar Maid*, still works continually at the mouth of the river.

Lyn Gallagher

Merganser

BLOCKHOUSE ISLAND AND GREEN ISLAND

Off Cranfield at the mouth of Carlingford Lough [J254097]

Blockhouse Island and Green Island lie in the generously wide bay at the mouth of Carlingford Lough, where, in the words of one Victorian travel writer, 'the whole navy of Britain might ride in perfect safety'. To the north are Greencastle and Cranfield Bay which is said to be washed with the warmest sea water in Ulster, with the magnificent jagged profile of the Mourne Mountains. To the south is Greenore and the fine, if less imposing, range of the Carlingford mountains. The twin islands are flanked by lighthouses at Hawlbowline and Greenore.

Designated an Area of Special Scientific Interest, the islands are of great importance for birdlife and their carboniferous rocks are rich in fossils. Leased to the Royal Society for the Protection of Birds, they are a vital breeding ground for terns – common, arctic, roseate and sandwich. There are problems with erosion on both islands and from time to time the nests are flooded. To add to the terns' difficulties, they share their crowded, precarious breeding sites with common seals. Although visitors may not land on these fragile and vulnerable islands, great views of the terns can be had from the shore.

Blockhouse Island, once called Nun's Island and also Inniscarry, takes its best known name from a strategically placed fort which defended the mouth of the lough in Napoleonic times. A romantic story of Blockhouse has come down to us from the eighteenth century. It centres around a successful and gallant privateer, Commodore Thurot O'Farrell, of French and Irish descent, who was the scourge of British ships on the Irish Sea, the North Sea and the English Channel. In 1750 he captured a packet ship and found he had also seized the wife and niece of the governor of the Blockhouse. With great chivalry he allowed the ladies to go on their way, but before he released the packet he had discovered that a well armed and equipped supply ship was due to arrive; he also learned that the Blockhouse held a buried treasure. As the dramatic story unfolds, O'Farrell was captured when stealing into the fort at night, but was helped to escape by the beautiful niece. In true swashbuckling style he attacked and captured the supply ship and daringly brought it into the teeth of the garrison. The governor tried to make his escape with the treasure but was drowned, his wife was shot and O'Farrell gained girl and gold. They settled down to live happily ever after in Carlingford, but the 'Maid of the Blockhouse' died within a year, and the commodore left to ply his trade again. The story goes that his reputation as a man of humanity, gallantry and bravery remained a legend among the British seamen who were his prey.

Lyn Gallagher

CASTLE COOLE

SE of Enniskillen (A4) [H260430]

In the plantation of Ulster Captain Roger Atkinson, an Englishman who had come to Ireland in the late sixteenth century, was granted in Co. Fermanagh an estate of 1,000 plantation acres, called Coole, where he built 'a strong bawne of stone and lyme' and inside it a defensible castle similar to many other plantation castles of west Ulster. This castle was destroyed by fire in the 1641 rebellion.

In 1656 John Corry, a prosperous merchant and freeman of Belfast who had come from Dumfriesshire, bought the estate, repaired the house and again made it defensible. He died in 1683 and at that time the renovated house, then occupied by his son James, was described as 'one of the best in the country'. In the Williamite Wars of 1689, however, it was totally destroyed. James Corry appears to have been absent from Castle Coole at the time but had left it defended with a force of about sixty horsemen and a hundred foot soldiers. In his absence the men of Enniskillen – fearing that the castle might fall into Jacobite hands, and anxious to increase the defence of their town – withdrew the garrison and burned the castle.

Curld's drawing for the 1709 house

In 1709 James (now Colonel) Corry erected about the site of the two previous buildings a new house which was quite unlike anything that had gone before. Shown here is a drawing for this house, by John Curld. It seems a surprising house to appear on the site of two burned-out fortified castles. With its heavy pediment, deep eaves, dormer windows and high chimney stacks, and featuring a doorway with segmented pediment, approached by a flight of curving steps, it is suggestive of a lost Osbert Lancaster cartoon of Queen Anne's England. But then, all over Ireland Queen Anne houses were being built in the first period of peace and stability the country had known for centuries.

Almost ninety years later, in 1797, this Queen Anne house was burned to the ground when a pan of ashes was accidentally left on the wooden staircase. Presumably the old family pictures and furniture were destroyed, as they are absent from Castle Coole today.

James Corry's great-grandson, Armar Lowry-Corry, was created Baron in 1781, Viscount in 1789 and Earl of Belmore in 1797. In October 1789, at his request, Richard Johnston, a brother of the more famous architect Francis Johnston, submitted signed plans and work was commenced on the foundations of the present house. But Lord Belmore then decided that the architect should be James Wyatt and he instructed him to build on Johnston's foundations. Wyatt's designs, dated from May 1790 to 1793, many of which can be seen in the house, were those used for this, his austere neo-classical masterpiece.

Unlike most Irish houses, Castle Coole has preserved a complete set of the building accounts, showing that when the joiners had finished structural work they turned their attention to furniture which is still in the rooms for which

17

it was made. Wyatt's designs for the ceilings and even for the curtains were closely followed. Castle Coole was described by the French *émigré* the Chevalier de Latocnaye, when he was shown round by Lord Belmore in 1796, as a 'superb palace', though he considered it too magnificent for the residence of a private individual.

The house is 280 feet long, including the wings and colonnades, and is probably the finest example of a neo-classical country house in Ireland. It took ten years to build. The Portland stone with which the house is faced was brought by a brig, especially chartered for the purpose, from Portland to Ballyshannon on Donegal Bay, where a quay was built for its reception. The great blocks were then carted by oxen to Belleek on Lough Erne, about ten miles distant; from there they were shipped to Enniskillen, more bullock carts being employed to cover the two miles to the site.

The stucco workers were brought over from the London workshop of Joseph Rose, who had worked with Robert Adam; the marble chimneypieces of the great reception rooms were made by Richard Westmacott in London; while the scagliola pillars in the hall and saloon and the pilasters on the staircase were executed from Wyatt's designs by the Italian Dominic Bartoli. In June 1791, when the building and decorating was at its height and window frames, doors, floors, and much of the furniture were being made on the spot, twenty-five stone-cutters, twenty-six stone-masons, ten stone-sawyers, seventeen carpenters and eighty-three labourers were being employed.

The house, with Ionic portico and hipped roof of cool grey-green slates, appears at first to be of two storeys only, but a balustraded roof conceals the second-floor attics. Beautifully placed windows, with narrow glazing bars and no architraves, look out south east across the lawn to the woods. The central block is flanked upon either side by pillared colonnades terminating in pavilions. In the middle of the north-west side of the house a great central bow, with fluted Ionic pillars, is a dominant feature; the terminal pavilions on this side have graceful Venetian windows.

The entrance hall is austere with an expanse of Portland stone flags, plain walls and ceilings, a screen of porphyry-coloured scagliola columns, and mahogany doors. It is relieved by a delicate Doric frieze, repeated in Westmacott's chimneypieces. As in the rest of the house, the quality of the plasterwork, chimneypieces and joinery is exceptional. The hall is almost as it was in 1800. However, there is a significant change in the colour of the walls. Wyatt appears to have left the room an off-white stone colour, but John Preston, a leading Dublin decorator, was employed by Somerset Lowry-Corry, the 2nd Earl, to make a complete programme of decoration between 1807 and 1825, and the present porphyry red matches a scrape of the colour Preston specified shortly before 1816. It is a warm colour and enhances the architectural features of the room, bringing the scagliola columns into relationship with the rest of the room. This colour continues up the staircase to the first-floor lobby and attics.

After the austerity of the hall, the splendour of the oval saloon is very

Regency opulence in the saloon, Castle Coole

The restrained splendour of Castle Coole, James Wyatt's neo-classical masterpiece

striking. The walls are articulated with Corinthian scagliola pilasters and there is a frieze of swags and delicate ornament on the ceiling. The saloon sweeps through to the drawing-room on one side and the dining-room on the other.

The library is on one side of the hall. Its bookcases have delicate reeded mouldings and fluted architraves. The chimneypiece was made by Westmacott, though its elaborate drapery is unlike his other work in the house.

The stairway rises in a single flight of light-coloured stone steps to a half-landing and then in a double flight to the first-floor landing, where there is a screen of yellow and brown scagliola Doric columns. From the landing you enter the large lobby, one of the most impressive spaces in the house. It contains portraits of the four Corry sisters – Martha, Mary, Elizabeth and Sarah, whose son built the house – and it looks up at second-floor level to a gallery, its ceiling supported by coupled columns. The lobby and the attic storey are lit by three domed skylights.

From the windows of the bow room, between the Ionic capitals in the centre of the north-west front, the view extends to Enniskillen and beyond. The lawn slopes gently to Lough Coole, home of the greylag geese whose forebears were imported here by Colonel James Corry about 1700. Sir Richard Morrison designed an elegant farm and stableyard in 1820. A tunnel from the house, flanked by vaulted storerooms, opens on the yard. The present Lord Belmore has generously donated the stableyard buildings to the Trust. The Trust has made them wind- and water-tight and hopes, finance permitting, to restore their interiors for some future suitable productive use.

The park today is largely the result of the work of Armar Lowry-Corry, between 1780 and his death in 1802, and of Somerset Lowry-Corry between 1802 and 1820. Somerset took in additional land in 1813. In the early eighteenth century the building of the Queen Anne house was followed by the planting of a magnificent four-row avenue of oaks. This, in keeping with the formal garden, traces of which still exist, was directed straight at the house from the former Coach Road and its line was continued on the other side of the house by an ornamental canal. The avenue is the most prominent surviving feature associated with the Queen Anne house. The Trust has now replanted those parts which storms and age have depleted.

The present main entrance to the demesne is by the Weir's Bridge Lodge on the Dublin Road. Built about 1860, the lodge is a red sandstone ashlar building with Romanesque windows. The drive winds through informal woodland and then straightens out through the oak avenue.

The lovely woods south east of the present house are mainly beech, oak and Scots pine. There were three walks known as the Beech Walks through these woods: one led past the ice house to the walled garden; the middle walk went up the slope and had fine views eastwards towards Topped Mountain; the third had a good view of the house. For the daughters of the 4th Earl these were favourite walks, and each daughter had her own seat beside a path. They had a passion for preserving the old trees and if a main branch broke, they would have an iron supporting brace fitted to hold it up. One of them, Lady Dorothy, besides being an authority on the history and contents of Castle Coole, was a distinguished antiquarian. She contributed notes on 208 ancient monuments (all in Co. Fermanagh) in *A Preliminary Survey of Ancient Monuments in Northern Ireland*, published in 1940.

Dick Rogers

CASTLE WARD

On the Downpatrick–Strangford road (A25), 1½ miles W of Strangford [J752494]

The Ward family owned the lands at Castle Ward from 1570 when they were purchased from the Earl of Kildare by Sir Robert Ward, Surveyor-General of Ireland. The family prospered, and by judicious marriages increased their estates and influence.

Michael Ward of Castle Ward, MP for Co. Down in 1715, was for many years a Justice of the Court of the King's Bench in Ireland. He married Anne Hamilton, whose Bangor estates came into his possession after her mother's death. They built the house that preceded the present one at Castle Ward. No trace of it now remains, but we know it was located on the brow of the hill facing the walled garden and just south east of the Temple Water. In 1744 Walter Harris referred to it, in his *Antient and Present State of County Down*, as 'a large and handsome improvement of Mr. Justice Ward'. The judge died in 1759 and the estate passed to his only son, Bernard, MP for Co. Down from 1745 until 1770 when he became Baron Bangor, being advanced to the rank of Viscount in 1781, the year of his death. He married the daughter of the 1st Earl of Darnley, Lady Anne Bligh, widow of Robert Magill of Gill Hall, Co. Down.

In 1760 the discerning Mrs Delany, wife of the Dean of Down, visited the Ward family and described the property as 'altogether one of the finest places I ever saw'. It was not long, however, until the family decided to rebuild, for three years later she wrote: 'Mr. Ward is building a fine house, but the scene about is so uncommonly fine it is a pity it should not be judiciously laid out. He wants taste, and Lady Anne is so whimsical that I doubt her judgment. If they do not do too much they can't spoil the place, for it hath every advantage from nature that can be desired.'

Bernard Ward wished to build a plain, classical house, but his 'whimsical' wife wanted something more adventurous, in the Gothick taste, in the manner of Horace Walpole's Strawberry Hill, though it seems probable that Lady Anne

Bernard's classical taste on one side of Castle Ward (left); Lady Anne's Gothick style on the other

The classical façade,
Castle Ward

got her inspiration from Inverary Castle in Scotland which she visited with Bernard around 1740. They agreed to differ, and the result is a house classical on one side and Gothick on the other. The Gothick side faces north east and has the finer view – over an arm of Strangford Lough, surrounded by woods, with Portaferry and the gentle hills of the Ards Peninsula beyond. The interior of the house reflects exactly the Wards' opposing tastes: on his side of the house the rooms are decorated in classical style; on hers they are Gothick, with pointed doors and plaster vaulting. The architect is unknown. There is in the house a portrait by Francis Cotes showing Bernard holding in his hand a drawing of the classical side of the house. It has been suggested that the Wards used an architect's pattern book and drew the plans themselves but this would require an exceptional measure of skill and co-ordination which, considering

23

their differing tastes, it is hard to imagine they possessed. The lovely Bath stone, with which the house is faced, was shipped from Bristol in Bernard's own vessels, which transported lead from his mine as ballast on the outward journey.

Perhaps they did not get on together as badly as has often been suggested. Lady Anne seems to have been a good wife to Bernard and she brought up a family of seven children. She did not finally leave Castle Ward until 1783, two years after the death of her husband, and by this time her children were all of age, the youngest being twenty-one and married. She died in 1798 and has been described as eccentric in her last years, delighting in acts of private generosity, yet extremely parsimonious with tradesmen. But if it had not been for her we should not have had the unique and delightful Castle Ward we have today.

In *The Bagshawes of Ford*, published in 1886, William Henry Gunning Bagshawe quotes Sir James Caldwell of Castle Caldwell, Co. Fermanagh, recalling his visit to Castle Ward in 1772:

A little before dinner I got to Castle Ward. Lord Bangor received me with great cordiality and . . . asked me to dine and stay all night. This was the greater compliment, as his house was full of company, and not quite finished. There was an excellent dinner, stewed trout at the head, chine of beef at the foot, soup in the middle, a little pie at each side, and four trifling things at the corners . . . This is the style of all the dinners I have seen, and the second course of nine dishes made out much in the same way. The cloth was taken away, and then the fruit – a pineapple, not good; a small plate of peaches, grapes and figs (but a few), and the rest, pears and apples. No plate or knives given about; we were served in queen ware . . . During dinner two french horns of Lady Clanwilliam's played very fairly in the hall next to the parlour, which had a good effect.

It has been suggested that the wooden floor in the hall is not original, as most halls in large Irish houses were paved, but Caldwell's comment seems to show otherwise: 'You enter by a magnificent doorcase into the hall. In the middle there are two grand pillars, and the floor all inlaid with oak and mahogany, and diced and kept so smooth with rubbing and beeswax that you are in danger of slipping every moment.'

One of the most interesting people to live in the house was Mary Ward (1827–69). Born Mary King, she was brought up at Ballylin, fifteen miles from Birr Castle, the home of her cousin William who became the 3rd Earl of Rosse, the famous astronomer. In 1854 she married Henry Ward and their youngest child became the 6th Viscount Bangor. An artist and a naturalist, she wrote and illustrated three books on subjects connected with the microscope, she made her own microscopic slides, and her illustrated articles on comets and the natterjack toad were published in the *Intellectual Observer*. She painted Castle Ward and its views, her family and friends, with delicacy and accuracy. Many of the pictures in the Gothick boudoir are hers and copies of more of her watercolours are on display to the public in the Trust's 'Victorian

The Gothick saloon, Castle Ward

pastime centre' in Castle Ward.

Few of the eighteenth-century furnishings have survived, but the contrasting decorative schemes devised by Bernard and Anne have remained almost unaltered. Bernard contributed the hall, with its Doric screen of scagliola columns and the plasterwork of the ceiling and cornice (but not the panels, bows and trophies which are part of a restoration that took place in 1828); the dining-room with its entablature and panelling; and the lovely staircase with mahogany rail inlaid with satinwood and ebony. Anne contributed the Gothick saloon and morning-room, and fan-vaulted boudoir. An oddity in the hall is that the plasterwork of 1828 encapsulates time by covering a real violin, keys, bonnet, basket and tricorn hat. It is believed that in an attempt to hurry the plasterers towards completion of their work in the house, where they had been employed for a year, the subterfuge of dipping and attaching real objects was adopted.

In later years some of the servants slept on the top floor, but in the eighteenth century it seems that no servants, except a valet and a lady's maid, slept in the house. An underground passage (called 'the tunnel') leads to the courtyard which contained the servants' living quarters as well as stables, barns, byre, dairy and laundry. The tunnel's atmosphere is eighteenth-century and the steps are worn in slanting fashion, as if by tired feet that sought an easier way to climb. It was built to keep the architectural integrity of the house so that it would not be cluttered with ancillary buildings. This is an Irish fashion; there are other examples at Castle Coole and Lucan.

The Victorian laundry at Castle Ward

In the stableyard the laundry has been reinstated in two rooms: one the original washroom, with sinks and boiler, manually operated washing machines and mangles; and a room for airing and ironing. There is an array of irons, from large flat irons to small goffering irons, and there is a display of beautifully laundered period clothes, table and bed linens.

There is a small but charming theatre in the large barn in the stableyard, where performances by Castle Ward Opera take place every year. Here concerts are also held and exhibitions mounted. A restaurant is alongside.

In the farmyard, a little distance downhill towards the shore, is Old Castle Ward, a massive and defensive three-storeyed tower house erected in 1610. The stairs rise by straight flights in the thickness of the walls. It has a clock commissioned by William J. Ward, who had the twelve letters of his name inserted in place of digits on the clock face. Here, also, are the hayloft, the sawmill, the corn mill and the slaughterhouse. The sawmill has been restored and the corn mill, with its elaborate machinery, is being prepared for display.

To the north, approached by an ancient lime avenue, now replanted, lies the Temple Water. This long rectangular lake was made in 1724 near Judge Ward's early eighteenth-century house, of which no trace now remains. The surrounding grounds have been restored to their eighteenth-century character and have been replanted with a variety of deciduous trees.

The Temple, situated on a steep bluff overlooking the Temple Water, is slightly earlier in date than the new Castle Ward and was no doubt used as a summer pavilion for the earlier house. Although the date 1763 appears on the keystone above the central door, the building was already in existence by July 1762, when it was drawn by Mrs Delaney and called by her *Lady Anne Ward's Temple*. It is built with Bath stone dressings and commands a fine view of Strangford Lough and the demesne.

To the north east of the estate, overlooking the lough, is the Anglo-Norman Audley's Castle, built in the fifteenth century with bawn, roof-level walk, spiral staircase, machicolation and murder-hole. It is in the care of the Department of the Environment.

The park was landscaped in the eighteenth century, much of the ornamental planting being carried out by Anne Ward, wife of Judge Ward, between 1710 and 1759. There was a deer park from at least 1770 and throughout the nineteenth century. The deer could be observed from the mansion house, as can be seen in one of Mary Ward's watercolours. By the 1920s the deer park had been neglected and the deer had dispersed. The Sunken Garden was created in the mid-nineteenth century and its luxuriance in 1858 can be seen in another of Mary Ward's watercolours.

There are three quays serving the estate: the coal quay; another which was used for importing wine and provisions, and for exporting lead and timber; and Audley's Quay which is usable at practically all states of the tide. The remains of the lead mine may be seen on Dickson's Island (now a peninsula). The Eagleson hide, for birdwatching, is along the shore, south towards the Black Causeway.

The Barn, which lies between the stableyard and the farmyard, houses an audio-visual show and interpretation display for the Strangford Lough Wildlife Scheme. It is much used by schools, especially those around the lough.

Dick Rogers

CLOUGH CASTLE

5 miles NE of Dundrum (A24) [J409404]

Clough Castle, in the little village of Clough in south Down, may look unprepossessing from the main Ballynahinch–Newcastle road, sitting a little incongruously behind a garage forecourt. It is, in fact, quite an important example of a Norman motte-and-bailey castle dating from the thirteenth century. It was willed to the National Trust by Robert Cromie Jordan in 1969, and is on long lease to the Historic Monuments and Buildings Branch of the Department of the Environment. In the 1980s the branch undertook a substantial reconstruction of the stone keep.

The remarkable thing about Clough is that it is a motte-and-bailey castle in the English Norman tradition rather than in the pattern of Norman castles generally found in Ireland. The bailey or outer courtyard has an earthwork quite clearly marked and raised, whereas most Norman castles in Ireland, which are rarely found so far inland even as Clough, do not have such a well defined bailey.

The motte was excavated in 1951–2, revealing evidence of the original wooden palisade of timber posts, with a single stone loop – a defensive and firing point for archers. Two coins from the reign of King John (1199–1216) were found. In the middle of the thirteenth century a single-storey hall was built on the diagonal to the north east of the motte, but it seems that it was burned shortly afterwards. The keep itself is the only structure to remain standing, and there is evidence that the main entrance was on the first floor where the socket for the bar of the door can be seen. Archery loops remain with fragments of a wall walk.

It is well worth taking the path across the grassy sward up to the keep where the full extent of the earthworks can best be seen and where the views of Dundrum Bay and the Irish Sea, the Mourne Mountains and Slieve Croob more than repay the effort.

Lyn Gallagher

COLLIN GLEN

From Glen Road (B38) to the foot of Collin mountain [J270720]

Collin Glen, about a mile from the city boundary of Belfast on the Glen Road, sits among housing estates, quarries and scrapyards. It follows the course of the Collin stream which, with many tributaries, runs rapidly down the cleft between Black Mountain and Collin. Its interest for geologists was marked in 1860 when a party was sent from the British Association for the Advancement of Science to explore the bed of the stream. The geologist will recognise the red marly boulder clay, spreading up towards the escarpment of basalt, will note the interesting landslips, will identify chalk, basalt and flint, and might even be able to compare the riebeckiteeurite in certain stream sections with that of Ailsa Craig; but the landscape lover will see the effects of the fast-flowing streams on these formations, in gorges, clefts and a waterfall.

There is a dense cover of vegetation and wild tangle of native trees. Robert Lloyd Praeger noted Collin Glen as a site for rare plants in his important pioneering botanical books, and no doubt he joined in visits there with groups such as the Belfast Naturalists' Field Club – the kind of organisation which supported the Trust's appeal for subscriptions to acquire the glen in 1947.

As early as 25 July 1868 the Belfast Naturalists' Field Club records a visit to the glen by kind permission of Finlay McCance JP, who also granted the privilege of removing specimens. At the end of the day members of the party bore away examples of elegant plants from 'the steep and rugged banks of this fine glen . . . richly clothed with ferns' – Victorian ladies and gentlemen were currently gripped by a 'fern fetish'. Others, provided with the implements of the geologist, had taken from the thin stratum at the base of the lias known as the bone bed, scales, shells and fish teeth of the Triassic period; and the party divided, some to the railway at Dunmurry, others to enjoy the fine evening by walking into town along the Hannahstown Road.

There are less scientific associations with Collin Glen. One concerns the 'Black Bull' which haunted a certain Den McGaw – not a teetotaller – who lived in the house at the top of the glen. The bull thwarted Den's attempts to cross the river, eventually chasing him across the stepping stones. Den, later doubting the existence of this bovine apparition, found the bull's hoof print in the stepping stone, where it can still be seen to this day.

The Black Bull may have been a figment of the imagination, but the thick cover of Collin Glen and the wide open spaces of Collin mountain were among the last refuges of the wolf in Ireland; the last recorded sighting there was in the 1660s.

Lyn Gallagher

CROM

3 miles W of Newtownbutler on the Newtownbutler–Crom road [H361245]

Deep in the meshy green and silver country of Upper Lough Erne lies Crom, a remote and rare place, set among winding waters and ancient woodland, lush meadows and plashy marshes. An inspired scattering of buildings merge perfectly with this mature, almost primitive, landscape, giving Crom its special quality. Angus Stirling, the Trust's Director General, expressing the essence of the property, felt that 'the scale and relationship of water, woods and buildings makes a landscape of extraordinary harmony'. The immense environmental significance of Crom is just as important as its scenic quality: the largest surviving area of semi-natural oak woodland in Ulster combines with one of the most important and least spoilt freshwater habitats in the British Isles.

A look at the number of place names around Crom which have the prefix derry-, from the Irish *doire* meaning oakwood – Derrylin, Derryvore, Derrymacrow – gives some idea of the continuity of oak forests in this area. A rich and varied habitat remains because of this long continuity, for lichenologists have shown that although the present oaks may be less than 200 years old, woodland of the same kind has been growing there for a very long time, perhaps back to the wildwood. Not only have the lichens survived but other woodland plants and animals from Ireland's distant past can be found. The wealth of wildlife is exemplified by the presence of two rare butterflies – the purple hairstreak can be found in the tree canopy and the silver-washed fritillary occurs at ground level. The timelessness of Crom was disrupted in the 1950s when its trustees clear-felled 200 acres of ancient woodland in order to plant a crop of coniferous trees. An important part of National Trust management will be the reinstatement of broad-leaves, with a special eye to the requirements of scenery and conservation. Felling of conifers has created raw areas on the estate, and opened up fine views in some parts, but new group planting of trees and shrubs, and natural regeneration, will soon give a softer aspect.

Less disturbed is the rich plant life which grows on and by the water. Yellow and white water lilies and dock abound on the open water, clumps of tufted sedge, greater water dock and water parsnip colonise the shore lines, and some marshes hold a bounty of colour with meadowsweet, yellow iris, purple loosestrife and wild angelica; these in turn are alive with bees, butterflies and dragonflies. Ian Herbert, Head Warden at Crom, has discovered the abundance of life in the semi-natural pastures and hay meadows of the estate, and in one small field he has recorded seventy-nine species, including the seldom seen marsh pea: 'If one rare plant was not enough, imagine our delight in finding another – the blue-eyed grass, a native of North America, and found nowhere else in Europe as a native species except Ireland.'

Such a fragile and precarious environment is a challenge to manage. In 1988, 1,350 acres came to the National Trust from the 6th Earl of Erne, in order to secure its future.

The subtle blend of buildings and landscape, with which his family enhanced Crom, is minutely chronicled in a detailed Landscape Survey commissioned by the Trust, and written by Terence Reeves-Smyth. His task was enlivened by the writing of Shan F. Bullock, the novelist, who grew up at Crom in the 1870s and who described it as a world of 'lavish magnificence, of endless goings and comings and doings . . . a civilisation, a little state, splendid, stirring with life; a great centre'. Terence Reeves-Smyth records:

> The paraphernalia on this demesne included the castle with its retinue of nearly forty servants, the stable yard with its grooms, postilions, coachmen and stablemen, the forge yard with its smiths, carpenters and painters, the laundry, the gas works, the indoor riding school, the turf house, the church, the chaplain's residence, the school and the alms house for estate widows. There was a boat house, a floating dock and a fleet of wherries, cots, yachts and steamers attended by sailors and ferrymen. There were dozens of gardeners looking after a walled garden with vineries, pine pits, stove and greenhouses as well as parterres and an arboretum near the castle. The woods were managed by foresters while keepers controlled the vermin, looked after the fish stocks in the lakes, managed the pheasantry, the kennels and the deer in the park. There was a thrashing mill, bone mill, saw mill, tilery and one of the first silos in Ireland. The Farmyard occupied around a hundred and forty people attending the horses, cattle, pigs, making hay and numerous other tasks. In addition there were masons, road keepers, a cobbler, engineers, a steward, overseers and many more besides.

The centre of this empire was Crom Castle, which is not owned by the National Trust and is the home of Lord Erne and is not open to visitors. It was designed by Edward Blore in 1834–6 and is finely integrated into the landscape with limestone towers and turrets, battlements and gables rising among woodland in true picturesque romanticism. Love of the 'picturesque' informed the landscaping work at Crom, when William Sawrey Gilpin, the watercolourist and garden designer, was commissioned by John Crichton, later the 3rd Earl of Erne. Followers of the picturesque movement sought to form a series of pictures to be viewed from path or carriage, creating 'alternate expectation and discovery', and often focusing on buildings of romantic antiquity. The unity of scale and texture was important, and the character of the original landscape was respected in contrast to the practice of making large scale 'improvements' which characterised the era of 'Capability' Brown.

It seems likely that Gilpin was consulted on the site for the building of the

Lady Anne's 'whimsical' Gothick boudoir at Castle Ward, Co. Down. When Sir John Betjeman visited this room he remarked, 'Ah, now I know what it i like to sit under the udder of a cow.'

The Boat House at Crom,
once the hub of a world of
yachts and wherries,
steamers and punts

The long façade of Florence
Court looks out over an
eighteenth-century
parkland. The fine view is
kept uncluttered by the
device of a ha-ha, or ditch
and sunken fence, which is
in the foreground.

new house in the 1830s and played a major part in landscaping the demesne, and although many of the eye-catching buildings date from after his death, their positions on promontories or islands, or charmingly set against water or foliage, respect the original concept. The formal parterres and ha-has, formerly to be found in the garden by the Old Castle, were probably designed by him, and it is in this garden that the famous ancient conjoined yews may be found, with a combined circumference of almost 380 feet.

Gilpin may also have been responsible for ornamental planting and the sham extensions to the Old Castle, with false towers and ruined walls executed to present an aged profile to be viewed from the castle, and to make a romantic venue for picnic parties. Another destination for

35

Crichton Tower on Gad
Island, Crom, against the
wooded slopes of
Inishfendra

refreshments was the Tea House, a pretty hexagonal building, which is set
on a little lawn on a rise above the water. It was apparently built for Lady
Florence Mary Crichton, wife of the 4th Earl, who added the azaleas and
rhododendrons which skirt the lawn.

Another lakeside building is the Turf House, designed by Blore. It stands
beside a dock which was cut out to ease the delivery of materials for the
building of the castle. After its use for the storing of turf, it became a
sawmill, which was kept in constant use providing wood for the estate.

Particularly demanding was the old wooden bridge, before its replacement by one made of concrete. Built to connect the castle with a new walled garden on Inisherk, it hungrily consumed wood for repairs. The workers at the sawmill and the estate carpenters maintained the buildings and fences and constructed and repaired the cots which were used on the lough. The estate kept two big cots for transporting cattle and machinery to the islands and a smaller one for ferrying people to church and children to school.

The school and church, both attractive buildings, played a large part in the lives of the people of Crom, and there are still memories of around eighty children travelling to the schoolhouse at Corlatt, and Sunday school picnics when Lord Erne's men would drive the pupils down to the rectory in Derrylin in ponies and traps. It is said that the church at Derryvore would always be full, as Lady Erne saw to it that attendance should be high.

Perhaps the most dramatic eye-catcher is Crichton Tower, a landscape feature visible from all parts of Crom, set on a patch of rock and bushes known as Gad Island, backed by the thickly wooded shore of Inishfendra. This round tower was built in the 1840s, and was used as an observation post for the lough races.

The importance of boats to life at Crom is reflected in one of the estate's most attractive buildings – the Boat House, which was designed by George Sudden between 1839 and 1842. The charm of its situation and design has made it a perfect focus for twentieth-century photographers, and the upper room was used as the headquarters of Lough Erne Yacht Club. Shan F. Bullock recalls the Sailor's Room as the 'Cuddy Hole', ruled by Sheridan, 'a gruff, humorous, reddish squat British tar, imported from Southampton or somewhere', who was in 'command of all the fleet, wherries, punts, steamers, yachts, the barge wherein the family rowed sedately to church by two sailors in white tunics and caps'.

Terence Reeves-Smyth records that the Boat House was 'closed in 1914, but because Lord Erne and so many members of gentry families around the lough were killed in the war, the boat races at Crom came to an end'.

Since the nineteenth century the level of the lough has dropped by about six feet. As well as radically affecting the waterfront as envisaged by Gilpin, it precluded the lovely large yachts with their deep keels from using the waters around Crom, while high-masted vessels were barred by the construction of the Lady Craigavon Bridge. Small yachts, known as snipes, continued to sail in large numbers throughout the 1950s and 1960s.

Some of the glory of life on the water was recaptured when the Duke of Westminster's family lent the motor yacht *Trasna* to the Trust for three seasons, during 1987–9. Built at Bangor Boat Yard to designs for a Victorian twin-masted steam schooner, it gave visitors a stylish view of the pleasures of Crom from the lough.

Lyn Gallagher

THE CROWN LIQUOR SALOON

Great Victoria Street [J738332]

The Crown Liquor Saloon, a high-Victorian public house of the most elaborate and ornate decoration, stands in Great Victoria Street, Belfast. It is celebrated as a rare and remarkably intact survivor of the gin palaces of the nineteenth century and it complements perfectly its 'big sister' across the road, the Grand Opera House.

The Crown Liquor Saloon was built about 1895 by Michael Flanagan on the site of the former Railway Tavern. The station of the Great Northern Railway used to be opposite the Crown, making the bar a distinctive first call for visitors to Belfast. Flanagan, a Banbridge man, had been an extensive traveller in his youth and his delight in the exotic was liberally indulged in the designs for his public house. This exuberant taste was satisfied by supplies from manufacturers' catalogues and the execution of the designs was helped by a ready pool of imported skilled craftsmen who were in Belfast because of the blossoming of richly ornamented Catholic churches. Every possible hard-wearing material was introduced – tiles, wood, painted glass and mirrors, mosaics, marble and stucco.

The bar of the Crown Liquor Saloon

In 1978 the National Trust acquired the Crown in co-operation with Bass Ireland, which manages the bars, and a major restoration programme was begun. A great mix of Belfast people use the bar: students, businessmen, journalists, or the current cast of the Opera House. A television slightly rocks the nineteenth-century integrity but provides important information for the daytime regulars who follow the horses and bet in the neighbouring bookmakers.

The work of restoring the pub was complex. The exterior, richly coloured with showy pilasters and columns and a frieze of black and gold, shared the effects of the many explosions suffered by the Europa Hotel opposite. The Crown's former owner, Edward McGeeney, had carefully taken down and stored the heavy doors, and although many tiles had disappeared from the outside, these were remade using traditional methods from the original moulds at the Ironbridge Gorge Museum in Shropshire. Lost windows were faithfully copied, handpainted, fired and replaced.

Popular tradition claims that the creator of the Crown, Michael Flanagan, was an ardent nationalist, while his wife was an equally fervent loyalist. While she insisted upon the name of the pub, he gained revenge by depicting the crown in mosaics at the entrance so that those who wished might wipe their feet on it.

Once past the entrance the whole fabulous Aladdin's cave opens up, an interior described by a rapturous John Betjeman as a 'many coloured cavern'. To the left is the long bar of granite, divided by decorated wood and mirrors.

Hand-painting glass for the restoration of the Crown Liquor Saloon

Behind the bar is a myriad of wood, painted glass and mosaics. At one end a painted mirror reveals an inviting female figure reclining among clusters of grapes. In the centre large oak casks gleam with brass taps.

Facing the bar are the snugs or boxes. Each has a letter and the customers could communicate with the barmen by bells which are marked on a board across the centre of the saloon. Nickel plates for striking matches are inserted in the woodwork, and each snug is surmounted by a heraldic griffon or lion bearing the inscriptions *Fortuna audaces juvat* – 'Fortune favours the brave' or *Verus amor patria* – 'True love of one's country'. One of these snugs was re-created in Pinewood Studios for its film *Odd Man Out*, in which James Mason plays a fatally wounded gunman on the run.

In 1988 Bass Ireland introduced the Britannic Lounge to the first floor of the Crown. One of Harland and Wolff's famous trio of White Star liners, the *Britannic* was ordered in 1927 to be fitted out to the finest standards of luxury and opulence, like its sister ships the *Oceanic* and the *Titanic*. Highly ornate pilasters and columns, which were prepared for the *Britannic*, form a central feature of the lounge, while surviving features of the old Crown Hotel, which was part of the original building, such as painted slate fireplaces, mouldings and decorated glass, were jealously guarded and incorporated into the overall design.

Perhaps the best time to visit the Crown Liquor Saloon is on a late autumn afternoon when the bar staff come round to light the gas lamps – reinstated by the Trust – with their long lamplighters, and the rich colours are reflected in the shining surfaces under a burnished yellow glow.

Lyn Gallagher

Cushendun Bay from the
Torr Road

CUSHENDUN

23 miles N of Ballymena at the foot of Glendun [D248327]

The Glens of Antrim contain some of the most beautiful scenery in Ireland. They are usually described as the nine glens, but you will find four or five more if you look for them. Everyone has their favourite glen, but mine would be Glendun. Its river, the Dun, starts on the moors below Orra mountain and tumbles narrowly through heather, mosses and bracken, whin and thorn, past small farms and under little footbridges, till it flows beneath the great viaduct built by Charles Lanyon in 1839 when he was only twenty-two. And so down the widening valley (with a tributary glen joining it on the south side) through small but fertile fields towards a bay that on a fine morning sparkles in the sun. Here you look across at the surprisingly near shores and hills of the Mull of Kintyre in Argyllshire.

As you come down the valley Craigagh Wood (generously covenanted to the Trust by Patricia English) is on your left, on a rocky hillside. Of mixed deciduous trees and pine, it is very beautiful in all seasons. It contains a souterrain, and near the road on the south-east side is the 'altar in the wood', a Mass rock used in penal times. The old stone altar has a carved crucifixion on a slab brought over from Scotland in the eighteenth century; it is similar

41

The Square, Cushendun

to carvings found on Islay and Iona. The present Catholic church, built in 1840 and rebuilt in 1865, is just down the road.

The village of Cushendun lies around the bridge over the mouth of the Dun: the name means 'the foot of the dark brown river'. On the south side are three hotels and the little salmon fishery; on the north side is the rest of the village, almost all of which, with the shore and the green, is in the hands of the Trust. The Main Street is all very black and white, nineteenth-century vernacular in style, modest and quiet. Number one Main Street has been refurbished by the Trust as an information point with a tearoom and a small shop. McBrides is a decent public house and there is a post office and shop. The Cornish-style square was built by Clough Williams-Ellis in 1912, commissioned by Ronald McNeill, Baron Cushendun, and his Cornish wife, Maud. It consists of two-storeyed terraces with mansard roofs and Georgian glazing, planned symmetrically around a courtyard entered between massive gate-piers; the terraces are linked by arches at the corners. Round the turn of the road to the right, and facing the sea, are the Cornish-style Maud Cottages built by the same architect in 1925 in memory of Maud. They also are whitewashed, with hanging slates on the upper storey.

Cushendun House, to the north, had been burned down in 1921 in the 'troubles', and so Clough Williams-Ellis built Glenmona set back from the middle of the bay in 1923: it is in neo-Georgian style with a five-arched arcade on Tuscan columns, and is now an old people's home.

Across the bay is whitewashed Rockport Lodge, a Georgian house built

42

about 1815. The front, facing the beach, is formed of three canted bays, set in a zigzag under the wide eaves, so that the triangular recesses between them make an attractive pattern. On the west front there is an interesting three-light doorcase with glazing of an ornamental geometric pattern. It was the home of Moira O'Neill (Nesta Higginson) who wrote the much loved *Songs of the Glens of Antrim*. Two more modern poets, Louis MacNeice and John Hewitt, also found Cushendun inspiring. Artists of national repute who have been captivated by the landscape around the village are James Humbert Craig, Maurice Wilkes, Theo Gracey and Deborah Brown.

In the grounds of Rockport Lodge are the ruins of the small, square Carra Castle, covered with ivy. It was here that the great Shane O'Neill was treacherously killed by the retainers of Sorley Boy McDonnell, in the course of a banquet in 1567.

The parish church (Church of Ireland), erected in 1839, is set quietly among trees between the village and Glenmona. It has a square tower with tall tapering hexagonal pinnacles.

Past the hotels is the way to Cave House. It is completely surrounded by cliffs and can be reached only through a natural cave twenty yards long in conglomerate rock, or 'pudding stones', in the old red sandstone. The house, at present occupied by a religious order, was built in 1820 by Nicholas de la Cherois Crommelin, a member of the Huguenot family instrumental in developing the linen industry in Ulster. John Masefield, the poet, married a member of this family and spent many holidays here. The cave has several offshoots formerly used for stores and warehouses. In 1830, at the entrance to this cave, Sir John Rennie proposed to build Port Crommelin harbour for the Crommelins, though nothing came of it.

Dick Rogers

DERRYMORE HOUSE

1½ miles NW of Newry [J056280]

Derrymore House, in Bessbrook, Co. Armagh, is perhaps the best example of the Irish 'cottage ornée', a concept partly of architecture and partly of landscape design. It looked to the romantic rural idyll, and rustic arbours in this tradition were dotted around demesnes in Ireland at the end of the eighteenth century. Often they were thatched, sometimes resembling Swiss chalets, sometimes elaborately and picturesquely trailed with ivy and rambling roses. The typical 'cottage ornée' was built as a garden ornament, as a landscape viewpoint or as an eye-catcher, but a few were designed to be lived in, and of these the earliest and most elaborate was Derrymore.

In this 'gentleman's vernacular' style, as Hugh Dixon calls it in *An Introduction to Ulster Architecture* (1975), there is a happy marriage of traditional materials and methods such as thatching, and sophisticated architectural features such as quatrefoil windows surmounted by mouldings. Derrymore is, in fact, a generously fenestrated house, including a polygonal bay window with no fewer than eighty panes running from ground to roof, helping to bind the house with the landscape and giving the occupants increased contact with the carefully moulded parkland view. These plentiful and distinctive windows have been a cause of wry remark, because the house was built for Isaac Corry, who, after he had succeeded Sir John Parnell as Chancellor of the Exchequer in the Irish Parliament in 1799, introduced the famous Window Tax. A contemporary verse commented:

> For the loss of Sir John we need not be sorry
> For his place is well filled by the keen Isaac Corry,
> Who the art of financing has brought to its height.
> Our taxes being heavy, he laid them on light.

The Corry family came to Derrymore some time before 1771, when Isaac and Edward Corry agreed to divide their lands, Isaac gaining Derrymore. Isaac was called to the Irish Bar, but never seems to have practised; instead he devoted himself to politics. At first he was an enthusiastic advocate of Irish parliamentary independence, being a member of the Irish Volunteers as Captain Commandant of the First Newry Company in 1778, and a keen supporter of Grattan's Parliament. Later, probably under the influence of Lord Castlereagh – who had been a fellow pupil with him at the Royal School, Armagh, and often stayed at Derrymore on his way to Dublin – Isaac's views changed and he voted for the Act of Union in 1801. It is popularly believed that the details of the Act of Union were drafted at Derrymore. There is some evidence to suggest that he came to regret his support of the Union, as his political career faltered after that; he represented Newry at Westminster only from 1802 to

Derrymore House

1804. His name is still remembered locally in the 'Chancellor's Road' which runs from the corner of the Derrymore parkland in a fairly straight line to the Dublin Road at Carrivenaclose. Made for his own use, at public expense, it bypassed the steep hills and possibly the hostile crowds of Newry.

Derrymore itself is single storeyed, with a rabbit warren of a basement, and is built around an oblong courtyard. A stone entrance hall, with a pillared porch, erected by Sir William Young after 1810, was dismantled by the Trust to restore the original 'U' shape of the building. The distinctive thatching covers the whole roof in three separate and complete pieces and has a hipped formation, rather than exposing the gables in the usual Ulster fashion. The interior of the house is simply decorated, with unelaborate plaster moulding in the hall, and egg moulding in the drawing-room which has a pleasant marble fireplace flanked by bookcases, with decoration to match the doorcase, and two curious niches, very high up in the wall, which held busts. Although some pieces of furniture were in the house and were associated with Derrymore when it was given to the Trust, the house was substantially furnished by outside purchases and loans.

The parkland at Derrymore was laid out by John Sutherland (1745–1826), one of the most celebrated Irish landscape gardeners and a firm disciple of 'Capability' Brown, who declined to become involved in the popular 'picturesque' school of landscape design. Sir Charles Coote in his *Survey of County Armagh* of 1803 is unreserved in his approval of Sutherland's work:

45

> The very fine improvements at Derrymore (built 1776) show the correct and elegant taste of Mr. Sutherland, who planned them and supervised their execution. The young plantations already display a fine appearance of wood, the cottage, which is as yet the only residence, is without exception the most elegant summer lodge I have ever seen.

The implication here is that Sutherland may have been the architect of the house as part of the overall scheme, and there is no doubt that the design of the house and landscape are as one. The house is set on the higher part of the land which forms a wide, flat, natural terrace to catch the fine views of Newry and of the Mourne Mountains beyond. Sutherland obeys the orthodox eighteenth-century rules, with belts of trees following the natural contours around the edge of the park and specimen trees sprinkling wide expanses of lawn. He uses two clumps of woodland to disguise the home farm and the walled garden. The smooth lines are interrupted by an escarpment which divides the high and low ground, but Sutherland has overcome this jarring element by planting a dense belt of woodland here which blurs the sharpness of the division and gives a pleasant backdrop to the house.

In 1810 Isaac Corry conveyed Derrymore to Sir William Young, a lieutenant colonel in the East India Company, who made improvements including the construction of the walled garden. Young sold the property to Edward Smyth of Newry in 1828.

In 1859 Derrymore was acquired by the Richardsons, a Quaker family of strong principles, humility and idealism. They had taken over the Nicholson linen mills in Bessbrook in 1845, and chose that village for their home and industrial base because, in the words of John Grubb Richardson . . .

> I had a rooted aversion to be responsible for a factory population in a large town . . . so, on looking around, we fixed upon a place near Newry . . . with water, power and a thick population around, and in a country district where flax was cultivated in considerable quantities. It had moreover the desirable condition in my sight of enabling us to control our people and to do them good in every sense.

It was this approach which led to the establishment of Bessbrook as a model village with the proud boast . . .

No { public house / pawnshop / police

It was not until 1897 that a police station was set up in the village, and before that the firm had employed its own 'private policeman', Joe Milligan, whose favourite threat was 'I'll hev ye on the carpets before Mr. Harris [the managing director] in the morning', and who was also known to exclaim 'What sort of a randyboo is this yer havin' on the corners? Y'er neither ornamental nor beneficial. Skedaddle.'

The Richardsons' brand of paternalistic care was much admired in the nineteenth century, and in 1882 John Grubb Richardson was offered a baronetcy by William Ewart Gladstone. Their correspondence is worth recording:

April 21, 1882.

Dear Sir,

I have received the permission of Her Majesty to offer you a Baronetcy. It gives me much pleasure to propose to you an honour which I trust will not be disagreeable to you; and your acceptance of which will I am confident gratify all those who have had an opportunity of appreciating your personal position and your public services.

I remain, Dear Sir,
Faithfully yours,
W.E. Gladstone.

The Woodhouse
Bessbrook,
4th Mo. 24,
1882

Dear Mr. Gladstone,

I have duly received your kind letter offering me by permission of our beloved Queen the title and position of a Baronet for which I feel grateful as if I could accept the honour. You are aware that I belong to the Society of Friends, some of whose members in early days resigned their titles for conscience's sake. I cannot say I feel as strongly as they did in this matter, but I feel as if the acceptance of your offer on the grounds of having tried to do a little for the benefit of my fellow men would detract from the satisfaction I have found in so doing . . .

Believe me to be
Yours faithfully,
John G. Richardson.

The Richardsons always lived in the Woodhouse, the largest house on the estate, rather than in Derrymore, and in 1952 John S.W. Richardson gave Derrymore, with the park of forty-eight acres, to the National Trust. During the time since then it has been cared for with great love and diligence by Edmund Baillie and his two sisters. During the 1970s, Derrymore suffered several terrorist attacks; on each occasion the house was restored and the restoration continues. At the time of writing Derrymore is not open to the public.

Lyn Gallagher

DOWNHILL

5 miles W of Coleraine (A2) [C758363]

When Frederick Augustus Hervey, Bishop of Derry and Earl of Bristol, was looking for a site for his latest building venture in the 1770s, he picked one of the least hospitable places in his diocese. While the average 'improver' in Ireland at that time was carefully creating tame landscapes in which nature was harnessed into the gentle curves advocated by 'Capability' Brown, the Earl Bishop deliberately chose Downhill because it was vast, rugged, dominated by the elements and inspiring. The demesne displays many of the qualities of the 'Sublime' which the philosopher Edmund Burke had praised in his *Philosophical Inquiry Into the Origin of Our Ideas of the Sublime and Beautiful* in 1757. Grandeur was the inspiration, not elegance, and the chief elements were vastness of dimension and a sense of infinity. Dread, mystery and 'a delightful horror' might also be present. The bishop, who had enjoyed himself with many building projects in Ireland and England, now chose this place to challenge nature with man's handiwork.

Hervey was one of the most colourful characters of eighteenth-century Ireland. He was a churchman by profession rather than by vocation, wealthy, a traveller after whom the Bristol Hotels throughout Europe are named. He was generous; a promoter of public works for unemployment relief; a liberal nationalist who kept his own company of Volunteers; a Protestant bishop who allowed Mass to be said for his Catholic tenants in the crypt of the Mussenden Temple; a collector, who travelled Europe in search of art treasures to bring

Downhill House: engraving by J.P. Neale (1823)

back to his houses; a builder and creator of effect. He had a wicked sense of humour, and there are stories of races run between fat and lean clergy after good dinners at Downhill. The course was across the soggiest sand and the prizes were the richest livings in the diocese.

He was above all an enthusiast, who rarely let his own lack of knowledge hinder his ventures, and who had the fatal flaw of an inability to finish projects, as his attention wandered to the next big scheme. In fact, he lost interest in 'sweet Downhill' in about 1787, when the building of Ballyscullion at Bellaghy claimed him; but the decade before had seen intense activity. Arthur Young, traveller and agriculturalist, had rather sneered that the Bishop of Derry was building 'a large and convenient edifice . . . on a bold shore where a tree is a rarity' and had thus provoked an invitation from Hervey. 'A tree is no longer a rarity since above 200,000 have this winter been planted in the glens around my house. Come and enjoy the rapidity with which I have converted sixty acres of moor, by the medium of 200 spades into a green carpet covered with white clover.'

The scores of men employed had also created some of the artifices beloved of eighteenth-century landscape gardeners, ha-has – or sunken ditches – cascades and lakes, and had dotted the demesne with buildings designed as eye-catchers. The most outstanding of these is Mussenden Temple, a building of the rotunda shape so favoured by the bishop. Working with Michael Shanahan, a long-suffering and patient architect, the bishop planned it as a library, and named it after his attractive cousin Mrs Frideswide Mussenden, with more gallantry than discretion. It is said to have been based on the Temple of Vesta at Tivoli and it is perched dramatically on the edge of a cliff, the ultimate challenge to the elements. The inscription round the dome is by Lucretius, translated by Dryden, and reflects an ambivalent but confident relationship with nature:

The clifftop demesne: engraving by J.P. Neale (1823)

'Tis pleasant, safely to behold from shore
The rolling ship, and hear the tempest roar.

Of the other buildings on the demesne, the mausoleum to the bishop's brother George also derives from a classical model. The Bishop's Gate on the Coleraine–Limavady road is a well known feature with its Gothick gate lodge and garden. The Lion Gate has lost one of its animals, which is in fact a leopard or ounce and not a lion; it stands beside the remains of a double walled garden with a dovecot and ice house still intact. Lady Erne's Seat, an ornamental viewpoint, or belvedere, looks across the fish pond out to sea.

At the heart of the demesne is the house, which the bishop called his 'Tuscalanum'. Even the most ardent of his fans cannot claim that it is in the first rank of architectural achievement. 'On the whole a most unpleasant place to live,' said Arthur Young in the eighteenth century. 'Never seen so bad a house occupy so much ground,' added Edward Wakefield, another travel writer, in the nineteenth century. 'It can never be said to have had an outstanding profile,' stated the Ulster Architectural Heritage Society in the twentieth. H.J. Bruce, who lived there as a boy, recalls its uncomfortable gloom and the difficulties of living on an exposed cliff. Servants had to enter on hands and knees when the wind was blowing in a certain direction, and while his grandfather ruled the establishment from his own rather gaunt quarters, his parents and family squatted in a dark smoke-filled room off the 'Curate's Corridor' giving way to the dogs before the fire.

Himalayan blue poppies, *Meconopsis grandis*, create a vivid corner in Rowallane's Walled Garden. Photograph by Jerry Harpur, courtesy of the National Trust Photographic Library.

The house had a spasmodic history of occupation. The bishop lived there erratically for a short period of time, it was burned and rebuilt in the middle of the nineteenth century but sold by the Bruce family and billeted in the Second World War. After that it was partly demolished and was used for livestock. Since then the winds and the frosts have taken their toll, fulfilling in an eerily uncanny way the prophesy made by Mr Justice Day in 1801:

> It is impossible not to regret the misapplication of so much treasure upon a spot where no suitable demesne can be created, where trees will not grow, where the North blast and the trade winds in the West almost forbid all vegetation, where the salt spray begins to corrode the sumptuous pile of Grecian architecture and the imagination, anticipating the distant period, weeps over the splendid ruin, a sad monument of human folly.

The spirit of the bishop lives on to some extent in the person of the present warden, Jan Eccles. She came to the Bishop's Gate in 1962 when it was derelict and the Black Glen was completely overgrown with weeds. Singlehandedly she reclaimed the property. In 1972, after a decade of achievement, she retired, but five years later, although a series of well qualified, energetic wardens had been employed, Downhill missed her and she was recalled to work her normal hours – dawn to dusk – earning recognition by an honorary degree from the New University of Ulster. Quite recently a Trust land agent, after a long day on the north coast, called late to visit her. He could see that she must be around somewhere, but when he could not trace her and was just wondering whether to alert emergency services and coastguards, he heard the crunch of wellington boot on gravel, and round the corner she came, secateurs in hand. When he confessed his anxiety she gave him a withering look and said, 'Don't you know I always prune by moonlight? You get the shape of the bush better.'

Lyn Gallagher

Jan Eccles, warden at Downhill

FAIR HEAD AND MURLOUGH BAY

3 miles E of Ballycastle [D185430 and D199418]

Fair Head is one of the great headlands of Ireland. It is magnificent when seen from Ballycastle or from any of the other headlands on the north coast, and it is a landmark from the sea and from the air. The massive basaltic cliff falls sheer from nearly 600 feet above sea level. Its base and face are so inaccessible that a pair of golden eagles was able to meet here and rear two young in 1953. (After that their nesting was intermittent and ceased in 1960.)

Fair Head, or Benmore (the great headland), looks across to Rathlin Island and to Kintyre. Lower carboniferous sandstones, lying in horizontal beds, were invaded by a mass of molten lava, which squeezed its way in between the layers, forming a bed of hard basalt (dolerite) about 300 feet thick. Having solidifed slowly between two cold surfaces, it stood up in huge polygonal columns, at right angles to the planes of cooling, as at the Giant's Causeway; but here at Fair Head the columns are some fifty feet in girth and hundreds of feet high. The sandstones which originally formed the cover of the sill have been removed by time and weather; only traces of them remain and the wide heath on the top of the head is the upper surface of the volcanic intrusion.

It is possible to walk round the foot of the cliff from the Ballycastle direction past the old coal-mine workings at Colliery Bay and Carrickmore, but it is a formidable scramble over fallen boulders, with overgrown crevices, and the only way up to the top of the cliff is by the Grey Man's Path – stiff enough to climb, but easier on the ascent than going down. The top of Fair Head is ideal habitat for the chough, which feeds here in flocks and is distinguished by its red legs and bill and by the gruff cry which gives it its name. The 'pruck' or deep croaking of the raven can also be heard, and the wild mewing of the buzzard, soaring high up with splayed wing-tips. The peregrine falcon patrols here with swift wing-beats followed by a glide, and its excited shriek can be heard as it careers out from the cliff.

There is a herd of feral goats which uses the Grey Man's Path to get up and down; in winter the woods of birch and rowan on the slopes of Murlough Bay provide shelter and sustenance for these hardy animals.

The easiest point from which to explore Fair Head is the Trust's small carpark at Coolanlough, with a walk of about a mile north to the clifftop. To the left as you go north is Lough na Cranagh, so called because of the crannog, or artificial lake dwelling, in the middle of it. The crannog is oval in shape and is faced with a dry-built revetment about six feet above the water level.

The Grey Man's Path is the home of the bright yellow Welsh poppy, and clinging to the cliffs is the sticky, hairy little rock sea spurry. The open plateau is covered in heathland vegetation, heather and grasses predominating, but in season you will see the pink flowers of lousewort and in wet places the modest bog orchid and the heath spotted orchid with its delicate spotted pink flowers. In dry places you may find the heath pearlwort. Sundew and butterwort supplement their poor food supply from the soil by catching small insects on their sticky leaves.

Murlough Bay to the south is best explored from the main carpark at the top of the steep, narrow lane down to the shore. The bay contains a great variety of rocks. To the north is Fair Head whose gigantic dolerite columns can here be seen from a different angle. In the centre of the bay there are high cliffs of white chalk, overlying bright red Triassic sandstone. The southern horn of the bay is made up of ancient mica-schists.

The wet surface of the red sandstone is the home of the yellow mountain saxifrage, showing well in July and August down to the level of the sea. In spring the sloping woods with their fresh leaves are carpeted with primroses, wild hyacinths, red campion and ferns. In wet places around the bay are the delicately marked grass of Parnassus and the modest white mossy saxifrage. In many places there are patches of the tall, bright pink rosebay willowherb.

Murlough Bay around 1900, photographed by R.J. Welch

MURLOUGH BAY CO.ANTRIM. R.W. 614.

There is a small lake, Lough Fadden, to the west of the road down to the bay. On a rocky knoll 525 yards south west of the lake is a mutilated horned cairn, almost entirely hidden in heather. There appear to have been three chambers totalling twenty-seven feet in length and opening to the north east. Archaeological sites of a more recent kind can be found nearer the shore. There are three entrances to long abandoned coal mines, and there are the ruins of some miners' cottages. Along the shore to the south of these are the very scant ruins of the tiny church of St Mologe. The spot is known as Drumnakill, 'the ridge of the church'.

There is a very pleasant walk from the main carpark, down past the memorial to Roger Casement, and turning right through the Breesha Plantation, to the bottom road. Go south from here, and immediately beyond the gate turn right, up through the wood, taking care to respect the privacy of the tenants of Murlough Cottage. Above the wood, follow the path to the Benvan farmhouse. It has been converted by the Trust into a 'base camp' to provide accommodation for groups visiting the area and in particular for those undertaking voluntary work on the property. These lands around Benvan once belonged to the McDonnells; it was therefore appropriate that this spot should be chosen as a memorial to the Earl of Antrim, the Trust's former Northern Ireland Chairman, who did so much to preserve the beauty of the Ulster landscape.

From the upper carpark at Murlough Bay, as from Fair Head itself, on a fine day you can see Carrick-a-Rede, Inishowen in Co. Donegal, Rathlin, Islay, the Paps of Jura, the Mull of Kintyre, Sanda Island, Ailsa Craig and the Ayrshire coast.

Dick Rogers

FLORENCE COURT

7 miles S of Enniskillen via A4 and A32 [H175344]

You should enter the Florence Court demesne through what the local people used to call the Grand Gates, along an avenue which follows the eighteenth-century approach to the house.

About 1780 the demesne was landscaped by William King, who worked for the Earl of Bristol at Downhill in 1778 and for the Earl of Belmore at Castle Coole in 1780. King replaced the existing straight drive with a new informal approach in the manner of Lancelot 'Capability' Brown. The park was entirely ringed with a belt of trees wide enough to contain a drive, and it is from this outer enclosure that you catch the first glimpse of the house, standing on a ridge in the inner park beyond the 140-acre lawn, with the Cuilcagh mountains to the left.

If, on the other hand, you approach the demesne on foot along the avenue from the village, with thick woods on both sides, it is not until the last moment, when the path takes a sudden turn, that you round the side of the house. Then the mountains of Benaughlin and Cuilcagh spring into view to the south, forming a dramatic backdrop. Majestic woods of beech, oak and sycamore complete the setting.

The tall, three-storeyed mansion is linked by corridors with open arches to low flanking pavilions. The central bays of the main block break forward and the centre of the house is given further emphasis by a pediment over the doorway and a Venetian window with flanking niches on the floor above. The elevation has an early Georgian appearance.

The stone pedimented exterior doorcase is repeated on the inside in plaster with more elaborate decorative detail. A bold entablature is supported by sophisticated Doric pilasters. In the drawing-room, dining-room and 'Venetian room' the ceilings are very beautiful, with fanciful and spirited rococo plasterwork. These ceilings and the plaster panels of the staircase hall are the most memorable features of the interior.

Sir William Cole, ancestor of the owners of Florence Court, came from Devonshire in the last years of the reign of Elizabeth I and raised a regiment for service in the Irish wars. By 1607 he was established at Enniskillen and was one of the 'undertakers' in the plantation of Ulster. The family resided in the castle of Enniskillen until 1710 when it was destroyed by fire. They then moved to Portora Castle, just outside the town, and lived there until a house at Florence Court was completed. Sir John Cole (1680–1726), MP, great-grandson of Sir William, was the first to build at Florence Court. In 1707 he had married Florence Wrey of Cornwall, and it appears probable that about 1719 he built a house on the present site and named it after her.

Sir John's son, Lord Mountflorence, altered and probably enlarged this house

Florence Court and the Cuilcagh mountains

in the 1740s, possibly employing the architect Richard Castle. He also initiated preparatory work for wings which by 1767 had not been erected; there is an estate map dated 1768 which shows only the central block. The wings and the pavilions appear to have been built by Davis Ducart for Lord Mountflorence's son, William Willoughby Cole. This was probably in the 1770s when Ducart was working on various canal schemes in Co. Tyrone.

William Willoughby Cole was created Viscount Enniskillen in 1776 and 1st Earl of Enniskillen in 1789; he died in 1803. With him the history of the building of Florence Court came to an end, and the house has remained substantially as he left it through successive generations of the long-lived Cole family. It was the 5th Earl who succeeded to the title and estate in 1924 and who, with his son, Viscount Cole, gave the property to the National Trust in 1953. Viscount Cole died in 1956, and on the death of the 5th Earl in 1963 the title went to a cousin, David Lowry Cole, who became the 6th Earl. He died in 1989 and was succeeded by his son, Andrew John Galbraith, the 7th and present Earl of Enniskillen.

At the beginning of the eighteenth century the Coles had a formidable task in developing this part of their estates. The Revd William Henry wrote in 1739 that about 1712 it had been overgrown with woods and had no sort of roads, but that by 1739 great improvements had been made. 'A very grand road passes from Enniskillen to Florence Court and thence through the mountains to Leitrim and Sligo . . . The common people are so accustomed now to these public works that they look on it as part of their yearly labour and in the months of June and July fall as regularly and cheerfully to the breaking of stones and gravelling of roads as in March to the plough or harrow.' The Coles were responsible for building and maintaining these roads.

John Wesley passed this way in May 1767 . . . 'We rode by a large seat [Florence Court] elegantly built and finely situated.' In May 1785 Wesley came on his second journey and wrote, 'I preached about ten in the court-house at Manor Hamilton, and then rode over the black mountain, now clothed with green, and through a delightful road to Florence Court.'

he 3rd Earl of Enniskillen – courtesy of Lord Erne

The agriculturalist and traveller Arthur Young visited Florence Court on 17 August 1776. 'The people increase considerably,' he wrote. . . . 'Their circumstances vastly improved in 20 years; they are better fed, clothed and housed; more sober and industrious in every respect.' He continued, 'Their food is potatoes and oaten bread and a bit of beef or bacon for winter, all keep cows, and most of them pigs, and some poultry; many turkeys and geese. No drinking tea.'

The Coles were largely responsible for the building of St John's Church on the demesne in 1791; schools were also built at Cladagh, Lisblake and Florencecourt. About 1840 Lord Enniskillen built a tilery near Florencecourt which produced tiles for roofing (as at the Cladagh school) and for flooring which can still be seen in some of the houses in the district.

There was a big social occasion at Florence Court in the 1880s when one of Lord Enniskillen's daughters was married to Viscount Erne. Model-maker Gordon Johnson, of Enniskillen, has created an 8 ft × 7 ft miniature of the basement of the house as it was on the big day. With exquisite models of staff, it shows the kitchen, bakery, servants' hall, housekeeper's room, butler's room, wine cellar, scullery, larder, lamp room, silver store, and the still room for the arrangement of flowers and table displays. The model can be seen in the Colonel's room. This octagonal room, which is in fact the north pavilion, is the first the visitor enters before commencing the tour of the house. For many years it was occupied by Lt Col. Henry Arthur Cole (1809–90), the bachelor younger brother of the 3rd Earl. He was MP for Enniskillen between 1844 and 1855 and for Fermanagh from 1855 to 1880 and, having served for a time in the 7th Hussars, returned to Florence Court to end his days. Finding himself at odds with the rest of the family, he moved out of the central block and into the north pavilion, where, with the exception of his manservant, he lived in isolation, only joining the family for silent meals in the dining-room.

The period between the two world wars is remembered as a happy time by some of the older residents of the Florencecourt district. Nigel Brady, sometime guide at the house, tape-recorded a chat with George Forde who worked at Florence Court for over fifty years . . .

I came down here to play with Lord Cole, me and my brother Thomas . . . and there was Christmas parties and there was Sunday School treats every year. They had a Christmas tree in the big dining-room and the 5th

Earl gave presents out to the men on the estate . . . He would then have a party for all the children of the estate workers, and they used to have scrambles for pennies, big swings in the hayshed, small swings for the wee tots. The band used to come up and play for them; they had tug of war, they had tilt the bucket, and potato races.

At one time there were 300 fallow deer on the estate; the deer park extended to 270 acres and had a six-foot-high wall. George Forde's brother, Billy, followed in his father's footsteps as gamekeeper at Florence Court. At the age of thirteen it was his job to look after the kennels where there were thirteen dogs: retrievers, setters, pointers, spaniels and terriers. Lord Cole and Billy established the record game-bag for the estate when they shot twenty-eight woodcock, seven snipe and six pheasants in one day.

A disastrous fire occurred at Florence Court during the night of 22 March 1955. The Earl was at his club in Belfast and Lady Mary was in bed when at 6 a.m. she noticed light under her door. She got up and opened the door to be greeted with smoke and flames coming up from the stair-well. She managed to make her way to her husband's dressing-room, donned his knickerbockers and tweed coat over her nightdress and ran to the dower house to give the alarm. Her husband being somewhat deaf, the following telephone conversation took place . . .

'George, are you there?'

Silence.

'George, can you hear me?'

Silence.

'George, this is important; the house is on fire.'

A pause.

'What the hell can I do about it in Belfast? I've an appointment with the dentist at half past ten.'

With that he put the phone down.

The Duchess of Westminster, Viola Grosvenor, as she was then, at Ely Lodge ten miles away, heard about the fire in the early morning and rushed to Florence Court. In her own words, 'the house had red eyes', and in the still and frosty air two columns of smoke rose up. She found no urgency about saving family treasures – she met the old butler on the stairs removing a pair of his master's well darned socks – so she got the servants cracking to form a human chain, and they saved many valuable paintings and furniture. George Forde recalls, indicating the dining-room ceiling . . .

> The Duchess of Westminster came over as soon as she heard the house was on fire, and Charlie Pierce came out from Enniskillen with the big long steps to see what he could do, and she recommended that the ceiling should be drilled in order to save it, so he got a few men in . . . and they bored holes in the ceiling to let the water down, otherwise the weight of water which the firemen were pumping in would have destroyed the whole ceiling.

A careful restoration, following old photographs as well as surviving fragments, was undertaken by Sir Albert Richardson. During the work the opportunity was taken to remove several nineteenth-century additions and alterations which had marred the appearance of some of the main rooms.

William Willoughby Cole, the 3rd Earl, had, as a young man, made a name for himself as an enthusiastic geologist and discerning collector of fossil fish. He had acquired many hundreds of fossils in the British Isles and on the Continent and arranged them in his private museum in the south pavilion under a glass lantern roof. His father regarded this activity as 'damned nonsense', but the young man's reputation grew, and when the leading geologists of the British Association for the Advancement of Science, after their meeting in Dublin in 1835, came to Florence Court, the 2nd Earl entertained them well. He liked them, made them stay a week and encouraged his son to lead them on geological expeditions through the limestone mountains of Fermanagh and the volcanic scenery of the Antrim coast. Thereafter, Viscount Cole was able to finish the building of his museum and for the rest of his life he pursued his geological hobbies. His collection reached nearly

10,000 individual specimens. It became one of the most important scientific collections of fossil fish in the world and remained at Florence Court for nearly fifty years until he transferred it to the British Museum (Natural History) in London, where it remains a prized research collection. In 1988 the Ulster Museum mounted a large exhibition ('Nonsense, Damned Nonsense') on the 3rd Earl's life and collection. The Trust participated in this exhibition and a reduced version of it is now housed in the south pavilion.

To the south of the house lies the Pleasure Ground, containing fine groves of beech, oak and sycamore, mostly planted in the early nineteenth century by the 3rd Earl. In these woods is the mid-nineteenth-century Ice House, which was the equivalent of a large modern refrigerator. It was packed with river ice during the winter and used to preserve meat, poultry, game and fish during the summer. Close by is the eighteenth-century Eel House Bridge over the Larganess river, containing a recess in which eels were kept for eating. Here, also, is the hydraulic ram which pumped water to the house from the river. Between Eel House Bridge and the Ice House is a ford over the river – a part of the track on which the family went to St John's Church.

In a clearing in the woods to the east of the Pleasure Ground is the original Florence Court yew (*Taxus baccata fastigiata*), the progenitor of trees now found all over the world. It is one of a pair found on Cuilcagh mountain about 1767 by a kinsman of my own, George Willis, a tenant of Lord Mountflorence, and it can be propagated only by cuttings.

On the south side of the house the cobbled foundations of the Summer, or Heather, House can be seen. It was thatched with peat sods and heather and when funds are available it will be restored. To the west of the house are the sawmill and the forge, which have been restored. In the farmyard the old staff quarters are being converted into flats for seasonal renting. On the east side of the house the Walled Garden and Rose Garden have been restored.

Dick Rogers

GLENARM

No public access

Glenarm is one of the famed nine Glens of Antrim, an area which is extremely beautiful and richly wooded. Richly wooded, that is, in Irish terms, because Ireland's natural deciduous woodlands are very scarce. In the seventeenth century about one eighth of the island was covered in woodland, but by the nineteenth century only about two per cent of the land was forested, and this original, natural woodland was limited to the remoter areas, such as the north west of Co. Donegal, Killarney and the Glens of Antrim.

In Glenarm, oak, once a dominant species in Ireland, grew along the wet valley bottom while the drier slopes and higher ground were clothed with the familiar native Irish trees, the hazel, holly, ash and alder. The saying, which is applied in different places throughout Ireland, that a man could cross any of the glens on the tops of the trees or that a bird could hop from branch to branch the length of the glen, was common in the early nineteenth century.

In the seventeenth century, Glenarm, like other communities close to good supplies of timber, was able to support a shipbuilding yard, which was capable of building a ship of forty tons in the 1660s. In the early eighteenth century timber in this part of Co. Antrim was used, among other things, for burning chalk for fertiliser.

While the lower glen is now in the hands of the Forest Service and is planted with conifers, the upper glen remains more intact. This is owned by the McDonnell family, the Earls of Antrim, who live in Glenarm Castle, and Lord Dunluce gave the National Trust protective covenants over 685 acres there in 1980. The management of the glen is in the hands of the Ulster Trust for Nature Conservation.

The area now protected includes the Lower Deer Park with its rich grassland on the valley floor and dense mixed scrub on the valley sides; an important oak grove stands here. Undisturbed hazel coppice and scrub, with woodland growing over the site of a rath, and marshy areas of significant botanical interest occupy the Middle Deer Park. Old specimen oaks are dotted over the High Hollow, and good woodland continues along the Cottage Park by the banks of the Glenarm river. The Plantation, an area of coniferous planting of mixed age surrounding most of the glen, has changed considerably since 1683 when landowner Richard Dobbs – later mayor of Carrickfergus – wrote: 'Above the town in the Glen through which the river runs, and is clad with underwoods, is the pleasantest hunting for buck that ever I saw, for you may ride on either side and have the dogs or Bucks or both, continually in view and stand in a manner still in one place for two hours together.'

Lyn Gallagher

GLENOE

8 miles SW of Larne (B99) [J397967]

Glenoe is a pretty little pocket of a glen, south of Larne in Co. Antrim. It is not numbered among the famous nine Glens of Antrim, which begin further north at Glenarm, but like most of them the valley through which the river Glynn runs lies north west.

The river Glynn has many waterfalls as it passes down to Larne Lough. A deep fall and a glen of four acres, which was given to the National Trust by Thomas Shaw and Lord Trevor in 1968, is right in the middle of the village of Glenoe. A steeply twisting road winds on both sides of this attractive place, which has whitewashed terraces of houses along the abrupt slopes of the basalt hillsides. The river runs down between rocks draped with ferns, ivy and bluebells. Beech trees cling to the steep sides and seedlings grow in pockets of earth. Steps are cut into the precipitous banks and a simple wooden bridge spans the water.

A low cliff of chalk is exposed to one side of the carpark, while a new plantation of woodland shelters it to the other.

Lyn Gallagher

The shop front, Gray's
Printing Press

GRAY'S PRINTING PRESS

Main Street, Strabane [H345977]

In the centre of the busy Co. Tyrone town of Strabane stands a remarkable, graceful survivor of the later Georgian period. From an indifferent scarred townscape, Gray's Printing Press stands out with its pretty, slightly bowed shop front, four slender Tuscan pilasters and a central door with elegant window tracery. Across the frieze, on a good shopboard with moulding, are the words 'Gray Printer' in a raised, slightly curly serif face.

Inside, the privately managed shop is a traditional stationers of great charm, full of paper, pencils and pens, books and artists' materials, cards and office requirements.

A long passage from the street leads to a flagged courtyard, and across the yard is a whitewashed two-storey building. In the upper room, reached by an outside stairway, is a printer's workshop. It is quiet now but it is easy to imagine the smell of ink, the heat of the cast-iron stove and the noise of the presses at work. Everything needed for printing is here, down to the wooden setting sticks, metal sidesticks, wooden galleys and the old mallet and shooters which

hammered in the wooden wedges to secure the type in the frame or chase. Indeed, there was a working press here right up until the middle of this century.

Grays owes its chief claim to fame to its associations with John Dunlap, the printer of the American Declaration of Independence, who was born in Strabane and emigrated at an early age to Philadelphia where his uncle was a printer and publisher. Dunlap later founded America's first daily newspaper, the *Pennsylvania Packet*. Another emigrant from Strabane, James Wilson, is said to have been an apprentice at this printery. In 1807 he too went to Philadelphia, where he became a judge and newspaper editor, father of ten children and grandfather of President Woodrow Wilson. During the time when these two emigrants were boys, Strabane was a thriving printing centre, surpassing Londonderry in importance: fifty books were published there in the period between 1779 and 1840. There were two newspapers, the *Strabane Journal*, founded in 1771, and the *Strabane Newsletter*, dating from 1780.

All of the presses in Grays date from the nineteenth century, and appropriately the most impressive is the American Columbian press, invented by George Clymer of Philadelphia, with a cast-iron American eagle, positioned on the cross-rod, acting as a counterweight. A similar large-scale hand-operated press is the Albion, but examples of the faster platen presses can also be seen. These were worked by treadle and could produce up to 1,000 impressions in an hour. A hand-operated guillotine, a perforator, stapling machine and lead-cutter make up the equipment, but experts in printing get really excited when they see the large selection of wooden type used for printing posters, and the old type in wood and metal which was used before the point system was introduced in 1886.

Lyn Gallagher

HEZLETT HOUSE

5½ miles W of Coleraine on the coast road (A2) [C772349]

A pretty thatched cottage sits just back from the road at the Liffock crossroads near Castlerock, Co. Londonderry. It is long and low with an elegant cobweb fanlight and twelve-paned Georgian windows. It is, in fact, older than its Georgian appearance would suggest and the dendrochronologists in the Palaeoecology Department at Queen's University, Belfast – those experts who can date wood by scientific methods – have placed the house around 1690. For its date alone it demands attention: very few dwellings in Northern Ireland date from before the eighteenth century, mostly because Ulster's earlier houses were made of poor material, and are largely undocumented.

Hezlett House is a cruck-built dwelling. The crucks are pieces of naturally curved timber acting as upright posts and sloping rafters. These crucks, or pieces of crucks, were placed together in arches to form the skeleton of the house, and then the walls were filled in with whatever material was locally available. It was a form of building more common in Great Britain than in Ireland and it has been suggested that these timber frames were carried over, ready for quick assembly. In the case of Hezlett House the five cruck frames were planted without foundations on a platform of rock, and filled in with clay and rubble, with a 'batter' – a formation of the wall in which the base is noticeably wider than the top. The outside was covered in roughcast and thatched, formerly in flax, now in wheat straw. This area of the country has, in fact, several other examples of this kind of construction, especially at Magilligan and Aghanloo.

Hezlett House may owe its origin to the enthusiasm of Bishop King who had just been appointed to the See of Derry in 1690 and who found the 'land almost desolate, country houses and dwellings burnt'. He was anxious to encourage clergymen to live within their parishes, and embarked on a scheme to provide local clerical residences. On the other hand, Hezlett House may have been an earlier farmhouse which was converted as a rectory. What is certain is that it was occupied by the Venerable Roger Fford, who served from 1693 to 1719, and by four rectors who succeeded him until the house was acquired by Isaac Hezlett, a local farmer. This family lived in the house for over 200 years.

Probably the most dramatic moment in the family's history came at the end of the eighteenth century. Of Isaac's two sons, one, Jack, joined the United Irishmen, and had to flee to America on the failure of 1798 rising. The other, Samuel, refused to join and was threatened with hanging from the Spanish chestnut tree which still shadows the house.

The Hezlett family are well known in the Coleraine district and the primary school up the road from the house is named after Hugh Hezlett, who was chairman of the local council and of Coleraine Regional Education Committee

Hezlett House

in the first half of this century.

When the National Trust acquired the house it was essentially because of the interest in the cruck construction, and so it was decided that one room be left completely open to the roof, with the crucks and walls exposed, so that all the details could be seen. A suspended walkway takes the visitor across the room, eye to eye with the highest level of the thatch, the oak beams, well finished with an adze, and the massive oak pegs.

In 1983 the National Trust wardens, Eric and Gloria Stewart, noticed ominous bending and sagging in the walls and ceilings, and investigations revealed that the building needed to be completely rethatched. Over the 300 years of the house's existence it appeared that no thatch had ever been removed;

Strangford islands – Co. Down's rolling drumlins spill into the lough. Photograph by Joe Cornish, courtesy of the National Trust Photographic Library.

a fresh layer had simply been added if it was thought necessary. The result of this was that at one end of the house the thatch had accumulated to a depth of seven feet; the weight being borne by the crucks was forty tons, or as someone helpfully calculated, the equivalent of four double-decker buses. The rethatching was done by Gerald Agnew of Ahoghill, while other professionals had to use all their expertise to adjust the uneven levels of the roof – revealed when the thatch was stripped – while keeping the cruck structure intact. In 1986 a fire consumed the south end of Hezlett House but damage was mostly confined to the nineteenth-century extension, and although the cottage had to be rethatched, the cruck trusses remained essentially unimpaired.

Inside, the house is furnished in mid-Victorian style, although some pieces of furniture are considerably older, including an oak cupboard in the servants' loft, dated 1701, which has been in the house since the mid-eighteenth century.

Most visitors remark on the small scale of the house, with tiny bedrooms and low doors. In fact, there would originally have been three even smaller internal wall-bed cubicles in the west wall. The two rooms now to be seen are the kitchen and the parlour. In the kitchen a turf fire usually burns on the open hearth with the cooking irons over the grate. The kitchen is painted a strong red and is comfortable and welcoming; a pantry and a narrow, winding stair to the attic lead off the back. By comparison, the parlour is prim and correct, with a piano in prime position, upright chairs, an aspidistra and Victorian paraphernalia, all in its Sunday best.

Lyn Gallagher

The distinctive whitewashed rear of Springhill, Co. Londonderry, shadowed by the Sperrin mountains. Mature trees grow around the house, and in the foreground are the young beeches which will replace an avenue planted at the end of the seventeenth century.

ISLANDMAGEE

[*J483958*]

'They are utterly inaccessible': this was James Boyle's description of the stretch of Antrim coastline called The Gobbins in the Ordnance Survey Memoirs of 1840. He recorded that this 'precipitous and unvaried wall or cliff of limestone and basalt' was 'far-famed for that boldness and grandeur of the scenery'. The quality of this scenery attracted the protection of the National Trust in the 1990s and a major part of Trust management will be to ensure that access is no longer a problem. In addition to some dramatic coastline near The Gobbins, the Trust has acquired the grassy headland of Skernaghan Point, in the north of Islandmagee, which has long been a popular and very accessible recreational area.

The Trust owns around forty acres of land at Ballykeel and Mullaghdoo, giving access to a stretch of grassland, cliff face and undercliff. It is said that the name 'The Gobbins' comes from the Irish *gob*, meaning mouth, beak, or snout, and *binn*, meaning high place. Cliffs rise to a lofty 200 feet above the sea, dipping into curving bays, where slopes covered in hazel, whin and fuchsia give a softer coastline than some of the more austere Antrim profiles to the north.

The fame of The Gobbins was firmly established when, at the beginning of the twentieth century, the enterprise of the Northern Counties Railway Company opened the cliffs to a wider audience by the construction of an elaborate cliff path in order to encourage greater use of their railway system to Whitehead.

The Gobbins Cliff Path was built by the engineer Berkeley Wise for the railway company and opened in 1902 just in time for the Belfast meeting of the British Association for the Advancement of Science. Cut into the perpendicular face of the rock, it ran along the base of the cliff for several headlands, and climbed and spanned the coast with a network of steps and bridges up to seventy feet in length. The sea-stack Man-o'-War was connected to the mainland with a tubular steel bridge. The bridges were floated out on barges from Whitehead. By 1927, however, the path system had fallen into such disrepair that local historian Dixon Donaldson hoped that someone might take an interest in the famous landmark and 're-create the amazing interlocking bridges more safely by modern methods'.

Now some of the charm of this part of the Antrim coast is perhaps enhanced by its solitude, as the Antrim Coast Road north of Larne has drawn away the motorists from this peninsula. Islandmagee is a very separate place, bounded by the waters of Belfast Lough to the west and of Larne Lough to the east, yet everywhere the horizons are enclosing. The gentle contours of the Antrim plateau, and the undulating pattern of fields and villages of Co. Down bound

Skernaghan Point from Brown's Bay

the landscape to east and west, while to the north is a magnificent front of headlands mounting on headlands – Ballygally, Glenarm, Garron Point and Cushendun, and beyond are the clearly distinguishable landmarks of the Isle of Man to the east, and further to the north, Galloway, Ailsa Craig, the Mull of Kintyre, and even the Hebrides.

The Gobbins have always been rich in bird life, providing nesting sites for some dozen varieties. Puffin, razorbill and guillemot come to breed, and fulmar have colonised the cliff. Gannet and Manx shearwater have been summer visitors, and in winter great northern divers may be seen.

Skernaghan Point lies to the east of Brown's Bay, and the Trust property, which was acquired with the help of a special Enterprise Neptune appeal sponsored by Gilbeys, takes in a flat plain and shoreline littered with huge basalt boulders. The Rocking Stone, a ten-ton basalt boulder once considered to be used in druidic priestcraft, is a well-known local landmark. For long it was a source of amazement because it was capable of easy movement if rocked from one point at a south-east angle. Skernaghan's crowning glory is the view of the Antrim coast to the north, a view regularly enlivened by the passage of ferries into the nearby harbour of Larne.

Lyn Gallagher

KEARNEY AND KNOCKINELDER

3 miles E of Portaferry [J650517]

A long narrow road, which ends at the sea, takes the visitor to Kearney, a cluster of houses right at the southern tip of the Ards Peninsula. It is a place of some beauty although, like much of the Irish Sea coast of the peninsula, there is no high ground close to the shore. Around Kearney well mannered farmland rolls gently down to the sea, giving way to little bays of shingle, skirted by ridges of rock, with the houses themselves sitting squatly on the point. It is the kind of place you find by accident and return to again and again.

Research by the Ards Historical Society shows that in the nineteenth century Kearney was a flourishing community, with fishing as the central occupation. Stories are told of a 'she-cruiser', crewed entirely by women, which set out to fish from those waters. The skipper of this unusual vessel was at one stage Mary Anne Donnan, a very well known character, six feet tall, a storyteller, midwife, layer-out of corpses and flowerer of linen, as well as a fisherwoman. She was born in 1841 and lived till she was ninety-nine, her home being the very small cottage on the extreme north of the village. The Ulster painter Sir John Lavery could not resist Mary Anne as a subject.

In the village there were three windmills – two for flax and one for corn – and a school. The villagers augmented their income by profit from salvaging wrecks, but the stories associated with the place, of enticing ships on to the rocks, and of smuggling, are typical of many Co. Down villages. A well documented story of the wreck of the *Snow Anne* on 14 February 1766 shows that the powerful local family, the Savages, had to pay eighty-two men 3s. 3d. each for twenty-four hours, for a total of 1,125 days and nights, to salvage the

Mary Anne Donnan: photograph courtesy of M. Armstrong

wreck; and the Savages still made over £100 from the job.

At the turn of the century there were seventy-five people living in the cluster of dwellings, with two rows of terraced houses in the centre. Only traces remain of the pattern of 'one door, one window' per house. Why the village became virtually deserted is not clear, though the mechanisation of agriculture substantially reduced the employment of farm labourers in the years to follow, and there was large-scale emigration. An intriguing attempt to revitalise the area was made in 1938 when a 'model farm' was set up on the road to Kearney, with altruistic new ideas which included a social club and cinema for the workers. Those ideas failed, but the farm itself still thrives on the rich agricultural ground around the village.

Kearney is now a place of recreation: a good coastal walk stretches two miles, towards Cloghy in one direction and right round to the National Trust beach of Knockinelder in the other. It is a splendid place for sea-watching, with constant views of ships passing on the Irish Sea, lighthouses and lightship and continually changing birdlife. Seals can be seen here regularly; perhaps the best place is the rocky shoal right on the tip between Kearney and Knockinelder, just at dusk.

Lyn Gallagher

KILLYNETHER

1 mile SW of Newtownards [J473723]

Under the bold hilltop and tower of Scrabo, Co. Down, are Killynether Woods, one of the National Trust's first properties in Northern Ireland, given in 1937 by Jessie H. Weir, and now leased to the Department of the Environment which manages the forty-three acres as part of a country park. These are fine old woods, mostly of beech and hazel, rising straight and well spaced up the hillside. In autumn they give that familiar landscape its reddish-brown skirt and in the late spring the ground below the trees is extravagantly clothed with bluebells.

The woods creep up to the well known rugged top of Scrabo, an important geological landscape, which owes its appearance to a thin capping of dolerite on Triassic sandstone pierced by Tertiary dykes and sills. There used to be a Killynether House here, but after it had been used as a youth hostel, dry rot claimed it and it was knocked down in 1966.

The hill is, of course, dominated by another building, and although it is not a National Trust property, it has close associations with Mount Stewart, which can be seen from the summit. Scrabo Tower was built in memory of the 3rd Marquess of Londonderry, Charles Stewart, the younger half-brother of Lord Castlereagh. In the post-1815 period Charles was an international figure of some reputation, dashing and extravagant in everything he did. He was married to the lively Frances Anne, a wealthy heiress. Both characters were larger than life, and this monument, devised by the 3rd Marchioness for her husband, is a landmark which can be seen for miles around and, in its showiness, is an extremely suitable tribute to them.

The views from Killynether are excellent. To the south the expanse of Strangford Lough opens up, changing with the tide as the mudflats are exposed or covered. The long strip of the Ards Peninsula, with its drumlins and the Irish Sea beyond, is to the south east, and to the south west is the rolling land past Comber to Killyleagh, Slieve Croob and the Mourne Mountains beyond. To the west lies the Dundonald valley and in the foreground is much-prized agricultural land. In 1744 Walter Harris, in his *Antient and Present State of County Down*, commented on the 'vast extended Prospect' from Killynether, adding that Scrabo was 'a fruitful Hill, and the Plowman's Furrows are carried up near the summit of it, where there was a fine Spring Well, but of late Years fill'd up with stones by idle Boys'.

Lyn Gallagher

LAYDE

2 miles N of Cushendall [D245289]

The National Trust owns only seven and a half acres at Layde, one of the little hidden corners of the Co. Antrim coast, just north of Cushendall, where a right-of-way protects a path to a tiny beach.

A fast-flowing stream falls before it reaches the sea in the little bay of Port Obe, sheltered by a long spur of rock jutting southwards. There is a rocky way along the cliffs and slopes, where the steep butt of Cross Slieve meets the water. To the east the view is dominated by the strong headland of Garron Point.

Outside National Trust property, near the path from the small carpark to the beach, are the ruins of Layde Church and a graveyard. The church was first mentioned in a taxation roll of around 1300, and although traditionally a Franciscan foundation, it was used as a parish church until 1790. The remnants of the structure show four phases of development during and after the Middle Ages; a stone dated 1696 probably marks one alteration. The church had a tower at the west end, with a stone vault over the ground floor; perhaps this chamber was a dwelling for the priest. Marks of wicker bands for retaining early plaster can be seen under the vault.

Around the churchyard are fine gravestones and vaults spanning several centuries; after Bonamargy in Ballycastle, Layde was the chief burial place of the McDonnells, including Dr James McDonnell, one of the organisers of the great festival of harpists in Belfast in 1792. Just at the churchyard gate is a curious holed stone cross. Normally such stones have pre-Christian, ritual associations, but this one has a cross scored on its west face; in the nineteenth century it was reused as a grave mark and has an inscription of that period on its base.

Lyn Gallagher

Lapwing

LIGHTHOUSE ISLAND

3 miles off the mouth of Belfast Lough [J596858]

There is now no lighthouse on this member of the Copelands, off the north-east corner of Co. Down. Walter Harris's *Antient and Present State of County Down* recorded that its former beacon stood on a round tower 'on which the Grate is fixed on a thick iron Spindel. Scotland supplies it with Coals, of which, in a windy Night, it consumes a Tun and a Half, Burning from Evening to Day Light both Winter and Summer.' Ships today are served by a modern lighthouse on the nearby Mew Island.

The Copelands, which are said to have derived their name from a family who came over with John de Courcy, were owned by John Ker of Portavo, and he gave Lighthouse Island to the National Trust as part of the Enterprise Neptune campaign in 1966. A bird observatory had already been started in 1954 by enthusiastic volunteers, and the management of the island is still in the hands of the Observatory Committee.

Lighthouse Island is a special place for birds and it offers some rare experiences for birdwatchers, who can apply for a permit for a visit which includes the boat trips, tours, and self-catering accommodation in the converted quarters of the former lighthousemen. Neville McKee, who has a long association with the observatory, describes a visit to the colony of Manx shearwaters – birds which breed in rabbit burrows and come in and out only at night because of the threats from predatory gulls:

A shearwater colony at night is an exciting place to be, with heavy, hurtling shapes swishing past, issuing a ghoul-like, raucous cry. Birds land with a bump, and take-off is a problem as the birds need a clear runway. Seeing all this is an experience worth having at least once in a lifetime.

Another rare opportunity is offered at Lighthouse Island, for this is one of the areas where birds are ringed and studied for purposes of identification, ageing, sexing, measuring and weighing, and, of course, for releasing again. Ringing operations are stringently controlled, and only highly trained, qualified ringers can take part, but visitors to the island can watch and become involved in the rare privilege of seeing birds in the hand. A favourite species to occur is the storm petrel.

There are plenty of opportunities for seeing birds in the wild; two sea-watching hides are provided and there are many vantage points for observing the island's breeding population, including eider, red-breasted merganser, shelduck, fulmar, black guillemot, oystercatcher, lapwing, stock dove, moorhen, water rail, the three larger gulls and the common gull.

An important part of the observatory's work – and it is one of only sixteen in the British Isles – is the monitoring of bird populations, especially the migrants. At the same time the committee is trying to improve the habitat of the island. In 1974 the only established tree was elder; rabbits and salty winds proved a great discouragement to efforts in planting other species but now twenty-seven varieties are growing, with the willows doing particularly well.

Lyn Gallagher

Oystercatcher feeding

LISNABREENY

Near Cregagh, 2 miles S of Belfast [J367703]

One hundred and sixty-four acres of National Trust property lie on the very skirts of south-east Belfast. These lands exactly fit the aim of Octavia Hill, one of the national founders of the Trust in 1895, who wanted to safeguard 'open-air sitting rooms' for urban populations.

Fields edged with beech and hawthorn hedges fringe housing developments at the top of the Cregagh Road, and give extensive views over central Belfast. It is a favourite local Sunday afternoon pastime to climb the steep hill of the Rocky Road and pick out Belfast landmarks. An attractive glen path, which begins at the busy dual carriageway, takes the walker alongside a stream, through a mix of native trees growing on steep banks, into rural Co. Down and the grounds of Lisnabreeny House.

Lisnabreeny was given to the National Trust by Nesca Robb, of the well known Robb family who had a large department store at Castle Junction. Nesca Robb was an historian, a prose writer and poet, and perhaps her poem 'The Glen in January' is recalling Lisnabreeny . . .

Here, by the singing waters,
Moist ferns and mosses deep,
Though winter make the woods all bare,
Spring's greenness keep;

And frost-clear moonlight, falling
Over cascade and lin,
Still by that cool, and secret verdure
Is folded in.

A further walk through the grounds of the house leads past a new plantation of varied woodland in the old walled garden and cuts between fields up a long straight path, to a wide open space covered with gorse. From this point, 400 feet above sea level, there are fascinating views, and on a clear day the panorama takes in Belfast Lough, the Lagan valley and the land right around to the Mournes, Strangford Lough and the Ards Peninsula.

A little further on, the walk leads to a well preserved hill fort. There are dozens of these scattered about the Castlereagh Hills and a drive through the winding roads of this area will reveal many, often on a hill top, sometimes slashed in two, but nearly always crowned with a ring of trees. 'Lis' means fort but the word is slightly misleading. The simplest of these Dark Age remnants would have been a raised earthwork with a wooden palisade to keep out predators, human or otherwise, but they developed into fortified farmsteads, and this fort at Lisnabreeny would probably have had a simple clay dwelling within. It is approximately forty yards wide, with a rampart twelve feet high in some places, surrounded by a ditch about ten feet wide.

Lisnabreeny House was the first youth hostel in an Irish city when it was loaned to the Youth Hostel Association of Northern Ireland in 1938, but its hostelling days were short-lived and it was used for military purposes during the Second World War. A graceful, unpretentious building of the early nineteenth century, with an entrance flanked by Ionic columns, an elegant Diocletian window in an arched recess above the door, and a five-bay front sitting on a low podium, it was reconstructed in 1986–91 by Lagan College, Belfast's first religiously integrated school, run by the All Children Together movement.

Lyn Gallagher

MINNOWBURN BEECHES

At S end of Shaw's Bridge, Lagan river [J325684]

Only three miles from the centre of Belfast is the area known as the Minnowburn Beeches, 128 acres of naturally mixed countryside, with prime agricultural land, a fine stand of beech trees and riverside walks, in a part of south Belfast handsomely provided with public parks and open spaces.

Although the property is very close to the city and is well used by its inhabitants, it has changed little over the years, and is still frequented by small boys, using the traditional tools of sally rod and bent pin, to catch the minnows which give the stream its name. In some ways, of course, it has to change, because the soil in the steep banks, which is so good for sending the beeches up straight and tall, is not so good for holding them there. Some of the trees which have lasted since the first half of the nineteenth century are now vulnerable, and new young trees can be seen among the more ancient specimens; thus a mix of ages will ensure that the whole stand of trees will not disappear in one night of a 'big wind'. Beeches have been planted throughout the property, fringing the side of the roads, skirting a field, often 'nursed' by larches which can be removed once the young hardwoods are strong enough to survive on their own.

The Minnow Burn, or 'Purdy's Burn' as it is also known, rises in the Castlereagh Hills and meets the Lagan at a point just south of Shaw's Bridge. It is a clean stream in comparison with Belfast's polluted river, and it supports valuable wildlife.

This National Trust property is well used. It is a favourite place for photographers and artists; canoeists use the landing stage, and walkers and joggers the stiles and paths. A Save the Children Fund city farm brings rural realities within the reach of the urban population, and in 1969 a massive 'Pop for Peace' concert was held in a natural amphitheatre when no one else would give access to the organisers. Despite official National Trust misgivings, the young people gathered the litter themselves at the close, and no damage was done.

Lyn Gallagher

MOUNT STEWART

5 miles SE of Newtownards on the Portaferry road (A20) [J555701]

Mount Stewart, more than any other National Trust property in Northern Ireland, is a family creation. When Alexander Stewart bought the estate in 1744 it was the beginning of a process in which each generation brought its own ideas, enthusiasm, taste and resources to the house and gardens. Layer by layer, Mount Stewart has been moulded and enhanced, in a story which comes right up to the twentieth century.

It was Alexander's marriage to his cousin, Mary Cowan, an heiress with wealth from the East India Company, which increased the family fortune and led to the purchase of what was then Mount Pleasant. This generation of Stewarts is recalled in the splendid Chinese Export armorial service, with the Cowan coat of arms, which is displayed in cabinets in the hall of the present house. Alexander never established a significant dwelling here; his grandson, Charles, said that 'there was an old barn, with a few rooms added'.

Alexander's son, Robert, who became the 1st Marquess of Londonderry, ensured the position of the family through his ambition and wisdom. He was a responsible resident, an improving landlord, and a man of impeccable taste. It is to him that we owe that perfect little building, the Temple of the Winds, created by James 'Athenian' Stuart between 1782 and 1785; it is a small banqueting house and a landscape feature, standing on a high point overlooking Strangford Lough. It is exquisitely decorated with plasterwork by William Fitzgerald and marquetry by the carpenter John Ferguson.

Alexander and Robert are represented in the house by busts in the hall, and Robert and his brother, Alexander Stewart of Ards, both brought home, as souvenirs of the Grand Tour, important portraits of themselves by Batoni and Mengs. Robert chose the fine architect James Wyatt to begin work on remodelling the house, but Wyatt's plans were never executed. Instead Robert Stewart's energies and resources were channelled into ensuring that his son, another Robert, later Lord Castlereagh, was returned as MP for Co. Down; the election cost the family an estimated £30,000. In 1804 George Dance designed what is now the west wing of the house to replace a temporary structure.

The 1st Marquess had two famous sons whose personalties were quite different. Lord Castlereagh was a leading European statesman, who was British Foreign Secretary and an influential figure at the Congress of Vienna. He was also an unswerving advocate of unpopular policies at home. A private person, of great ability, he was a poor communicator, and he became an object of hatred in Ireland. The only major change which the National Trust made in the house was to identify Lord Londonderry's study as a 'Castlereagh Room'. Handsome cases hold leather-bound copies of the fascinating

The staircase at Mount Stewart, with George Stubbs' *Hambletonian*

Castlereagh and Londonderry papers, which were handed over to the Public Records Offices in Belfast and Durham.

Castlereagh's half-brother, Charles, who became the 3rd Marquess after the statesman's suicide in 1822, was quite different – flamboyant and extravagant. The 'Soldier Marquess', as he was called, firmly established the family when he married Frances Anne Vane Tempest, a double heiress with fortunes in Co. Antrim and in the coal mines of Co. Durham. It was this influx of funds which encouraged the building programme at Mount Stewart to go ahead, with plans by William Vitruvius Morrison. The new house, replacing everything except Dance's wing, was on a considerable scale, designed to impress, and was dominated by a large central hall lit by a dome, providing an area in which to display collections.

When Frances Anne first met Charles, her mother asked her what she thought of him. 'Not much,' she replied. 'He seemed finnikin, and looked as if he had false teeth.' But these first impressions mellowed and the couple were married in 1819, Castlereagh writing of his sister-in-law, 'She is not a beauty, but she is extremely well-looking, mild and intelligent . . . and for her time of life, she seems to have a great deal of decision and character.'

The couple became celebrated figures in Europe; they travelled widely and led a glittering life in the highest circles. Frances Anne had an intense friendship with Tsar Alexander, and Disraeli, who described her as 'half great lady, half ruffian', said that at the coronation of Queen Victoria she 'blazed among peeresses' and 'looked like an Empress'.

Mount Stewart owes many of its treasures to Charles and Frances Anne. The magnificent *Hambletonian*, the masterpiece by George Stubbs, depicts a racehorse which was owned by Frances Anne's father. The painting was exhibited at the Royal Academy in 1799, and hung at Wynyard in Durham, where the horse is buried. Furniture and *objets* were collected throughout Europe and brought back to Mount Stewart. In the drawing-room, for example, an enormous inlaid walnut writing desk of the Biedermeier period, and an earlier card table with a marquetry top, are both Austrian and were probably brought back by Charles, while Frances Anne contributed to the same room an eighteenth-century tea caddy with chinoiserie motifs. Perhaps the most spectacular piece of European collecting was the retrieval of the twenty-two chairs used at the Congress of Vienna. Each chair was later embroidered with one of the coats of arms of those present and of the country they represented, so it is possible to identify the chair of Talleyrand, Metternich and the Duke of Wellington among others.

On the death of Charles, his son Frederick Vane Tempest inherited the title; he complained that Mount Stewart had become run down and he spent some time putting things to right and supervising the erection of Scrabo Tower in memory of his father. He also contributed the neo-classical nudes by Lawrence Macdonald and the Carrara marble font which stand in the hall. He married Elizabeth, widow of the 6th Viscount Powerscourt. She was converted to the Roman Catholic faith by Cardinal Newman, and later built the Catholic

The dramatic colours and ornate furnishings of the Rome bedroom at Mount Stewart, seen as a reaction against the drabber Arts and Crafts movement of the turn of the century. Photograph by Peter Aprahamian, courtesy of the National Trust Photographic Library.

In the Italian Garden at Mount Stewart: from left, Nigel Marshall, head gardener, Lady Mairi Bury and National Trust gardens advisor Graham Stuart Thomas

church and school in Newtownards. The couple spent a considerable amount of time at Powerscourt, while in later years the 5th and 6th Marquesses used the London, Welsh or Durham homes in addition to Mount Stewart.

Nevertheless, it was during the time of the 6th Marquess that Mount Stewart enjoyed perhaps its most glittering occasion – the visit of King Edward and Queen Alexandra in 1903. Theresa, the 6th Marchioness, was a *grande dame* in the line of Londonderry hostesses. A scrapbook in the sitting-room documents the elaborate organisation which went into the royal visit, and records every detail – where the guests slept, how the rooms were arranged and what the band played. One menu reads like this:

The interior of the Temple of the Winds, Mount Stewart, designed by James 'Athenian' Stuart, with plasterwork by William Fitzgerald and marquetry by John Ferguson. Photograph by Peter Aprahamian, courtesy of the National Trust Photographic Library.

Dîner du 26 Juillet.

Tortue Claire.
Consommé de Volaille froid.
Petits Cendrillons de Soles en Aspic.
Saumon Ecossais, Sauce Hollandaise.
Timbales de Volaille à l'Ecarlate.
Cailles à la Demidoff.
Quartiers d'Agneau.
Jambon de York braisé au Madère.
Poussins rôtis.

83

Epinards à la Crème.
Parfait Esterhazy glacé et Fruits à la Melba.
Caviar et Biscuits au Parmesan.

The number of staff required to keep the important guests happy is equally impressive.

Sunday, July 26th. 1903.

Steward's Room.	Servant's Hall.
6. House Servants.	18. House Servants.
1. His Majesty's Valet.	4. Royal Footmen.
2. Her Majesty's Maid & Dresser.	2. Hired Footmen.
1. Princess Victoria's Maid.	2. Visiting Footmen.
2. Royal Detectives.	2. Pantry and Steward's Room Men.
1. Royal Footman. (Sergt. footman.)	8. Detectives.
4. Hired Waiters.	2. Boatmen.
1. Standard Reporter.	8. Firemen. (2 Drivers & 6 Firemen.)
2. G.P.O. Telegraphists.	42. Bandsmen.
1. Bandmaster. R.I.C.	2. Gate Attendants.
12. Valets.	1. Tent Man.
1. Lord Selborne's Messenger.	10. Dollars Men.
1. King's Messenger.	5. Motor Drivers.
1. Lady Dudley's Hairdresser.	1. Motor Washer.
6. Lady's Maids.	3. Electricians.
1. Post Clerk, from G.P.O. Belfast.	2. Plumbers.
1. Mr. Morris, clerk to Capt. Holdford.	2. Men helping in Hall.
	4. Carmen for Band.

Dining Room.	Lunch	34
"	Dinner	48
Steward's Room.		44
Servant's Hall.		118
Kitchen.		10

When Edith, wife of the 7th Marquess, came to Mount Stewart in the 1920s a new era dawned. She was a beautiful, talented and charming hostess, who was acclaimed in smart London society but who clearly had a warm affection for her Irish home. She made vast improvements to the house, adding the soft furnishings and the warm, rich colours, giving the place the comfortable atmosphere of an Edwardian house party. The leading names of society, of literature, the arts and politics, were entertained here. Sean O'Casey, for example, writes warmly in his autobiography of the kind reception he was given, and records that the Londonderrys 'sponsored' his trip to the United States.

Lady Londonderry's taste is best reflected in the drawing-room, with informal arrangements of sofas and armchairs mixing happily with formal furniture of an earlier period; soft warm creams and peach colours, huge bowls of pot-pourri, a well stocked jardinière, and alabaster and Carrara marble urns and vases fitted with electricity, giving a soft glow. Many of the bedrooms – called after European cities – reflect her taste, and were refurbished in the 1920s, when bathrooms were also installed. The Rome bedroom was decorated in 1961 by Lady Mairi Bury, who gave the house to the Trust.

Lady Londonderry's own sitting-room in the house is full of her personality and her interests: mementoes, books, photographs, workbaskets are everywhere, and so is a large, functional set of scales used to weigh out seeds, for if she is remembered for her transformation of the house, her work in creating the gardens has now deservedly gained an international reputation. When she first came to Mount Stewart on a visit in the winter some time before her husband succeeded to the property, she thought 'the house and surroundings the dampest, darkest and saddest place I had ever stayed in'. The first thing she did was to cut down the huge ilex trees which almost touched the house in places, and then she began to garden in the grand style. Mount Stewart's gardens combine formal terraces and informal glades; they blend classical proportions and Celtic whimsy; they mix pavilions, topiary, statuary and dovecotes. They are a scrapbook of Lady Londonderry's life and loves, and they are blessed by the temperate climate of the Ards Peninsula, sitting between Strangford Lough and the Irish Sea. Their strength is derived from Lady Londonderry's talent as a plantswoman, and her remarkable ability to collect specimen plants and to take advice.

The first garden to be laid out was the Sunken Garden to the north west of the house, a project started from the St Leger winnings by a horse called Polemarch. In late spring the garden is a blaze of vivid orange and yellow from the azalea *Coccinea speciosa*, with orange, yellow and blue herbaceous plants and bulbs. Purple clematis climbs above tree heaths which flank the paved steps, and climbing roses and honeysuckle trail through the pergola along the raised walk. Steps lead out to Mount Stewart's most idiosyncratic 'compartmentalised' garden, the Shamrock Garden, designed in the shape of Ireland's emblem, with the Red Hand of Ulster blazing in scarlet begonias and a splendid topiary Irish harp above it all, with a colour scheme of red flowering plants, in decorative beds and pots.

To the south west of the house is the Italian Garden, based partly on villas near Florence and Caprarola and on the garden of Lady Londonderry's mother at Dunrobin in Scotland. In high summer there is a magnificent array of roses and choice herbaceous plants in symmetrical beds laid out on the terrace. On stone pillars squatting, smiling monkeys, cast by local man Thomas Beattie, look out towards the ornamental pools and the clipped bays which, with the others around the house, were imported from Belgium in 1923, already grown to maturity, for less than £100. Beyond is the Spanish Garden, named after the Spanish tiles in the little pavilion and laid out to reflect, in the pattern of the pool and beds, a ceiling in the Temple of the Winds. It is planted with glaucous foliage and flowers and shrubs, including a delicate, foaming hydrangea of a soft, peachy colour.

The Mairi Garden follows the shape of a Tudor rose. Pretty in white and blue, its theme is that of 'Mary, Mary, quite contrary', for it is here that Lady Mairi Bury sat in her perambulator. A huge New Zealand cabbage tree (*Cordyline australis*) dominates one side, and there is a dovecote, a little fountain, and also 'pretty maids' (*Saxifraga granulata* 'Flore Pleno') and silver bells in the form of a variety of campanulas.

A path from the Mairi Garden leads to the Dodo Terrace, which recalls the atmosphere and style of the Ark Club, an élite society of First World War officers, politicians and friends who met at Londonderry House. All were given names of birds, beasts or mythological creatures, with Lady Londonderry, the hostess, known as Circe the Sorceress. Arthur Balfour was 'Arthur the Albatross', Churchill was 'Winston the Warlock', and so on. At Mount Stewart they have been re-created, with the ark itself, all cast in concrete and set among huge eucalyptus and majestic Irish yews. This whimsical society is also commemorated in the Trust's 'Ark Club Tea Room' inside Mount Stewart House. The decoration of the room derives its inspiration from the colour scheme of the 'Moscow' bedroom with its Chinese wall-paper, pink background and traditional willow-pattern-type birds, trees and flowers. Against this fantastic backdrop the aristocratic animals of the Ark Club disport themselves. Garden, house and history are thus brought to-gether in an amusing way by Naomi McBride, a local artist.

In contrast to the formal terraces are the natural 'wild' areas – the Lily Wood, and the Peace Garden, carefully planted meandering glades, mixing herbaceous plants, shrubs and exotic and native trees in perfect harmony. One of the most beautiful places in Mount Stewart is the lake. The romantic turrets among the trees rise from 'Tir Nan Og' – the land of the ever young – the private burial ground of the Londonderrys. The planting around the lake looks natural, yet it has been carefully contrived to display a long vista here, a specimen tree there, perfectly placed by the water's edge, a sweep of autumn colour planned to reflect in the lake, a walk among flowering shrubs with delicious heady scents in June, or the contours of treetops against a skyline.

Lyn Gallagher

MOURNE MOUNTAINS

[*J358277*]

The landscape of the Mourne Mountains is essentially romantic. Their fame does not depend on their height, but on their beauty, their strength and their power. They lie gracefully on the horizon when viewed from many parts of Co. Down and from day to day they always look different: swathed in bands of mist or standing out against a brilliantly clear sky; blanketed by clouds or windswept with small white sails skudding across a background of fields, walls and heath.

For many exiles the Mournes are best remembered by Percy French's ballad, but the Chinese poet Shelley Wang saw them

> . . . like a team of bears
> tumbling into the sea,
> the embroidered fields like a monk's patched cloak
> spreading their skirts to every door . . .

There are some fifty peaks in all, the highest of which is Slieve Donard, rising to 2,796 feet. It is only twelve miles as the peregrine falcon flies from Saint Donard's shrine on the top of Slieve Donard to the summit of Slieve Meen above Rostrevor, and it is only seven and a half miles across country, north to south, from Kinahalla to Knockshee. But what an area these prosaic measurements contain! And how much walking is there up and down the intervening slopes, for the oscillations of the Mournes are closer and steeper than most mountains in the British Isles.

The raven, as he squawks darkly across his hunting ground, can pick out no human being except perhaps an occasional rucksacked hiker on the Brandy Pad, the old smugglers' route that climbs steeply from the sea at Bloody Bridge, and having crossed into the sanctuary of the hills, winds discreetly on an even contour. During the eighteenth century and the first quarter of the nineteenth, the Mourne shore was a favourite place for smuggling, often via the Isle of Man. In addition to wines, spirits and tobacco, contraband included spices, tea, coffee, sugar, leather and silk, landed on the coast between Glasdrumman and Bloody Bridge and carried to Hilltown or Trassey Bridge. Like the modern hiker, these smugglers knew the importance of keeping on the contour.

The mountains were not always so empty. Eighteenth-century inland farmers brought their cattle up to their summer quarters in the Deer's Meadow and made a booley or summer village there, and according to E. Estyn Evans, sheep, too, were brought from the lowlands for 'the summer's run' to various locations, including Ballaghanery, which means 'the shepherds' pass'. And it is only about seventy years since the Happy Valley was populated by a few small tenant farmers. A deep glacial trough, this valley's waters rush down from the slopes of Slieve Muck, Carn, Slieve Loughshannagh, Doan and Ben Crom, and empty southwards between the precipitous sides of Binnian and the Mountain of the Goats. The Belfast Water Commissioners renamed it Silent Valley when they built their reservoir there.

A well-known feature in the Mournes is the massive granite wall, built between 1910 and 1922 by the Belfast Water Commissioners to define their catchment area. The Mourne Wall runs like a ribbon for twenty-two miles over the tops of fifteen mountains and encloses about 9,000 acres. The Mourne workmen walked to work every day and, as the wall progressed, their walks grew longer. Constructed of stones quarried on the mountains, the wall is, on average, five feet high and between two and a half feet and three feet at the base, tapering slightly towards the top; cement was not used except in a few difficult places.

Being a comparatively young group of mountains made of granite, with poor, acid soil and steep slopes, the Mournes do not have a rich flora, but there is much of interest nevertheless. You will find the small rosettes of the starry saxifrage; in a few rock crevices, the yellow rose-root; in one or two of the gravelly lakes, the pale lilac water lobelia. Much more widespread among the heather and boulders blue-black bilberries will be found in autumn, and on the summits the scarlet berries and evergreen leathery leaves of cowberry. The summits also have swards of moss and frequently also dwarf mountain willow; juniper occurs more sparingly. Much of the

The Mournes and the sea, from Newcastle beach

area is dominated by grassland, with mat grass abundant; among the other grasses is the tall wood fescue. There are many boggy stretches with bog asphodel, and also sundew, the species with the rosette of red leaves. Other damp sites yield sedges, including the slender-leaved sedge.

The elegant Irish hare is frequently seen in the hills; unlike its European counterpart, it does not turn white in winter. Occasionally a fox may be encountered, even high up in the hills, and smaller mammals such as wood mice and pigmy shrews may be found in wooded areas around the fringe; they provide a source of food for kestrels.

The most common bird is perhaps the meadow pipit, a shy bird which in spring will try to divert you from its nest in the mossy grass. In May and June the larks are in full song. An attractive seasonal visitor is the wheatear, and during the spring and summer it may be seen flitting from rock to rock around the Hare's Gap, or Pigeon Rock Mountain, named after the rock pigeons which favour it. Not far away, Eagle Mountain has a commanding view of the White Water with its patchwork of fields and white houses down to Kilkeel and the coast and its towering precipice has attracted the peregrine falcon from time to time.

Where the Mournes fall into the sea around the Bloody Bridge, the cliffs provide nesting grounds for fulmars, black guillemots and herring gulls. Linnets and stonechats can be seen among the whins. Out at sea, divers and grebes can be seen in winter, and auks, terns, gannets, cormorants and gulls in summer and autumn.

Strange things have been seen in the mists of Irish mountains. In Cronicum Scotorum we read of Irish horse-riders passing on the clouds in AD 851 and Lieutenant Murphy of the Ordnance Survey relates that he and his company, climbing Slieve Snaght in Co. Donegal in 1825, were 'shadowed in the clouds'. Such descriptions are almost certainly manifestations of the Brocken Spectre, a phenomenon first recorded in 1780 on Brocken, the highest peak of the Harz Mountains in Saxony. It is the magnified shadow of the observer, often surrounded by coloured bands, cast upon a bank of cloud in high mountain regions when the sun is low.

The Mournes are no exception. In the *Irish Mirror* of 1805 Dr Edgar tells of a similar observation recorded on Slieve Donard in 1795 and, more recently, the *Belfast News-Letter* reported the experience of two men early one morning in 1942 when mist was lying in strata on Slieve Foye:

> It was when we turned to look into the mist-filled glen above Rostrevor that we saw the spectre. The sun was climbing over the low hills to the east of us, for we were now on the top of Slieve Martin. It was difficult to think that those gigantic shadows, surrounded by a band of the prismatic colours, were thrown by our small selves. However, when we raised our hands, so did the spectre; when we took off our hats and waved them, so did the shadows.

In her book *The Mountains of Ireland* (1959) Dr Pochin Mould describes how she saw the spectre from the top of Bearnagh. She had climbed the mountain from the Hare's Gap and, with the sun behind her, looked across the glen below the ridge of Bearnagh to the opposite slope of Meelmore which was still veiled in cloud. On that cloud she first saw a small circular rainbow, and then, as the sun gained strength, the full Brocken Spectre became visible: as she stood leaning on the Waterworks wall, she saw her shadow, encircled by concentric rainbows, projected across the valley on to a bank of mist.

David McFarland, a Belfast solicitor and scout leader, sighted the spectre on 27 December 1991 when he and another troop leader walked into dense mist. They were engaged on a search and rescue exercise at the back of the Mournes and were making their way up towards Pierce's Castle. Suddenly it cleared; the sun was low and beneath was a carpet of mist. The air was full of water droplets, plainly visible as they caught the rays of the sun. They stopped and then they saw the spectre.

> It was cast on the layer of mist over the valley of the tributary to Shanky's river, about 200 yards away. Because of the short distance the shadow was not large, about twice my size. Surrounded by a halo of the prismatic colours.

The Trust's Mourne Coastal Path follows the line of the sea for three quarters of a mile south of the council carpark at Bloody Bridge, but also climbs up beside the Bloody river at one of the best access points by foot into the heart of the Mournes. The Bloody Bridge is a single-span bridge,

Walkers on Bearnagh, with Slieve Donard and Commedagh in the background – courtesy of David McFarland

constructed in the eighteenth century or earlier. It derives its name from a massacre of a number of Protestants of Newry, including their minister, ordered by Sir Conn Magennis during the 1641 rebellion. Nearby, on the sea side of the road to Annalong, are the ruins of the ancient church of Ballaghanery, which was one of several chapels attached to the mother church at Kilkeel. The foundations of a nave and a small chancel have been traced. An interesting feature was the semi-circular chancel arch which was still standing in the 1930s and has now been rebuilt in rudimentary form. Near the river on the north side, the Trust maintains an unobtrusive pebble path for about a quarter of a mile. Beyond that, if you want to climb Donard, make your own way up to the Saddle and the wall, and then climb north along the wall to the summit.

The Trust has now acquired the large northern portion of Donard up to the summit, including Thomas's Mountain, Millstone Mountain and the whole of the upper Glen river valley with the Eagle Rock cliffs. The area also takes in the top and eastern half of Slieve Commedagh, the Pot of Pulgarve, the eastern half of Shan Slieve and the whole of Slievenamaddy. In fact, viewed from Newcastle, the Trust area forms the whole of the mountain landscape above the Donard Lodge plantation. To climb Donard from Newcastle, walk up from Donard Park, along the Glen river, and at the edge of the woods cross the stile and follow the Glen river to the col between Commedagh and Donard, then follow the wall south-south-east to the summit.

Though so compact in area, these mountains are extensive enough to be dangerous for climbers and walkers when conditions deteriorate, for the heart of the Mournes is a wilderness, cut off from the outside world. But on a misty day you can always wander among the foothills and talk to the farmers or search for the abundant archaeological remains. On the fringe, too, there are two areas of great beauty: Tollymore Forest Park, which provides a variety of sylvan walks for young and old; and to the south-west, the wonderful fjord of Carlingford Lough, where the mountains roll down to its warm shores, this time more slowly and in luxuriance and peace.

Dick Rogers

91

MURLOUGH NATIONAL NATURE RESERVE

2 miles NW of Newcastle [J410350]

Murlough, Co. Down, is as beautiful as it is interesting, and it was because of its scientific importance that it was recognised as Northern Ireland's first nature reserve. Sand-dunes merge into heathland, with the calm, narrow lagoon of Dundrum Inner Bay to the north and the wide sweep of the Irish Sea to the south. In the distance is the imposing profile of the Mourne Mountains, while closer by, among old woods, stands the round Norman keep of Dundrum Castle.

The large sand-dune system was built up at the end of the last ice age and it is one of three significant systems in Northern Ireland. Early man found the dunes an attractive place to live, and disturbed sand now occasionally uncovers evidence of dwellings and pottery, implements and weapons from the Stone and Bronze Ages.

John de Courcy invaded the area in 1177 and the Normans established their presence there at the beginning of the thirteenth century. They brought rabbits with them and that set the pattern for centuries of vegetation at Murlough. Rabbits were used as a crop, farmed in warrens and providing a useful source of meat and hides; and warrening continued for centuries, more recently under the control of the Downshire family who built Murlough House at the north end of the property. Rabbits contribute to the production of very short turf, in which wild flowers flourish but in which shrubs and trees are allowed no opportunity to grow.

About 1900, Lord Downshire, concerned about the sand blowing around Murlough House, introduced sea buckthorn in an effort to stabilise the dunes. Sea buckthorn is an attractive plant with bright orange berries enjoyed by birds, and at first it did a good job as a stabiliser in a limited area, but when myxomatosis decimated the rabbit population in the 1950s, the sea buckthorn – because the seeds and young shoots were able to grow – became rampant and started to invade the dunes. Sycamore, too, began to colonise further areas.

In the 1950s the landscape of Murlough attracted the attention of the Forest Service, which saw in this seemingly barren site an ideal place for commercial planting and laid out a trial plot of 1,000 Corsican pines; the trees grew well and are still to be seen, a landmark on the skyline. At this stage there were protests from conservationists and eventually in 1967 the property was acquired by the National Trust. It was specifically the dunes which needed protection. Sand-dunes, with the complicated system of wild life which they support, are extremely fragile, and in the 1960s the Murlough dunes were already becoming degraded and eroded, with the development of recreational pressures and the spread of the caravan sites near Newcastle. The fragility of the property, combined with the needs and effects of the visitor, has made Murlough the Trust's most intensely managed coastal or countryside property in Northern Ireland.

Jo Whatmough became the first warden in 1967, and since that time she has developed a sustained programme of management to help visitors enjoy Murlough National Nature Reserve while causing minimum damage to the property itself. The first priority was to control access to the main high dunes, so a large sensitive zone was made a restricted area crossed by specially designed paths. Threaded fir board-walks are employed in some places, simple wire-netting in others. Fertiliser is used to encourage vegetation in selected areas, and buckthorn is held down with wire as a thatch to deter walkers from worn patches which need regeneration. The management strategy of Murlough is based on assessing what the visitors want to do and trying to fulfil their needs in the way most appropriate for the property. For example, it is unrealistic to expect a party of small children, out for the day to the seaside and coming to a beach edged by sandhills, to resist the temptation to slide and jump. So one big dune has been sacrificed for this traditional seaside occupation.

Another instinctive human reaction on a windswept beach is to dig in to a sheltered bank of sand, which of course would be damaging to the structure of the dune system, so the wardens have constructed little 'family nests', scooped out of the low fore-dunes and lined with wire and saplings, perfect for windless picnics. In the same spirit, carefully sited bridle paths for horses have been designated. However, because the efforts to ensure that Murlough National Nature Reserve is an enjoyable place to visit result in increased satisfaction and return visits, the volume and intensity of visitor pressure also increases.

Marrying conservation and amenity requires a carefully planned and sophisticated approach to education and interpretation. Murlough has long been regarded as an important site by botanists and zoologists, and the fact that it was originally managed jointly with Queen's University, Belfast, reflects the academic importance of the site; it is well known to groups of advanced students as a good case for field-study exercises, but the wardens have been well aware that most visitors to the reserve have only the haziest idea about the value of a dune system. The interpretation work began gently, with simple display boards along the walks indicating local points of interest, such as a nearby badger set. Now there is an ambitious and well used interpretative programme. An information centre, guided walks, leaflets and residential weekends make Murlough one the liveliest nature reserves in the country.

The wardens have no doubt that the best way to communicate is on a one-to-one basis, so visitors can be led to the best places to get face to face with creepy crawlies, to discover the truth about life in the mud, to watch seals, or to see the 'anvil' which hooded crows use to smash the mussels they have gathered in the Inner Bay. By all these means the Trust hopes that a gradual understanding and respect for the dunes will be built up.

To understand the importance of Murlough it is best to imagine the whole

area under some twenty-five feet of water about 8,000 years ago just after the ice age, when pebbles left by the retreating ice were thrown up by the advancing sea to form storm beaches, now under the dunes. By 5,000 years ago the oldest dunes were well developed, but towards the sea these were covered by fresh dunes, rising to a height of a 120 feet or so, and this last change may have taken place as recently as the twelfth to fourteenth centuries, a period of storm conditions.

The younger dunes and shoreline shingle are richly covered by plants in most summers, with sandwort, saltwort, sea rocket and the rarer frosted orache. In the fore-dunes are sea couch and marram grass. Because the more stable dunes on the landward side are rich in lime, a characteristic series of plants flourishes here – mosses, spurges, the bird's-foot-trefoil, orchids, carline thistle and viper's bugloss. The change of species continues with the development of the dunes as rain leaches out the lime, and increased acidity favours a new vegetation where heaths and heathers, burnet roses, bracken, primroses, tormentil, bluebells and lady's bedstraw flourish over a large area.

As the plants vary, so of course does the habitat for animals. There is a wealth of moths and of butterflies, including the meadow brown, common blue and the rare dark green fritillery and grayling; study into other insects continues. Badgers and foxes flourish and the common lizard, Ireland's only reptile, has been seen here.

Because of its varied habitat, Murlough National Nature Reserve has a wide range of birdlife. The heath and woodland areas support skylark, meadow pipit, sandmartin, stonechat, wheatear, willow warbler, grasshopper warbler, whitethroat, blackcap, linnet, bullfinch, reed bunting and pheasant, as well as sparrow hawk, kestrel and long-eared owl. In the late spring Murlough is alive with the sound of the cuckoo, and in winter flocks of fieldfares, thrushes and redwings gather.

Summer is not a good time for watching the birds of the Inner Bay. The great change in tidal levels makes it a difficult area for nesting for most species, but some birds do breed here. Shelduck nest down disused rabbit holes and provide an opportunity for birdwatchers to see twice a day, morning and night, 'the changing of the guard' when the male escorts the female down to the shore to feed during incubation. Moorhen also nest around the Inner Bay along with mallard and kingfisher. Although the red-breasted merganser can be seen here nearly all year round, flocks of up to 400 arrive offshore to moult, reaching their peak in July and August, when the males exchange their glossy green, black and white plumage for a dull reddish brown like the females.

The bay is rich in fish, including sand eels which attract the terns, coming from Carlingford and Strangford Loughs to feed. There is some competition for these fish, which bury themselves in the mud or the sand, both from man and from the Murlough foxes which have been seen digging them out at low tide. Gulls, cormorants and shags are common in the bay. Sometimes gannets travel from their breeding grounds in Scotland and Wales to feed, crash diving from a height of forty-five metres.

In winter the mergansers can still be seen in appreciable numbers quite close to shore. The common scoter prefers to be further out and the velvet scoter occurs in very small numbers; identification of this rarity is difficult and may require a telescope. Razorbills and guillemots are winter visitors, as are small numbers of red-throated and great northern divers, and puffins and little auks have been recorded. Waders may be seen on the mudflats of the estuary and there are plenty of gulls about the bay throughout winter.

Lyn Gallagher

THE NORTH COAST

From Runkerry [C935435] to Carrick-a-Rede [D062450]

As a small boy I was brought to see the Giant's Causeway and I was disappointed that Finn McCool, that great giant, had not done better; the piles of hexagonal stones were not large enough and their continuation at Staffa in Scotland seemed very far away. When I later read Dr Johnson's comment that the Causeway was worth seeing but not worth going to see I was inclined to agree with him. But I have never ceased to wonder at the great cliffs that rise in pillared majesty above the Causeway and stretch away to the east, rising and falling, above the sea all the twenty miles to Fair Head.

The Causeway attracted so many visitors in the eighteenth and nineteenth centuries that, like the Lakes of Killarney, it built up a small industry. There was an old woman looking after the wishing well and there were jarveys and boatmen, and huts and stalls for souvenirs. There were also gates, and an entrance charge was made. In 1962 the Trust removed the gates and huts, and admitted the public free of charge. The less pleasant of the two hotels on the cliff, the Royal, was pulled down, a Trust information centre opened, and a small café provided. Now the Trust occupies part of a larger centre built by Moyle District Council in 1986, where the cultural and natural history of the Causeway coast is exhibited. There is an expanded Trust shop and restaurant, and educational facilities are provided.

There was at one period considerable pressure to build a road to the top of Aird Snout, a headland overlooking the Causeway, but the Trust successfully resisted this on the grounds of its intrusion into the landscape. To help invalids and the infirm to get down to the Causeway, the access path was strengthened sufficiently to enable the Trust to operate a shuttle service by minibus.

When the Trust acquired the Causeway and its approaches it started to obtain access from the farmers along the cliffs and shores. The Ulster farmer loves his land and farms the headlands right to the cliff edge, either by sheep or cattle-grazing or in barley. Where the farmer would not sell the strip of coast or cliff the Trust negotiated a covenant or agreement with him and provided fencing and stiles. In this way the Trust completed a path from Runkerry (one and a half miles west of Causeway Head) to Carrick-a-Rede, a distance of about twelve miles. In 1963 the International Voluntary Service cleared paths over two miles to Hamilton's Seat and extended the under-cliff path and fencing. Since then the rest of the work has been done by the Trust with the help of government schemes, largely using unemployed countrymen whose native skill accounts for the excellent finish of the stonework and step-making. In many places hexagonal stones appear in the steps; this is not a philistine use of the Causeway stones, for they came from an inland quarry.

The place names of this coast are particularly evocative. The older name

Work on the cliff path at the Giant's Causeway

Basalt formations in the
Grand Causeway

of the Giant's Causeway was Clachanafomhaire, the stepping stones of the Fomorians, the small dark people who inhabited Ireland before the Gaelic-speaking peoples arrived. The Stookans are stacks of rock, like stacks of corn or flax, the same Irish word being used. Port na Callaigh is the port of the old woman, while Port na Traghan is the port of lamentation – so called from a moaning sound made by the wind through a fissure in the rock. Bengore is the peak of the goats, and Portmadadh Ruadh is the port of the red dog, i.e. the fox.

A group of place names had Spanish references and in 1968 these came alive. It was known that in October 1588 the *Gerona*, one of four galleasses in the Spanish Armada, laden with men and treasure, had sunk off the Causeway. Many bodies were washed up in an inlet east of the Causeway called Port-na-Spaniagh. In 1968 the *Gerona*'s story was pieced together by the Belgian underwater explorer Robert Stenuit. On an Ordnance Survey map he found 'Spaniard Rock', 'Spanish Cave' and 'Port-na-Spaniagh'. Deciding to trust local names, obviously handed down by generations of fisherfolk, he searched the seabed in these areas. He found nothing at Port-na-Spaniagh, or at Spanish Cave, but at Lacada Point (lacada meaning 'slab'), a large flat-topped point between those two inlets, he made the first important find which led to the recovery of the valuable *Gerona* treasure now lodged in the Ulster Museum, Belfast.

Bold cliffs of black basalt, from Runkerry to Dunseverick, are varied by white limestone at Port Braddan, White Park Bay and Ballintoy Harbour. The black cliffs show the sequence of the successive lava-flows, with a red band in the middle which marks a long pause in volcanic activity. White Park Bay is in limestone, but out at sea stacks of black rock rise from the water, showing how the surface of the land has cracked and portions have dropped down hundreds of feet as a result of disturbance.

On the coast there is an abundance of wild flowers. You may remember most the blaze of whin and broom, but on the high tableland you will find the cross-leaved heath, ling and blaeberry, and the violet flower of the carnivorous butterwort. The rocky shore supports sea aster, sea-lavender and sea pink. In more protected parts there are red campion, bird's-foot-trefoil, silverweed, lady's bedstraw and sheep's-bit-scabious. A Scottish influence can be traced in the presence of the wood crane's-bill, the wood cow-wheat and the tea-leaved willow. This stretch of coast offers much besides: the 'pruck' of the raven, the gruff cry of the chough; the sight of the kestrel, sparrow hawk and peregrine falcon; razorbills and guillemots nesting on the cliff edges; puffins in burrows; black guillemots tumbling in the sea below; and the ever-present fulmar gliding on the cliff updraughts, master of the air.

The cliff path starts from Runkerry round the less spectacular cliffs to the west of Causeway Head. Down low, the Trust has reconstructed the Brenther slip. Two caves, Pigeon Rock and Runkerry, are accessible only from the sea, but the long narrow Portcoon Cave can also be entered from the land by a side passage. (The entrance to this passage is at high water mark at the end of the

lower path to the Portcoon inlet.)

The path climbs up to Weir's Snout and Aird Snout, and as it continues between Aird Snout and Benbane Head many dykes can be seen. Their dark dolerite rock is very hard and resistant. They can be seen on the foreshore at Port Noffer (the Giant's foot), Port Reostan and Port-na-Spaniagh, while another cuts through the basalt above Port na Tober (the port of the well). Fine hexagonal basalt columns at Portfad and Bengore can be seen after you pass the magnificent series of bays, amphitheatres and stacks that make up the Causeway. The path is on top of the middle basalt layers that contain the typical hexagonal columns; the lower basalts have no columns. The two series, lower and middle, are separated by the very distinctive reddish interbasaltic bed, along which the lower cliff path runs. This layer is the result of the weathering of the top flow of the lower basalts, which took place during a period of quiescence in volcanic activity. The bed is thirty to forty feet thick and contains fossil plants.

Portfad and Port Moon are still actively used for salmon fishing. The net used is known as a 'bag' net, a Scottish invention introduced to north Antrim in the 1830s. After these ports the path comes to Benadanir (the Dane's peak), to Portnahooagh (port of the cave) and Port na Hastul.

Dunseverick Castle, like other castles on the north coast, depended for defence on being perched at the edge of a promontory. Their names –Dunseverick, Dunluce, Dunanynie – suggest that these sites were in occupation long before the days of castles, and formed the promontory forts of older peoples. The pear-shaped rock on which the ruin of Dunseverick Castle stands was fortified from earliest times. Its name, Dún Sobhairce, is said in the *Annals of the Four Masters* to be derived from the chieftain who first fortified it. One of the five roads that radiated from Tara terminated here and the name occurs in many of the ancient Irish tales. It was stormed by the Danes in 870 and 924. It became the focal point in the McDonnells' kingdom of Dalriada which covered north Antrim and Argyllshire.

The path continues from Dunseverick round the coast past stacks and tiny inlets from Portnaweelan, the port of Dunseverick village, to the Sandy Ope (ope, meaning a bay, is a word of Norse origin), Portninish, the March Foot, Portnabrock (the badger's port), Portachornan and Portacallan. It passes Templastragh (the church of the flame), goes through Port Braddan, a very pleasant fishing village, and so enters White Park Bay. This is a magnificent natural amphitheatre of limestone, with a mile of golden strand, flanked on the west by Port Braddan's snug harbour and on the east by a 'raised beach' (with caves) leading on to Ballintoy Harbour. On the top of a small hillock near the centre of the bay is a small circular cairn thirty-six feet in diameter. Two Neolithic sites have been explored, one just west south west of this cairn and the other near the east end of the bay. Some of Ireland's first inhabitants made their homes here five or six thousand years ago. Their kitchen middens have yielded large quantities of flints and pottery. During archaeological excavations in the Potter's Cave on the 'raised beach' in the 1930s a clay figurine four inches high was found, and is believed to be the only 'mother goddess'-type figure ever to be found in Ireland.

The kitchen middens yielded many bones including those of the great auk. This was a cousin of the razorbill and the guillemot, and like the penguin it had rudimentary wings and stood about three feet high. The only known Irish specimen is preserved in the museum in Trinity College, Dublin; the species became extinct in 1844. On the grassy slopes in spring there are masses of primroses and wild violets and through the summer can be found the maritime orache, the purple carrot broomrape and a profusion of the lovely blue meadow crane's-bill; the grass of Parnassus is plentiful in its dwarf form (*Condensata*).

In 1939 the small white cottage in the centre of the bay was a youth hostel and the Youth Hostel Association of Northern Ireland raised a public subscription to buy the surrounding farm which consisted of 179 acres. The target was met with help from the Pilgrim Trust and the bay was handed to the National Trust just at the start of the Second World War. Groups of islets, including Long Gilbert, Carricknafurd and Island Lean have since been

Carrick-a-Rede, showing the rope-bridge and the fishery

acquired by the Trust, as has the larger offshore Sheep Island, a perpendicular stack with a flat grassy top. This is a great breeding ground for ten species of seabird, including cormorant, razorbill and guillemot, but for some years it was infested by rats. However, the Army and the Marines landed National Trust wardens on the island by helicopter to lay poison in suitable places, and the birds are now breeding in peace.

You will have to make a slight detour by road, through the village of Ballintoy, to get to Larrybane (the ancient white site). This was a magnificent headland of white limestone which appeared in one of Paul Henry's best known paintings. Owing to the weakness of planning law in the 1950s the headland was quarried away, but the Trust acquired the land and also the neighbouring basalt quarry and has made this stretch of coast available to the public, with an information point, lavatories and an overnight camping area. A fishery is still in operation there.

The track goes on by the cliff path to the exciting island of Carrick-a-Rede, and its rope-bridge. There has been a rope-bridge here for over 200 years, but in earlier times it had only a single hand-rope. It was to reach this important fishery that the bridge was first erected. Before 1830 the fishermen used a fixed draft net, but in the 1830s the bag net was introduced. Most of the salmon are going westwards, trying to return to the Bann or the Bush. Entering the bay below Carrick-a-Rede (the rock in the road, i.e. the road of the salmon), they do not swim through the narrows below the bridge, but are deflected northwards by the island into the net which the fishermen set daily (Monday to Friday) in the fishing season.

Dick Rogers

PATTERSON'S SPADE MILL

3 miles E of Templepatrick on the Belfast–Antrim road (A6) [J262855]

Patterson's Spade Mill at Templepatrick, Co. Antrim, was acquired by the Trust with every machine intact, with shavings on the floor, and shafts standing ready to be fitted to spade, shovel or fork. The fact that this workplace was the last surviving working water-driven spade mill in Ireland and complete in every detail made it a very significant site.

The National Trust commissioned the artist Jack Crabtree to paint the mill, before the Trust began the job of restoring the building and accomplishing the difficult task of marrying a working environment with accessibility to the public. He was struck by a sense of a workplace just vacated:

> What I was looking at was a situation that the lads making the spades had left at the end of an ordinary working day . . . the fact that in this day and age something which is really medieval in character, full of early industrial revolution machinery, remained intact . . . spades, shovels, forks, beautiful pieces of sculpture – the pride the men must have had in turning out objects of great physical beauty and yet working implements.

The Pattersons handed down the art of spade-making from generation to generation. John Patterson was the fourth successive oldest son to be engaged in spade-making when he moved to Antrim from Tyrone just after the First World War, attracted by the good water supply for powering the turbine. His grandson describes the importance of the hierarchical line:

> There are no gauges or measurements for making a spade, a piece of steel four inches by two inches by three quarters of an inch can be made into any type of spade. At the last count there were 171 different types of spade throughout all of Ireland, and for a man to know all those different types of spade, with no template, just shows the skill involved, and the task always fell to my father, because he was the oldest brother. It was a hierarchical line. My grandfather learned from his father, my father learned from my grandfather, and just as the older men passed away, so the younger men came up the line.

When John Patterson was interviewed for the BBC Home Service in 1940, he was asked about the different types of spades which were made.

> Our work ranges from light spades only about eight inches long for flower gardens up to the big mountain drain spades which I daresay few of you have ever seen. They're seventeen inches wide and seventeen inches long and are roughly heartshaped. They're used for cutting drains up in the sheep country. Another spade for a special purpose is the turf

spade – this is what we call a wing – really another blade – forged in one piece with the rest of the spade but at right angles to it. It's used in the bogs for cutting out the neat blocks of peat that you have seen stacked up to dry.

The tilt, or trip, hammer at the heart of the mill – courtesy of the Patterson family

Blades ready for fitting to shafts at Patterson's Spade Mill – courtesy of the Patterson family

The farmers in different districts use different spades. This depends partly on the work or the ground they're required for, but far more often, I think, on custom. For instance, in Co. Fermanagh they use a very long, narrow spade, only about five inches wide with a sharp bend in it. In Kilkeel, in the south of Co. Down, the spade they like tapers at the end and has a long shaft with no hilt – and everyone on this side of the water has heard of this description of a man that was a bit down in the mouth, 'He'd a face on him as long as a Lurgan spade.'

At the heart of the spade mill is the tilt, or trip, hammer. Patterson's trip hammer is about five hundredweight and water-powered, and each spade is forged in one piece. The device, designed to stamp or beat, was in use in Ireland from the seventeenth century, but when the population rose in the nineteenth century, local blacksmiths could not cope with the growing demand. A greater variety of spades was needed for the extended cultivation of areas which were not suitable for ploughing. At the peak of the activity over forty sites were recorded in the north-east corner of Ireland, but most spade mills collapsed after the Great Famine of 1845–9.

The Pattersons evolved systems to suit new conditions very gradually. When machines needed new parts, they tended to bring them in from cannibalised machines which they heard about on a network of communication

105

from all over the country. For example, when the mill had to be handled by one man, some smaller pieces of machinery were introduced, which made the work lighter; a mechanical cutter replaced a hand guillotine; and an electrically powered sander replaced a machine which had been water-powered. The old coke furnace, with three fires in the finishing shop and one in the main hall, disappeared when an oil-fired system was installed in accordance with new clean-air laws. In essence, however, so little has changed that a spade-maker from the 1920s could find his way about the workshop blindfold.

Members of the family recall the warmth of the mill – and the noise. Apart from painting the spades or pasting on the labels, everything else was noisy, as the massive trip hammer went down onto hot hard steel, slightly softened by the heat, or a hand hammer beat the plates to the right thickness, or to fashion the right bend – it was metal on metal. The wooden lathe whined as the square shafts were turned into rounds; and when it was in operation, the grinding of the sander was heightened with 'belts going and wheels going and water coming past'.

Prospective buyers who turned down the lane to buy a tool found a courteous and friendly welcome, combined with a justifiable pride in product, from a family who had very strong Christian principles. An early advertisement read:

> Reputation puts a seal upon any article of manufacture.
>
> To uphold a 'good reputation' the producer must be square and sound in business methods, ever alert to improve whenever possible, and always to acknowledge mistakes and to profit by them.
>
> W.G. Patterson & Sons is the name of excellence which we have for years striven to achieve, and we are to-day 'on the jump' to hold and improve our years of endeavour. Whenever you buy our Specialities you may rest assured you are buying the best that human endeavour can accomplish.

Lyn Gallagher

STEEL SPADE
HAND MADE
Guaranteed

Phone:
32227

"CALL A SPADE
A SPADE"

W.G. PATTERSON & SONS
TEMPLEPATRICK
CO. ANTRIM NORTHERN IRELAND

PORTSTEWART STRAND

[C720360]

'Portstewart, popularly known as the "Health Mecca" lies in a sheltered situation facing the west, and overlooking one of the most beautiful bays in Northern Ireland. Protected from the bitter east winds, the air here is delightfully cool and soft, with just enough crispness to produce a delightful sense of exhilaration.' So enthused the writer of the Ulster Tourist Development Association's guide of 1929. It was the reputation of its health-giving airs which first brought holidaymakers to Portstewart, but when a local landowner refused to let the railway pass over his land, because of his fears of the rowdy element it would bring with it, Portstewart stood still while Portrush developed into the north coast's most important resort.

Thackeray enjoyed Portstewart in 1842, but he laughed at the 'demure heads in crimped caps peeping over blinds' at him. 'The sea is not more constant roaring there, than scandal is whispering,' he reported in his *Irish Sketch Book* (1842).

The twentieth-century motorcar brought a much more mobile tourist and Portstewart Strand, with its firm sands, became one of the few places to which Ulster families could drive and enjoy picnics and recreation without having to leave the car. The strand can accommodate up to 1,200 cars on a hot day, and for about fifteen years there was much anxiety about the state of the beach, and more particularly about the survival of the dunes which were being run threadbare by the criss-cross paths of motorbikes. At last it was agreed that the National Trust should take over the strand, and despite the fact that it is almost a contradiction in terms for the National Trust to allow cars on to a beach which is to be protected, it was decided to allow this traditional practice to continue, although motorbikes were banned from the first day of National Trust management. Wardens sleep on the site to ensure vigilant enforcement of this rule.

Portstewart is a stunning strand: a rocky outcrop, overlooked by hotels and houses, gives it one boundary; the training walls of the Bann provide the other. To the west is the romantic profile of the Mussenden Temple, clearly etched against the skyline, with the Donegal hills fading into the distance. The links of Portstewart Golf Course run along the back of the dunes to the south east, while the bracing waters of the Atlantic, which are generally good for bathers, can deliver waves on a grand enough scale to attract surfers. The whole three miles of the strand are edged by dunes. The further they are from the popular end of the beach near the road, the better preserved they are, and the change in vegetation is noticeable. The same variation can be seen as the dunes run in from the sea. The fore-dunes suffer erosion through the wear and tear by beach-users but it seems that few visitors wish to penetrate too far into the sandhills. The Trust keeps a close watch on the effect of the visitor on the dunes, and paths have been designated to allow walkers and anglers to get through to the Bann.

Portstewart's sand-dunes had an important and intriguing role to play in the great gold ornaments trial of 1893. A man ploughing at Broighter, near Limavady in Co. Londonderry, came across some beautiful Celtic gold ornaments, including a torc, a necklace and an exquisite little gold boat complete with oars, and they were sold to the British Museum. A complicated legal case ensued, revolving around the 'treasure trove' principle, when the Royal Irish Academy tried to bring the treasures back to Ireland. Were they hidden at Broighter, or deposited as a votive offering to a sea god? The British Museum wished to prove that they had been cast overboard and subsequently found on dry land which had been lifted up to form a 'raised beach'. Robert Lloyd Praeger, the writer, geologist and botanist, and antiquarian and archaeologist George Coffey were asked by the Royal Irish Academy to prove that this geological uplift had been of a much earlier time, probably Neolithic. After much searching, they finally found the evidence they were looking for in the hollows of the dunes at Portstewart. Undisturbed Neolithic land surfaces, with implements and pottery, were found to go down to a point two feet above the high water mark, and so they were able to prove to the judge's satisfaction that the objects were buried, not lost. The case was won, and these most precious and beautiful objects were returned to the National Museum in Dublin.

Lyn Gallagher

ROUGH FORT

1 mile W of Limavady on the Derry road (A2) [C658230]

The earliest National Trust property in Northern Ireland, given in 1937 by Marcus McCausland, then Chairman of the Trust's Northern Ireland Committee, stands to the south of the Limavady–Derry road. Rough Fort is a ring fort, a farmstead of about 1,000 years ago. There are estimated to have been more than 30,000 of these forts in Ireland, and this one is complete and substantial. It is crowned with an imposing ring of trees – Scots pine, oak and beech –which make it a landmark in this part of Co. Londonderry.

Generally the earthen bank of a ring fort would have been built by using material dug out of the ditch, or fosse, on the outside and piled up on the inside. The fosse was often filled with water and crossed by a causeway, with an entrance gap in the earthwork. In the case of Rough Fort the structure is bivallate, or twin-banked.

Rough Fort has never been excavated, but where archaeologists have investigated similar sites they have found evidence that these ring forts were occupied over a considerable period of time, occasionally as late as the Middle Ages. Examination of post holes has given experts some idea of the kind of structure which would have been built inside the fort. At Rough Fort the banks were formed mostly of earth, not stones (in which case the structure would more strictly be known as a cashel), and the dwelling within would have been a wooden, or mud-and-wattle, thatched farmhouse. The rest of the enclosure was a sort of farmyard, and the earth bank, which acted as a protection against wolves and marauders, may have had a wooden palisade around the top.

Lyn Gallagher

A view of Rough Fort as it might have looked around 1,000 years ago (Artist D. Crone, copyright Ulster Museum)

ROWALLANE

1 mile S of Saintfield on the Downpatrick road (A7) [J409575]

Rowallane is a garden for all seasons and for all people, with appeal both for the connoisseur of rare plants and for those who just like to wander through a beautiful landscape. Although late spring may find Rowallane at its most spectacular, it is a fascinating place to visit in summer, too, when part of its attraction is a fine herbaceous display in the Walled Garden. Autumn sees the rich reds, russets, golds and browns in banks or single flames of colour, and a heavy frost or a fall of crisp snow will highlight the fine conifers and specimen trees throughout the garden.

In 1903 Hugh Armytage Moore inherited the Saintfield property from his uncle, the Revd John Moore, who had planted shelter belts of mixed woodland, had constructed a walled garden, improved the house and added the stableyard. He had also started to plant conifers in the Pleasure Grounds, had set the rhododendron 'Altarclarense' along the drive and had added the idiosyncratic stone seats, cairns and ornaments to the avenue. When Hugh Armytage Moore took over then, some progress had been made, but Rowallane was still an unlikely landscape in which to create one of the great gardens of the British Isles. A thin, peaty soil on Co. Down drumlin country seemed to fight a losing battle with the whinstone outcrops, but a sympathetic understanding of the quality of the landscape, together with Hugh Armytage Moore's great skill as a plantsman, have made Rowallane unique. The plants hug the contours of the hills and valleys, and the outcrops are perfect natural rock gardens.

Rowallane takes full advantage of its surroundings: a view of countryside will open up, a dry stone wall will be drawn quite naturally into the garden, or a bank of shrubs will easily turn back on itself in a dog leg to follow the lie of the land.

The garden is perhaps best loved for the spectacular arrangement and variety of the rhododendrons and azaleas. The way in which the plants gradually break into a gentle gradation of colour is magical; and they have been planted with an expert eye to shade, shape and form. In early April an abundance of daffodils sweeps from the top of the Spring Garden as the first rhododendrons come into bloom, with banks of mauve and blue; later the brilliant colours of the azaleas break out. There are magnificent specimens here, and as most of them were planted by Armytage Moore, they are fifty to sixty years old and are showing their age. In some cases the stunning displays are formed from the tops of giant rhododendrons which have fallen over. A private gardener might propagate, take them out and start again with the new plants, but this familiar Ulster scene is too well loved by too many thousand visitors to try that, so the Rowallane gardeners are attempting – with a very sanguine view of their hopes for success – to regenerate these species from

Mike Snowden, head gardener at Rowallane, leads a party around the gardens

old wood at the base, in a long, tedious, but kind approach to the mature plants.

The Rock Garden at the foot of this magnificent hill is another area which is demanding a lot of attention from the gardeners. It was abandoned during the Second World War and is only now really coming back to its prime of pre-war days. The clever ways in which the area is planted and in which the paths wander around the rocks make the scale seem deceptive, but in fact it covers an impressively large area. Dwarf daffodils and dwarf rhododendrons are tucked into pockets or spread on the grass. Sedums and saxifrages spread over smooth shoulders of rock; azaleas and meconopsis, primroses and aquilegias provide some of the prettiest blooms, and choice species nestle in crevices. A dozen varieties of primula seed themselves around the rocks. One of these is the primula 'Rowallane Rose', an elegant long-stemmed variety which was an accidental seedling, and which also grows in rosy pink drifts along the Primula Walk in the Walled Garden, where it was originally found.

The most famous Rowallane variety is the *Hypericum* 'Rowallane Hybrid' (*H. leschenaultii* × *H. hookerianum rogersii*) which was a seedling self-sown in the Rock Garden. It has a large, deep yellow cup and glossy green foliage, and is considered the most beautiful St John's wort in cultivation. Other varieties which carry the name of Rowallane to garden experts in all parts of the world are *Viburnum plicatum tomentosum* which can be seen in the Walled Garden, and the *Chaenomeles speciosa* 'Rowallane Seedling' the original of which is now a big bush growing in the Outer Walled Garden.

From the Rock Garden a path winds up through the Old Wood, where specimen rhododendrons sit among clefts of rock, and continues through a gate in a dry stone wall into the 'Hospital', where weak calves were nursed when the Rowallane land was farmed. Here is another favourite with visitors, a magnificent handkerchief tree (*Davidia involucrata*), an elegant spreading tree with hanging, creamy white bracts which flutter gently and give the plant its familiar name.

The Walled Garden is lovely throughout the year, from the spring when the cherry trees are heavy with blossom, framing the walks along the paths, through to autumn when the colourful berry-bearing shrubs, like the *Schizandra grandiflora cathayensis* and *s.g. rubiflora* come into their own, and the colchicums, or autumn crocuses, provide a display to brighten any October afternoon. The Walled Garden now has a collection of hybrid penstemons of national status. An impressive variety of these plants, with their open-mouthed flowers, is nurtured through the winter and displayed in beds here in spring and summer. Hostas do well in the Walled Garden, with roses, lilies and astilbes, but the most popular plant is probably the Himalayan blue poppy, *Meconopsis grandis*, which grows in vivid blue and purple drifts.

Although Hugh Armytage Moore is normally associated with the spring-time shrubs, he did, in fact, plant many summer-flowering species and philadelphus, eucryphia and hydrangeas can be found throughout the garden; the National Trust has added a new collection of hydrangeas around the lake.

Contemporary photographs show that Armytage Moore did not put neatness first in a garden; and a niece remembers picking blackberries from brambles scrambling among some choice azaleas in the Spring Garden. Now the Paddock and Pleasure Grounds have mown paths through areas which have been allowed to grow more naturally, so that the wild flowers can flourish – six varieties of wild orchid have since come to light – and as the flowers multiply, so do the insects and butterflies.

A happy recent arrival at Rowallane is the bandstand from the promenade at Newcastle, which for many years had provided a stage for pierrots and seaside entertainers. Its future was in doubt, and the Trust had always felt that the stump for the bandstand in the Rowallane Pleasure Grounds needed finishing off, so the two problems were solved together. The bandstand arrived at Rowallane a tangled mass of iron-work, to be reassembled for future entertainments in the garden.

Rowallane, like any great garden, is a continuing story, and a gardeners' garden. Armytage Moore – to whom great collectors like E.H. Wilson, George Forrest, and Captain Frank Kingdon Ward sent back rare specimens – was awarded the Victoria Medal of Honour by the Royal Horticultural Society in 1942. His first head gardener, William Watson, entered his service in 1903 and was with Armytage Moore for twenty-four years. John Hanvey succeeded his father, James, as head gardener in 1934, and was made an Associate of Honour by the RHS in 1965, in recognition of the achievements of his very special partnership with Armytage Moore. John Hanvey junior, his son, represented the third generation of the gardening family when he came in 1971 to work with garden manager Lady O'Neill. In 1981 Mike Snowden brought his expertise to Rowallane from some of the Trust's great gardens in England and Wales.

Lyn Gallagher

The approach to Springhill

SPRINGHILL

Near Moneymore on the Coagh road (B18) [H869828]

It may be fanciful to say that a house is friendly and welcoming, but if any house fits that description, it is Springhill, just outside Moneymore in Co. Londonderry. A straight avenue leads to the simple, open façade, flanked by two long, broad pavilions, with curved gables which look as if they are holding out arms of welcome. The house has an immediate claim on the affections of the visitor; it is something to do with its age – 300 years of one family's occupation – and something to do with the scale and the charm of small details, like the arched gateway, with a curly iron gate, at the top of a flight of worn steps leading from the carpark into the wide enclosed forecourt, with immaculately raked gravel.

Springhill is essentially an Ulster house. Architectural historians have commented on the slightly hesitant way in which the basically classical front is treated – with narrower, two-paned windows in the centre, a typical seventeenth-century Ulster feature – and have noted how the eighteenth-century bow extensions give it more assurance. One commentator, Alistair Rowan, describes it as 'one of the prettiest houses in Ulster, not grand or elaborate in its design, but with very much the air of a French provincial manor

113

house'. Its lack of pretension is its hallmark, and the rear of the house is described as 'a comfortable jumble of roofs, slate-hung walls and chimneys . . . with a big round-headed window on the staircase the most prominent feature'.

The Lenox-Conyngham family came to Ulster from Ayrshire in the seventeenth century, and it seems that the building of Springhill was first thought of in 1680, when 'Good' Will Conyngham married Anne Upton of Castle Upton in Templepatrick. The marriage articles required Will to build 'a convenient house of lime and stone, two stories high . . . and with necessary office houses'. Good Will began the house and planted trees which still stand in the grounds, and the Lenox-Conynghams began three centuries of life there which lasted until 1957 when Captain William Lenox-Conyngham left the property to the National Trust in his will.

Like men in many generations of the family, the seventeenth-century Good Will was a soldier, commanding a regiment in the Jacobite War, and there are numerous military reminders in the house. The gun room has a variety of weapons, all now inoperable; four flintlocks, later converted to muzzleloaders, were used at the Siege of Derry. Bulky blunderbusses recall eighteenth-century coaching days, and swords hang on the early-eighteenth-century oak panelling. A long pike was said to have been used in combat at Vinegar Hill, Co. Wexford, during the 1798 rebellion. It was quite by accident that the fine Chinese eighteenth-century wallpaper was discovered when the panelling was being restored, and now its faded blue, delicate pattern softens this sturdy, masculine room.

The library would have been another male stronghold, and in Springhill it contains a first-class collection of books, including rare volumes of John Gerard's *Herball, or Generall Historie of Plantes*, Thomas Hobbes's *Leviathan* and Sir Walter Raleigh's *History of the World*. A lovely seventeenth-century round oak table usually bears a bowl of flowers of warm colours. On either side of a cabinet for books and papers hang slightly sombre portraits of William and Mary by Sir Godfrey Kneller, given in recognition of services rendered by Sir Albert Conyngham, who commanded the Inniskilling Dragoons. Another soldiering kinsman, the 3rd Viscount Molesworth, who was ADC to the Duke of Marlborough during the War of the Spanish Succession, brought back one of the most fascinating items in the house, a medicine chest full of drawers and bottles for a whole range of medicaments which would have been useful for an Iberian military campaign.

The extent to which a house like Springhill is less a museum than a family history book is typified by a set of chairs in the library – four nineteenth-century copies of Jacobean originals, in fine oak with carved back and apron. It was Olivia Lenox-Conyngham who destroyed all but one of the originals which she had found uncomfortable and had detested. One chair escaped, and whether she regretted what she had done or whether someone else took a hand, they were remade by the estate carpenter, Maxwell. We know quite a lot about Olivia, and it is not all favourable. She was the second wife of George Lenox-

114

Conyngham, who was the first member of the family to use the hyphenated version of the name, and an active figure in the exciting political period at the end of the eighteenth century, colonel of the 'Springhill Union' volunteer unit and opponent of the Act of Union in 1800. In the family bible an entry by Olivia states:

> George Lenox-Conyngham, being in a melancholy state of mind for many months prior, put an end to his existence by a pistol shot. He lingered from 20th November 1816 to the 22nd, and died, thanks to the Almighty God, a truly penitent Christian.

No words of regret or mourning for her husband from Olivia, who was a severe enough stepmother to lock up a small boy in a dark closet. It is Olivia's name which is most often associated with the Springhill ghost. Over the years since George's death there have been regular sightings of a small, dark woman, perhaps Olivia filled with remorse for any part she may have played in George's suicide. These sightings are often connected with children, and Diana McClintock, the sister of the donor of Springhill, recalls an occasion when she and the other children were sleeping with a governess who asked Diana's mother, Mina, at breakfast, why she had come into the room in the middle of the night and looked at each of the children in turn. Mina had smiled and passed it over. There may have been a gentler Olivia, the one who had achieved the considerable feat of nursing six children successfully through smallpox and who was reliving that exhausting time.

Whatever the truth, there is nothing in the least unnerving about Springhill, and there are plenty of attractive ladies about the house. A favourite is the pretty portrait of Harriet Molesworth, painted by Cote. She lost her leg – it was replaced by a wooden one – trying to escape from a fire at her home in Brook Street, London, but she received a pension from George III, and seems to have managed to live a very full life. The ivory cane which she used lies on a small Chinese cupboard. Her picture hangs in the drawing-room, a lovely, light and airy room, using one of the later bays and decorated with a simple eighteenth-century cornice and a black marble chimneypiece with Tuscan columns of about 1820. Some William-and-Mary chairs are arranged in a formal manner against the wall, while French Empire sofas occupy the centre of the room. A fine eighteenth-century glass hangs on the wall, and a showcase has a collection of family memorabilia – seals, insignia, silver buttons and a little silver whistle.

A door leads from the drawing-room to the dining-room, a nineteenth-century room lit by long windows which give pleasant views over the parkland, the replanted beech avenue and the belvedere to the rear of the house. The marquetry walnut chairs are from the William-and-Mary period, and the room has some handsome old-fashioned conveniences, including a good eighteenth-century plate bucket of mahogany and a six-sided wine cooler. Some fine Irish glass sits on a sideboard, with good examples of Wedgewood basalt and biscuit ware.

The gun room,
Springhill

The core of the house is the hall and staircase. The hall is panelled in a late-seventeenth-century style with bold moulding, and contains a simple oak chair of the same period and brass-bound treasure boxes used for travelling. The oak stairs are five foot wide and rise gently, two banisters to a tread, one plain, one with spiral flutes, and a handrail of yew. At the foot of the stairs is an unsophisticated carved oak cupboard, bearing the message 'John Smith made this in 1714'. Upstairs two pictures tell a story – one of a blooming bride, the other of a grey, drab widow.

At the half-landing is a recreated nursery with a happy jumble of toys, mostly Victorian and Edwardian – cots, china dolls, slates and chalks, baby carriages, a scaled-down piano, books and much loved teddies. Still there is the high chair of little Wims, the child who was locked in the closet. The 'blue bedroom', scene of most of Springhill's mystery and of George's shooting, has been recreated, with pretty bed hangings, an elegant dressing-table and all the paraphernalia of a lady's toilette.

In the old laundry of the house is one of Springhill's best attractions. The display of costumes began in 1964, when a number of items which had belonged to Lady Anne Beresford formed the nucleus of a significant collection including some fine eighteenth-century garments. The gem of the collection is a lovely dress known to have been worn at a costume dance at Buckingham Palace around 1900, and it was always thought that it had been made at that time, until the Trust's costume adviser, Judith Doré, came to examine the collection and exclaimed that was nearly 150 years older than that. It is an exquisite court mantua of around 1760 in cream Spitalfields silk, woven with gold threads, sprigged with pink roses and foliage, one of about a dozen left

116

in Britain, and in immaculate condition. It is part of a display which changes every year, following themes such as weddings and sportswear, and showing off the best examples of different items.

The offices and outbuildings of Springhill were extensive and comprehensive. Mina Lenox-Conyngham in her thorough and affectionate picture of Springhill's history, *An Old Ulster House and the People Who Lived In It* (1946), paints a picture of a pleasant nineteenth-century rural existence . . .

> The girls organised a sewing class for cottage girls which was held every day in the upper room of the Eastern side-building . . . In the long summer days it was the custom to engage in making preserves and cordials, and we can imagine these charming girls, in their thin muslin gowns and sandalled shoes, fluttering from garden to still-room, like bees depositing their loads of sweets. There still remain jars of pot-pourri and a few bottles of elder-flower-water over a hundred years old, and the story lingers that once, after the making of black-currant whiskey, the squeezed currants were thrown out to be eaten by the fowl, which promptly became intoxicated and reeled unsteadily about the yards.
>
> Another old custom was the yearly filling of the Turf-house in the laundry yard, which also contained the slaughter house and the brew-house. This was achieved by a number of the tenants, who every year each supplied a cart of turf and a day's free work, and after piling up the turf in the long shed, they were given dinner on long tables set out on the grass-plot in the middle of the yard.

The gardens and grounds of Springhill hold the character of 300 years. A grove of ancient yews to the back of the house leads to a series of walled gardens. Lord Macartney brought back a new rose, *Rosa bracteata*, from China in 1793 to grow up the side of a grand stone barn. A small square shelters a herb garden with many of the plants which would have been used for culinary and medicinal purposes down the years. One of the Trust's gardens advisers, Graham Stuart Thomas, adds a new story to the house's repertoire . . .

> *Artemesia angustifolia* is a silvery sub shrub which gives off in warm air a distinct fragrance of curry – a character which is only known to the more experienced botanist and gardener. 'Do you smell anything special just here?' asks the very Irish custodian. The visitor sniffs appreciatively and says, 'Why yes! curry, I think.' 'Ah,' says the guide, 'I have often wondered about it. They tell me there was once an Indian cook at the house. He died one day and no one seems to know where he was buried . . . '

The storytelling custodian was Teddy Butler, Springhill's administrator and the owner of a much photographed one-eyed Irish wolfhound. He and his successor, Eric Napier, did much to make Springhill a delightful and popular Ulster house.

Lyn Gallagher

STRANGFORD LOUGH

[J560615]

A fast and awesomely powerful current brings the tidal waters through the narrow inlet between Strangford and Portaferry. This is the tide which runs up the twelve miles of the lough, eventually covering the broad flats under the rocky face of Scrabo Hill. Within these waters there is a rich store of marine biology; around the lough, feeding at the water's edge in winter, or nesting on the islands in summer, there is a wealth and variety of changing birdlife; seals and big fish swim in the waters; and there is a range of botanical and geological interest for the specialist and casual observer alike.

This magnificent environmental and scientific resource has been much used and enjoyed by people. In Neolithic times they were attracted by the ready supply of wildfowl for hunting, and early farmers discovered the fertile and easily cultivated land of Comber, Scrabo and the Ards Peninsula. Celtic monks sought the isolation and security of Nendrum from the fifth to the tenth centuries, and later, in the twelfth century, the Cistercians came to the wooded sanctuary of Greyabbey. Norse seamen took refuge in the lough, substituting their name – 'the violent fjord' – for the former name, Cuan. In the late Middle Ages landowners began to defend their rights with fortifications, and stone tower houses, like Audley's Castle, mostly associated with the Anglo-Normans, stand guard on tongues of land or promontories overlooking the lough. As times became more peaceful, the landed families chose handsome sites to build their impressive eighteenth and nineteenth-century houses in landscaped parks. The villages also developed, dominated by the market town of Newtownards. Now the unspoilt environment of Strangford offers recreation for the population of half a million or more who live close to its northern stretches. They come to play golf, fly, sail, fish, dive with sub-aqua equipment, to watch birds, to follow the sport of wildfowling, to swim, or just to drive, look and picnic.

Strangford Lough's beauty is readily accessible to the motorist, with a road running down most of its eastern shore. At the narrows, a long line of whitewashed and colourful houses at Portaferry looks across to the clustered village of Strangford, nestling among the rocks, meadows and woodlands of the western shore. This is the most dramatic and picturesque part of the lough, where its steeply sloped fjord-like inlet opens inland to a wide bay. The work of humans entirely complements that of nature here, with the stone tower houses and piers, the stump of a windmill on a hill, the pretty villages and the graceful prospect of Castle Ward above its lawns and parkland. Much of this landscape is protected by the National Trust, and the contoured sweep of the broad-leaved woodlands on both sides of the water is carefully tended to survive for many years. On the west is the 800-acre estate of Castle Ward,

Brent geese on
Strangford Lough

and on the east the Walter Meadow and the woods which fringe the Nugent
estate and add their grandeur to the landscape. This part of the lough has much
variety and subtle change, and new views open from a rewarding walk along
the western edge of the water, from the Strangford Bay path to Audley's Castle
and beyond.

Further north the lough develops into a wide expanse studded with islands;
some are inhabited, others are grazed by livestock. There are trees on some,
and on others the barren shingle makes an ideal habitat for breeding birds.
Lovely views of the pattern of islands which is this middle section of Strangford
can be had from behind the Temple at Castle Ward, from the higher points
around Killyleagh and Whiterock in the west, and from Savage's medieval
mound at Castle Hill, Ardkeen, on the east side. The Trust now owns a number
of islands in the lough, acquired for different purposes according to
conservation-management and recreation needs. Ballyhenry, a rocky five-acre
island near the narrows, is of great ornithological interest, as are Horse Island
and Salt Island. Gibbs Island, on the other hand, is a well known Strangford
landmark with its stand of Scots pine, but it was acquired because it makes
a good place for yachtspeople to picnic, so saving nearby and more ecologically
fragile islands. Green Island provides amenity use, while Darragh combines
both conservation and recreation interests.

Taggart is one of the most interesting islands of Strangford Lough. Its rich
wildlife includes badgers, foxes and otters; porpoises have been seen feeding

119

off the eastern shore; and the sheltered mudflats and salt marshes give feeding and breeding ground for waders and waterfowl. Scenically it is important, and its ninety-four acres were traditionally used for agriculture. The farm buildings had fallen into disrepair, but a new life is promised when the old house and barns are made into a field centre designed to help parties of young people to explore the lough and to work on conservation projects.

The key to Strangford Lough's spectacular wildlife lies in a unique combination of tidal currents and their associated sediments lying in the bed of the lough. The currents, some of the fastest in north-west Europe, create a stream of whirlpools and upwellings in the narrows, whilst further north they gradually slacken, until finally, in some particularly sheltered areas, there is virtually no movement at all. Associated with these different currents is a variety of sea-bottom types, ranging from bare bedrock swept by the most turbulent waters, through a succession of different areas covered by boulders, gravels, sands, and finally very soft muds. Added to this complex picture is the effect of winds and waves, the whole combining to produce a greater variety of natural habitats than is seen in almost any comparable sea area.

The result is a rich mosaic of animal communities, each with its own range of individual species capable of thriving in the conditions of each area. Almost 2,000 species of marine animal have been identified in the lough and it is likely

Whooper swans near the Maltings, just outside Newtownards

the list is far from complete. Many are filter feeders, siphoning their food in from the stream of microscopic particles being swept past. Transparent sea squirts, brilliantly coloured sponges, and a great variety of molluscs all feed this way, whilst brittle stars, in places up to 1,000 in a square yard, trap food in their delicate arms. Animals like the sea urchin and a number of snails graze on algae and other deposits, whilst active predators, like the deep red sunstar, crabs, and even octopus, make life hazardous for the other inhabitants of this dim world. It is possible to find out more about these fascinating creatures at the Northern Ireland Aquarium in Portaferry and at the special Strangford Lough interpretation centre in the Barn at Castle Ward.

The wealth of bottom-dwelling animals attracts a wide variety of fish. Little silvery sand eels enter the lough in their millions. Large predators, mackerel and pollack, chase after these shoals, and sometimes the water seems to boil as the whole shoal streams up to the surface and back down to escape, whilst seabirds fight and dive for the sudden harvest. Cruising over the bottom of this restless world are tope and skate; feeding on many of the communities in the lough, these relatives of the shark can weigh over 180 pounds and live for forty years. They are an exciting challenge for the sport fisherman, but faced with a decline in their populations in the whole Irish Sea, the Trust instituted a scheme whereby the fish were weighed on board and certified by the skipper before being immediately returned alive to the water.

With such stocks of fish as these, it is not surprising that the lough is one of the most important areas for common seals in Ireland. The numerous pladdies (reefs) and small islands provide sites for seals to haul out and bask at different stages of the tide. At present numbering over 600, seals can be seen diving for fish almost anywhere in the lough. One of the best areas to view them is in the narrows, particularly at Cloghy rocks.

Strangford Lough is perhaps most famous for its birdlife, and justly so, for not only are its bird populations spectacularly large, but they also vary with the seasons as different species arrive from areas as far apart as the Arctic and the Tropics. The winter birds are the most numerous, and indeed the most easily observed. As they settle along the shores in their thousands, or as different flocks rise and circle in the crisp air, they create a spectacle that startles even non-birdwatchers into enthusiasm. Particularly important are the pale-bellied Brent geese. One of the world's most northerly breeding birds, these geese leave their summer grounds in the high Arctic of Canada, flying east over Greenland, and by early autumn are settling on the northern mudflats of Strangford Lough to feed on the swards of eel grass. Often numbering up to 15,000 birds, they may account for about two thirds of the whole west-European population at this time.

A wide range of other species attracts interest and delight from both specialist observers and amateurs. Flocks of widgeon arrive from Russia, whooper swans from Iceland, waders, like curlew and golden plover, from highland moors, and knot from Greenland. All these, and many other species, arrive to feed on the eel grass and on the vast numbers of small worms,

The view northwards from inside a birdwatching hide at Castle Espie

shellfish and crustaceans burrowed in the mud. These immense flocks of wintering birds are easily seen – even by motorists travelling southwards from Newtownards to Portaferry – at almost any time between September and March, but they are at their best in autumn, particularly when a rising tide forces the birds to concentrate on the few remaining areas of exposed shore. In addition to guided birdwatching walks provided by National Trust wardens, there are a number of excellent hides at Castle Espie, Island Reagh, Mount Stewart and Castle Ward where the birds may be observed in relative comfort without disturbing them. Lay-bys at Greyabbey and Ballyreagh also provide excellent viewpoints.

The birds coming to breed in summer are hardly less spectacular. Terns, fresh from their winter quarters in west Africa, arrive to nest on island banks of shingle and grass; the lough holds about a third of Ireland's population of these beautiful white birds, and they can be seen almost everywhere plunging into the sea for small fish. Other nesting species include wildfowl like mallard and shelduck, with their carefully hidden nests, and waders like the oystercatcher and the ringed plover, depositing beautifully camouflaged eggs on the bare stones.

The islands are immensely important to the birds as secure nesting grounds. Lack of disturbance to parents, eggs and young is critical to their success, and the Trust asks people to avoid landing on those islands where nesting notices have been posted.

The National Trust's role in Strangford Lough is unusual in that it is not based solely on land ownership. Initially, Trust management was based on leases of the foreshore, which enabled control of shooting to be enforced through a permit system. The two great estates of Mount Stewart and Castle Ward gave protection to part of the important landscape of the lough but gradually more land, including significant islands, was acquired, and in 1982 over 5,000 acres of the bed of the lough at the north end was acquired, giving vital control over this essential part of the Strangford habitat, which is of National Nature Reserve status.

The Strangford Lough Wildlife Scheme, started in 1966, is based on an attempt to bring all the groups with interests in Strangford Lough to work in co-operation for the overall and long-term good of this wonderful resource.

Lyn Gallagher

TEMPLETOWN MAUSOLEUM

At Templepatrick on the Belfast–Antrim road (A6) [J228859]

The work of Robert Adam, the great Scottish exponent of neo-classicism, is hardly represented in Ireland. There were a few interiors, now gone, at Langford House in Dublin, and some fine rooms at Headfort, Co. Meath, while of the work he did at Castle Upton only the elegant mausoleum truly reflects his accomplishment.

There are other fine neo-classical buildings in National Trust care: both the Temple of the Winds at Mount Stewart and Mussenden Temple at Downhill are sophisticated attempts to follow classical models, only slightly adapted for their Irish regeneration. The incomparable Castle Coole perfectly demonstrates James Wyatt's interpretation of classical design proportion with serenity and restraint.

Robert Adam's best classical work is also chaste, crisp and elegant, and in the Templetown Mausoleum some of his great strengths are illustrated. The Mausoleum was erected in 1789 by the Hon. Sarah Upton to the Rt. Hon. Arthur Upton. Adam's original design had been for a much larger version with three decorated sides and one blank side; the building which was finally constructed was smaller and had only one decorated face. All Adam's assurance and skilful handling are there, with the solemnity appropriate to the subject and to his later years. Classical urns, sarcophagi, leafy swags and circular reliefs surround the arched door to the vault, above which in perfectly carved Roman letters is the simple inscription 'Sacred to the memory of the Right Honourable Arthur Upton'. A shallow roof of flush limestone flags covers the whole.

Templetown Mausoleum, which was given to the National Trust in 1965 by William Henderson Smith and Sir Robin Kinahan, stands in the graveyard at Castle Upton, off the main road through Templepatrick, Co. Antrim. Castle Upton, which is privately owned and not open to the public, is nearby. Originally a plantation castle, it was given a new look by Adam, and became a structure dominated by crenellated towers with conical roofs, linked by parapets with battlements. In 1837 much of Adam's work was lost when it was thoroughly remodelled by Edward Blore.

Mausolea, or monumental tombs, are quite common in Ireland; a good place to see examples roughly similar to that at Castle Upton is Knockbreda churchyard, where the sturdy 1747 parish church by Richard Castle looks down on an array of mausolea dating from the late eighteenth century, some elegant, some eccentric.

Lyn Gallagher

TONREGEE ISLAND

[*H330282*]

Upper and Lower Loughs Erne between them present a stretch of about forty miles of water, all except the lower half of the lower lough full of islands, points and lakelets connected by channels with the main waterway. One of the most interesting island groups in the upper lough is that which belongs to the Belle Isle estate, and one of the islands in this group, Tonregee, has been purchased by the Trust. It lies between Staff and Deal and south of Inishcreagh. It is one of a series of drowned drumlins left by the last ice age and as you sail up the lough you can see that it is now entirely covered with trees.

There are no grazing animals on Tonregee and landing is difficult, so it is a natural sanctuary. The shore is fringed with small trees: willow and alder, buckthorn and guelder rose, with its fragrant white flowers in June and shiny red berries in autumn. These are growing on the land left exposed by the successive lowerings of the level of the lake. Behind this outer fringe is a ring of Scots pine. The centre of the island, the slightly higher ground, is dominated by ash, with some oak, Scots pine and sycamore. There is much natural regeneration, particularly of ash and buckthorn, and under the canopy grow aspen, swaying in the slightest breeze, hawthorn and many wild roses.

The island has a frieze of common reed, interspersed in summer with marsh marigolds, purple loosestrife and the aromatic lilac-flowered water mint. In spring, near the shore there are primroses, violets and sanicle.

The centre of the island is a dense thicket of brambles and nettles, but amongst and around these in the spring and early summer there is a lush flowering of bluebells, cow parsley, goosegrass, hogweed, meadowsweet, pignut, wood sorrel and violets.

The dense woodland is alive with song. At quieter times the regular, contented murmur of wood pigeons can be heard. The deliberate heron, not nesting here but on a nearby island, flaps around, considering where to fish. The great crested grebe, which does nest here in the reeds, dives for its food and emerges several yards away. All the small woodland birds are breeding here including the goldcrest and, amongst warblers, the blackcap, with its short, mellow warble, and the willow warbler with wistful, descending song.

The bright yellow brimstone butterfly can be seen here; its larvae feed on the abundant buckthorn. Other butterflies which enjoy the island are the large white, small white, orange tip and speckled wood.

The island is rightly treated as a sanctuary and no active management will be undertaken. The present landing arrangements, which are of the Robinson Crusoe variety, are quite sufficient.

Dick Rogers

TORR HEAD–COOLRANNY

[*D243375*]

It is only thirteen miles from Torr Head to Scotland, and this narrow promontory is supposed to have been the last place in Ireland where Scots Gaelic was spoken; it died out about 1920. The people of this area have a strong identity with their Scottish neighbours on the Mull of Kintyre, which lies just across the Sea of Moyle, stretching out below the steep, twisting road to Cushendun. In 1899 Robert Lloyd Praeger described Torr as a 'boss of rock standing boldly out on the edge of the sea with a little whitewashed coastguard watch house perched like a doll's house on its summit. This was once a primeval stronghold of great celebrity, and the natives lit their warning fires on the neighbouring heights of Ballylucan to warn their Scottish friends.'

Another expert on the Glens of Antrim, Charles E.B. Brett, writing seventy years later, describes a contrasting scene on the headland – 'The ugly brick lookout station on the point is built on the site of the very ancient cashel of Dun Varagh, and itself replaces an earlier watch house of 1818. The burnt-out ruins of the coastguard houses have yet to attain the charm of antiquity.'

Above the road the summit of Carnanmore rises to 1,250 feet. Below the road the land rushes steeply down to the sea at Torr, the vivid green grass giving evidence of chalk on the high slopes. The narrow road winds between hedges rich in fuschia, brambles, honeysuckle and wild roses. In spring, sheltered hedgerows are edged with primroses, wild hyacinths and occasional orchids.

The National Trust has only seven and a half acres of land between Torr and Coolranny, just a toehold in this lovely corner of Co. Antrim.

Lyn Gallagher

WELLBROOK BEETLING MILL

3 miles from Cookstown on the Omagh road (A505) [H750792]

In a remote and green valley of Co. Tyrone stands Wellbrook Beetling Mill, now a lone reminder of the flourishing linen industry which once operated around Corkhill, near Cookstown. It was not unusual for a beetling mill to be isolated. For one thing, this final process in the manufacture of linen was often handled independently from the main mill or bleachworks, and for another, the deafening roar of the engines made it preferable that the beetling should take place at some distance from the other activities.

Beetling was the process which finished off linen, giving the damask cloth its characteristic smoothness and sheen, and closing the weave for special items like umbrella cloth, interlining, holland cloth or bookbinding strips. The sheen was achieved by the action of the beetles, or heavy hammers, pounding down with relentless rhythm for anything from two days to two weeks.

Two hundred years ago there were six beetling mills serving the Wellbrook bleachworks, but while the main mill ceased to operate in the middle of the nineteenth century, this beetling mill carried on working until 1961. When it was given to the National Trust in 1969 by Samuel John Henderson, the

William John Black, beetler at Wellbrook, between the water-wheel machinery and one of the frames of the beetles

machinery and workings were virtually intact, so that restoration with the help of the Landmark Trust was possible.

Today the few linen mills which still operate in Ulster are concentrated in large units, but in the eighteenth century the production of linen was a dispersed activity. Linen processing was no longer a cottage industry carried out to supplement the agricultural economy: industrial technology had brought scutch mills which prepared the flax for spinning at home; mills for weaving fine linen were beginning to spring up in large units west of Belfast, and bleach greens with beetling mills were found on many northern rivers.

Linen manufacture started at Wellbrook after 1764 when Samuel and Hugh Faulkner were looking for a site for bleach greens. Hugh was a linen merchant, or 'draper', as they were called, and he wrote detailed letters to his brother Samuel, describing the progress of the work and the development of the trade. He recalled taking a fishing rod when he went to examine the site 'in case anyone might suspect his design', but the work at the bleachworks went on well. Capturing the excitement and sense of achievement in the making of the weir in May 1765, he wrote:

> Finish'd the whole at 8 o'clock at night, turn'd the river into its usual course and let it down the race, which went very cleverly home amidst several shouts & acclamations. From 8 to 9 o'clock we drank whiskey & from 9 to near 11 fought yet by my management, no blood drawn, but several shirts and weastcoats torn. The Mountain Men when they got drunk fell

out. Thus you have the compleat history of the wyer making, which took
110 men and 20 hours and 15 gallons of whiskey.

Later in the year he wrote of the work on a beetling engine:

On 21st October, 1765, John Blear and he went up to the bleachyards
at 4 o'clock in the morning where they continued till 8 the next day. They
set the beetles agoing, they answered extremely well. They single beetled
66 pieces last night but Hugh was so fatigued thro' the want of rest and
labour that he could only say that in his opinion they had the best and
compleatest mill in the County Tyrone.

Wellbrook takes its power from the fast-flowing Ballinderry river. A path
follows the wooded banks of the river a few hundred yards to the west and
along by the mill race and flume – the wooden trough, carried on piers of
Coalisland brick, which takes the water for fifty feet to hit and drive the water
wheel on the gable of the building. This impressive wheel, sixteen feet wide
and four and a half feet deep, is made mainly of wood but has a cast-iron shaft
and shrouding which bears the name of the Armagh Foundry. Within the mill
is a sluice gate which is operated by hand and efficiently starts and stops the
action of the wheel.

When the beetler starts up the engines there is a tremendous roar and a
rhythmic thundering as the beetles rattle down. They look like organ pipes
in their arrangement, thirty-two to a frame, and are designed in such a way,
with mechanisms known as 'drunkens', 'gloys' and 'eccentrics', that they do not
hit exactly the same place more than once, and thus they avoid leaving marks
on the cloth. There are seven engines in the mill, standing over seven feet high.
Pine is used for the framework and wiper beams, while the beetles are made
from the harder beechwood.

Louvred wooden windows on the first floor of the mill reveal its former use
as a loft where the damp, beetled cloth was left to dry in the circulation of air.
Now this floor houses a display about the making of linen.

Like many beetling mills, Wellbrook had a cottage for the beetler close by.
Beetling, a tradition which was passed on through families from generation
to generation, was a craft of some skill, requiring the maintenance of tensions
and the ensuring of the correct level of processing for the different finishes
required. It was not unusual for beetlers – subjected to the great noise of the
engines within a limited space for a normal working day of 6.30 a.m.to 9 p.m. –
to become completely or partially deaf.

Lyn Gallagher

HISTORY
of the
National Trust
in
Northern Ireland

1
1935–9

One day in October 1935 the postman from Comber, Co. Down, dismounted from his bicycle at a house known as The Forde, a mile from the town, on the road to Ballydrain and Mahee Island near the head of Strangford Lough, and delivered a letter addressed to George Chester Duggan, Esquire. Appropriately – for Strangford Lough was later to become one of the National Trust's most important spheres of interest – the postman's country call put in motion a chain of events which was to bring the Trust to Northern Ireland.

The letter came from McLeod Matheson, secretary of the National Trust in London. He wrote that the Trust – whose organisation was so far confined to England and Wales – had been offered two properties in Northern Ireland, Killynether House near Newtownards and Ballymoyer House and Glen in mid-Armagh. These properties had been inspected and he wondered what should be done. The letter was addressed to Duggan as Principal Assistant Secretary in the Ministry of Finance at Stormont. He was a distinguished graduate of Trinity College, Dublin, who held the key financial position in the Northern Ireland Civil Service, and he had an independent mind. It is probable that, in addressing this letter to Duggan, Matheson was guided by Dr Alfred Chart who was in charge of public records and ancient monuments in the same Ministry and was an enthusiastic historian and antiquarian. Why the letter was addressed to Duggan's home is not clear. One can only speculate that Matheson feared Stormont would be obstructive, whereas events proved otherwise.

Duggan consulted Sir Arthur Quekett, Parliamentary Draughtsman, who confirmed that the National Trust – by then in its fortieth year of existence – legally 'ran' in Northern Ireland. He then showed the letter to Hugh Pollock, the Minister, who had no objection to acting upon it, so Duggan sent a helpful reply suggesting the setting-up of a small local committee to advise the Trust on the acceptance of property and generally to look after the Trust's interests in Northern Ireland. He said he would be prepared to suggest names of local people who might take an interest in such a movement.

The Trust's executive in London agreed such a committee should be set up before any properties in Ulster were accepted, so the Ministry then asked the Belfast Natural History and Philosophical Society to supply the names of three suitable members. The society nominated Senator Samuel Cunningham, a UK Privy Counsellor, a naturalist and a keen member of the Trust; Dr Dickie Hunter of the Department of Anatomy at Queen's University, a man of experience and energy in many fields (including the management of an annual circus in Belfast); and William Crawford, an entomologist who had graduated from Cambridge and had returned to Belfast after a career in the Indian Civil Service. To these the Ministry added the following: Dr David Barcroft, of The Glen, Newry, a medical practitioner whose family had an interesting house with a garden and wooded glen to which the public had access; Sir Thomas Dixon, His Majesty's Lieutenant for Co. Antrim; Marcus M. McCausland, His Majesty's Lieutenant for Co. Londonderry; Captain John R. Perceval-Maxwell, of Finnebrogue House, Downpatrick; John Seeds, a Belfast architect; Thomas Joseph Campbell, the Northern Ireland Nationalist MP, author of the acclaimed Wild Birds Protection Act (Northern Ireland) 1931, and former editor of the *Irish News*; Alfred Chart; and L.E.G. Laughton, secretary of the Rural Development Council, a voluntary body funded by the Carnegie Trust. Laughton was suggested for the honorary post

Marcus McCausland, first
Chairman of the Northern
Ireland Committee, from
1936 to 1938

John Perceval-Maxwell,
Northern Ireland
Committee Chairman from
1938 to 1939

of secretary of the new committee. All agreed to let their names go forward, so after a meeting between Duggan and Matheson in London, the Trust's executive appointed all those who had been nominated.

The Northern Ireland Committeee met for the first time on 1 May 1936 in the Law Courts building, Belfast. Marcus McCausland was elected Chairman and John Perceval-Maxwell Deputy Chairman.

The Committee considered the offers of Ballymoyer and Killynether and decided that members should view and report on the two houses. It was also proposed that Lady Mabel Annesley, whose family owned estates at Donard Lodge and Castlewellan, Co. Down, be asked to serve on the Committee, and she agreed.

The second meeting was held on 26 May 1936, when Laughton resigned as Secretary – because he was leaving for Scotland – and was succeeded by George Loxton, also his successor in the post of secretary to the Rural Development Council. Loxton convened the next meeting and the Committee's address from then on was that of the Rural Development Council at 29 Wellington Place, Belfast. A press conference was held on 11 September 1936, explaining the aims of the Trust to the public. At a meeting on 12 November 1936 the Chairman, Marcus McCausland, offered the Trust ownership of the **Rough Fort** near Limavady, and his offer was accepted. This first acquisition in Northern Ireland was a particularly happy start, for the one-acre ring fort contains, as well as beech and Scots pine, a grove of oak, the tree from which the county and city of Londonderry (*Doire*) take their name and which incidentally provides the acorn symbol for the Trust as a whole.

In March 1937 the Committee considered an offer from Nesca Robb, the scholar and writer, of the early-nineteenth-century **Lisnabreeny** House, in the Castlereagh Hills near Belfast, with a cottage, a steward's house and 157 acres of farmland including a glen and waterfall. With the approval of headquarters, in 1938 the offer was accepted. As the house was already being used as a youth hostel, the Committee decided to give the Youth Hostel Association a ten-year lease and Lisnabreeny continued to be used as a hostel until the outbreak of war.

In the spring of 1937 Loxton, although remaining on the Committee, resigned as Secretary and was succeeded by R.J. Wright.

In 1937 Jessie H. Weir made a gift of her family home, **Killynether** House, along with forty-two acres of mixed woodland on the side of Scrabo Hill, overlooking the most fertile land in Co. Down. The Victorian house combined Gothic and Tudor elements and had minarets on its many slender turrets. The YHA, which had already been using the property, was given a tenancy and Killynether was well used as a hostel until the war. With the house came an endowment of £2,000.

Ballymoyer House in mid-Armagh belonged to the Hart-Synnot family, on whose behalf Major Ronald Hart-Synnot, fellow and bursar of St John's College, Oxford, had offered the property to the Trust. In 1900 the estate had been of 7,100 acres, but under the Land Acts of 1899 and 1902 the bulk was sold to the tenants, leaving demesne land of 325 acres. Most of this was later sold to neighbouring farmers, leaving only the house and glen. From 1935 to 1938 the Georgian part of the building, erected in 1782, was occupied as a youth hostel. In 1937 the Committee accepted the glen, but decided not to accept the house, which was in a bad state of repair, and it was eventually demolished by the owner in 1938. A trout stream runs through the wooded glen which contains an ancient sweathouse, and in the old churchyard nearby is the grave of Florence MacMoyre. He was the last hereditary Keeper of the early Irish manuscript Book of Armagh, now held in the library of Trinity College, Dublin: the parish of Ballymoyer takes its name from his family.

In March 1938 a number of new members were appointed to the Committee: Randal McDonnell, Earl of Antrim, Alfred E. Brett, Wilfrid Capper, Professor Gregg Wilson and Northern Ireland MP Major Graham Shillington. In April Marcus McCausland died, and John Perceval-Maxwell was appointed as Chairman, with Samuel Cunningham as Deputy Chairman.

White Park Bay on the north Antrim coast – consisting of 179 acres of sandy shore and limestone cliffs – was offered to the Trust during 1938. The bay had been purchased by the YHA by means of public subscription. YHA members, notably John Calvert, Wilfrid Capper, Harry Dunlop and Sidney Stendall, had been entirely responsible for buying the bay, with assistance from the Pilgrim Trust – of which Lord Macmillan of Aberfeldy, the eminent Scottish jurist, was chairman – but they recognised that the Trust would make the most suitable holding body. It was decided that there should be an official opening on 6 September 1939 by Lord Macmillan. The minutes of a joint meeting of the YHA and the White Park Bay sub-committee of the Trust record: 'Lord Antrim as Chairman of the White Park Bay sub-committee would introduce Lord Macmillan who would accept, on behalf of the National Trust, the conveyance of the bay from the Youth Hostel Association. Lord Macmillan would take seisin of the bay by cutting a sod' – a nice medieval gesture, symbolic of the transfer of an important property. In medieval times, freehold estates could only be transferred by 'livery of seisin', that is a form of public ceremonial transfer. Delivery of the 'seisin', accompanied by words, written or spoken, was the means whereby the owner of a feudal possession might at any time thereafter be known to all the neighbourhood.

But war was declared on 3 September and so no sod was cut and there was no opening: Lord Antrim was called up to the Navy and Perceval-Maxwell to the Army.

There is no record of the Committee's financial position in the prewar period. In 1936 it had a few membership subscriptions and headquarters allowed these to be spent in Northern Ireland and also guaranteed an income of £50 per annum for the first two years. The number of members had increased to about forty by the outbreak of war. No government grant was paid or sought. In 1939 there was an income of £220 from Lisnabreeny rents, and expenditure on that property was £240. The Committee consulted L'Estrange & Brett on legal matters, but their charges were nominal.

The achievement of the Trust in this period was to hoist its own flag and, by acquiring five properties, to establish itself firmly in Northern Ireland. Headquarters in London was very sympathetic to the Province. There were no regional committees on the mainland, administration being by small local committees set up where necessary for individual properties; so the Committee set up in Northern Ireland was unique in that it covered what was later recognised as an administrative region.

2
1939–47

The outbreak of war was a serious blow to the Trust. The departure of the Committee Chairman, Perceval-Maxwell, and of Lord Antrim was an immediate loss. Petrol rationing reduced the visiting of properties by members of the Committee; some people had to dispose of their cars. The membership, small as it had been, was diminished; the black-out made communication difficult.

The Committee met twice before the end of 1939, eight times in 1940 and only five times in 1941. However in 1942 there were ten meetings, thirteen in 1943, fifteen in 1944 and eleven in 1945. Samuel Cunningham stood in as Chairman for three meetings and was then succeeded by Gregg Wilson from April 1940. R.J. Wright ceased to be Secretary and George Loxton again took over. The Committee met in his office in 29 Wellington Place and later high up in Ocean Buildings in Donegall Square, Belfast, after a trip in a tiny rickety lift in which you held your breath lest you disturbed its equilibrium.

Lisnabreeny House was requisitioned by the military immediately on the outbreak of war. Some damage was done, but the Army paid compensation and derequisitioned the house, which was then let to the YHA. However, in August 1940 the military again requisitioned it. A field in the estate was also requisitioned early in the same year for use as an anti-aircraft gun site, and during the air raids of 1941 the booming of the 'Lisnabreeny gun' gave some cheer to the local citizens. In May 1942 the first of two fires damaged the back part of the house and on 2 July the military derequisitioned it for the second time; then they offered to buy it outright, but this was refused. The Ministry of Home Affairs, which was responsible for civil defence and evacuation equipment, asked for a lease, and the Committee agreed, subject to the tenancy being terminated not more than two years after the end of hostilities. The Ministry was also allowed to set up Nissen huts in the stack-yard. In the event the Ministry took a long time to leave and the tenancy eventually expired on 1 August 1949. Even then it took longer to clear away the Nissen huts.

The Committee's third
Chairman (1939–47),
Professor Gregg Wilson

In 1942 the United States Government sought a site for the burial of service casualties in Ireland and chose a ten-acre field at Lisnabreeny: the Committee granted the use of the site free as a contribution to goodwill between the Allies. Over 100 simple wooden crosses were erected and an avenue of trees planted. Later the bodies were removed for interment in the USA, the site was reinstated and the young trees were removed and replanted in the nearby glen.

Killynether House, outside Newtownards, was also requisitioned by the Army on the outbreak of war and continued in occupation until its end. The lands were not finally released, and Nissen huts removed from the grounds, until 31 May 1949, and even then the bases of the huts remained and were the subject of claims by the Trust for compensation. The Committee was anxious that the house and grounds should be fully used, so a group representing four bodies – the YHA, the Federation of Boys' Clubs, the National Council of YMCAs and the Civil Service Social Service Society – was set up and the Trust granted this body a short lease. Killynether was used partly as a youth hostel and partly for the activities of the three other societies.

In July 1944, on Matheson's suggestion, three people were added to the Trust Committee: Dorothy Robertson, of Dogleap, Limavady, a progressive farmer; Ian Stuart, former headmaster of Portora Royal School; and Kathleen McCormick, of Cultra. In August 1941 William Crawford died and in January 1942 Charles McKisack, a retired Belfast businessman, attended his first meeting and at once started to help Loxton with book-keeping.

Loxton was anxious to give up his job as Secretary, and in July 1942 he approached me. In June 1939 I had been made an Assistant Principal in the Northern Ireland Civil Service, but on the outbreak of war I applied for permission to join up. This was refused, and then one evening in December 1940 I was appointed to the post of Private Secretary to Major John MacDermott, Minister of Public Security (later Lord Chief Justice). For the next two years I worked long hours, first for him and then on civil defence work through the air raids and their aftermath. It was in July 1942 that Loxton first asked me if I would join the Committee and do the job of Secretary, but it was 2 December when I attended my first meeting. On 19 February 1943 I was made Secretary. In July that year Austin Brown, an estate agent, was appointed Treasurer and he and I worked together for several years. In March 1944 we got another new member, accountant John Adams, who shared the secretarial work with me for a year.

John (now Major) Perceval-Maxwell returned to the Committee after the end of the war. He had been elected as an MP in the Northern Ireland Parliament and when he became a Junior Minister he offered to resign but the Committee prevailed on him to stay. On 14 November 1945 Lord Antrim, back from naval service in the Pacific, was present at his first meeting since 1939.

In 1946, Kathleen McCormick and John Adams having resigned, John M. Mogey of Queen's University and Dr Nesca Robb (donor of Lisnabreeny) were appointed to the Committee. In August 1946 Austin Brown agreed to act as Estates Secretary as well as Treasurer, leaving me with the job of Committee secretaryship and publicity. In February 1947 Gregg Wilson stepped down as Chairman and was replaced by Lord Antrim. It was clear to us that more members were needed and to get these we needed publicity. In the middle of the war this was almost impossible, but by 1943 we began to see some light. At my first meeting Wilfrid Capper, Charles McKisack and I were appointed as a sub-committee to arrange an exhibition for March 1943 in the Belfast Museum and Art Gallery at Stranmillis, in co-operation with the Ulster Society for the Preservation of the Countryside (USPC). The exhibition, called 'The Ulster

Participants in an
International Youth Rally
at Killynether House in
August 1947

Countryside To-day and Tomorrow', was a success; 7,323 people attended and we decided to show it in those country towns where we had some contact.

The purpose of the exhibition was to show the unspoilt countryside and the dangers of unrestricted development after the war, particularly along our beautiful but vulnerable coastline. I had recruited two young architects to do some extra posters to show what modern architects could do by way of necessary development and, as so often happens, they produced their work at the last moment. The exhibition in Bangor was to be opened on a Saturday afternoon but I could not attend, and as I left Stormont at 1 p.m. that day and ran for the bus I was handed a rolled-up poster. I in turn handed this to a friend who was going to the opening and asked him to put it up, which he did.

On the following Tuesday we held our monthly meeting. Perceval-Maxwell said the opening had been well attended and the exhibits admired: one poster, however, showed a proposed new hotel on a part of the Co. Down coast which he himself owned, and while he would make no comment on the architectural style, he did object to having his property thus developed. It was by far my worst moment in the Trust. I took full responsibility and said the offending poster would be taken down forthwith. At the end of the meeting I went to Bangor and removed the poster, which was in fact quite horrible.

We showed the exhibition in Portrush, Portadown and Derry, and finally it was shown in Mackie's Foundry, Belfast, where there was a captive assembly of over 1,000 workers. Lectures were also given to secondary schools by Denis Winston, an architect/planner, but it was the issue of letters to lists of potential members which was perhaps our most rewarding effort. The number of paid-up members in 1943 was sixty-three, compared with eight in 1942, and we had twenty associates (paying reduced subscriptions), a class which did not exist in England but which we had decided to recruit. By the end of 1944 we had ten life members, 109 ordinary members and twenty-four associates. By 1945 there was a further increase to eleven life members, 132 ordinary members and twenty-seven associates.

The Northern Ireland Government had shown an early interest in postwar development by setting up a Planning Advisory Board in 1942, and John Seeds had been appointed as the National Trust representative. We submitted a memorandum recommending the establishment of national parks and nature reserves and the protection of buildings of architectural or historic interest. The amenities committee of the board made an excellent report in August 1945, which was published in 1947 and formed the basis of subsequent Amenity Lands legislation.

Unaccountably, there was a movement in the Committee in 1943 in favour of independence from the parent body. It was sufficiently strong for Robin Fedden to comment on it in his book *The National Trust Past and Present* (1974, p. 51). The Northern Ireland Committee had always been treated with generosity by the Trust nationally. Busy London officials had given unstintingly of their time and headquarters had even been somewhat over-indulgent in deciding to accept at least two properties – Lisnabreeny and Killynether – which later experience would suggest were not fully up to the high standards which the Trust had set itself. So we had no need to complain, yet we created this impression of wanting independence.

In reply to an inquiry from me, Matheson wrote on 12 October 1943: 'Everything, broadly speaking, should be done by your Committee locally, except: decisions about accepting or declining offers of property; decisions on general amenity policy; initiation of opposition to or promotion of Bills or making of parliamentary representations; such formal acts of sealing, investment, etc. as must be done by the [Executive] Committee under the Acts or by the Secretary; appointments to your Committee.' At the meeting on 10 November 1943 at which this letter was discussed, it was resolved 'that the Northern Ireland Committee should take powers to enable them to take action in urgent cases affecting property of the National Trust in Northern Ireland by making representations to the Departments of the Government of Northern Ireland or by questions in the Parliament of Northern Ireland'.

A special meeting of the Committee was called for 25 January 1944 to meet Anthony Martineau, the Trust's headquarters solicitor, but he was stranded at Heysham on that day and the following day because of the presence of German U-boats in the Irish Sea. A month later Martineau visited Belfast, and in a subsequent letter of 14 March 1944 he suggested that 'the present Northern Ireland Committee be converted into a properly constituted Committee under the National Trust Act of 1907 and that the Committee should include two if not three members of the Council [the Trust's governing body]'. This and other suggestions were debated by the Committee, but we decided to settle for a Bill which would correspond to the English 1937 and 1939 Acts, bringing our legislation into line with that across the water.

Accordingly L'Estrange & Brett were asked to prepare a Bill on these lines. Being a private Bill, it was referred to a Joint Unopposed Committee of both Houses of the Northern Ireland Parliament, and it became law on 19 February 1946 as the National Trust Act (Northern Ireland), 1946. Its principal effect was to provide for the conveyance of property to the Trust by limited owners and trustees. It also enabled a local authority to hand over to the Trust land or buildings and to make contributions to the Trust. The Trust was made a sanitary authority under the Public Health Acts, a move which had the effect of enabling it to make bylaws. In the Finance Act (Northern Ireland), 1944, provision had been made, at the request of the Committee, exempting settled land bequeathed to the Trust from the payment of estate and succession duties. The effect of these two enactments was to make the Trust law in Northern Ireland similar to that in England. Charles A. Brett was mainly responsible for drafting the Bill, but Perceval-Maxwell helped with it, as did Thomas Joseph Campbell (now a judge) and Anthony Martineau.

The first property to be acquired by the Trust after 1939 was **Coney Island** in Lough

Neagh. Viscount Charlemont, a trustee of the island, was interested in its preservation, and in September 1943 I was asked by the Committee to report on the island. I rode my bicycle to the Great Northern Railway station in Belfast and took the train to Annaghmore. From there I rode through the flat boggy land, full of willows and reeds, to Maghery, where I met Lord Charlemont's occasional boatman who put up a sail and we rode the waves to this delightful island. It appeared as a shallow dome, completely covered by deciduous trees and pines. The lower parts were surrounded by willow and alder trees and a ring of yellow reed grass, from which emerged coots, little grebe, great crested grebe and a family of mute swans.

Lord Charlemont's tentative offer had to be declined for lack of funds, but early in 1945 the USPC offered to buy the island. At a meeting between the Trust, the USPC and the Portadown and District Scouts Association it was agreed that the USPC would buy the island and hand it to the Trust, which would lease it to the Scouts as a training place for their members. Fred Storey, chairman of the USPC, himself purchased the island from the trustees of the Charlemont estate. At the opening ceremony on 30 May 1946 he handed the deeds to Gregg Wilson who in turn handed a lease to the Scouts Association, which became responsible for maintenance. The Chief Scout, Lord Rowallan, was welcomed by a monstrous eight-legged beast, but he was rescued by a noisy and highly painted band of natives armed with spears and bows and arrows.

In June 1945 the **Minnowburn Beeches**, a stand of trees along the Minnow Burn, which joins the Lagan near Shaw's Bridge, were threatened with destruction when a permit for felling was sought from the Ministry of Agriculture. The Shaw's Bridge area had been a special place for the citizens of south Belfast for generations, being at the end of the tramlines and providing walks along the Lagan towpath. It seemed, however, that a permit could not be refused on grounds of interference with natural beauty. We had discussions with county council officials, but it was clear that once the trees were down it would be impossible to prevent building. The Committee decided to consider purchase of the ten acres containing the trees and we negotiated with the owners. We were already embarking on a public appeal to buy **Collin Glen** on the western edge of Belfast, so we could not start another public fund-raising campaign. Instead we made a personal written plea to a number of residents in the Malone Road area, but without success. Then one morning there came into Austin Brown's office in Donegall Street a man called Bennett Sergie who said he would like to help. Brown was delighted at the prospect of getting perhaps £5, but Sergie said he wanted to give the full amount required – £1,400. We pressed the owners for an option to purchase, and the Ministry of Agriculture was marking time so far as a tree-felling permit was concerned. Before we could act, though, we learned that Sergie, who had given generously to hospitals and other charitable works, had taken his own life. He had not fulfilled his offer owing to financial difficulties, but although the land was not finally transferred to the Trust until 1952 (and then thanks to a rescue by the Ulster Land Fund), publicity had been given in the local press to Bennett Sergie's generous gesture and in our annual report for 1947 the Minnowburn Beeches were, somewhat hopefully, recorded as a National Trust property.

Collin Glen, the deep gorge of the Glen river, three miles west of the tram terminus on the Falls Road, had also formed a useful lung for the citizens of Belfast. Here picnic parties, Scout troops and naturalists had forgathered for many years. The glen, divided in two by the Glen Road where it curved round the foot of the hills, had been purchased by a businessman and the trees in the lower section were cut down. The more picturesque upper glen was likely also to be despoiled, so we decided to obtain an option to purchase it and to appeal to the public for funds. We formed a committee, representative of outdoor organisations in the Belfast area, and towards the end of 1945 issued an appeal for £2,000. This sum was subscribed, by small amounts, in 1946, and a full list of subscriptions totalling £2,364 was published in May 1947. It included a generous subscription from the Pilgrim Trust.

The achievements of this period were that we kept the Trust going through the war years; acquired two more properties and saved a third; and completed a statutory base for the Trust in the Province which was similar to that in England and Wales.

3
1947–60

When Lord Antrim attended his first meeting as Chairman on 12 February 1947 we were an extremely amateur committee, only three or four of us being in a position to do any work apart from attendance at meetings. Lord Antrim told me that too many of us were from the Belfast area and not enough country people were on the Committee – a consequence of wartime with its transport difficulties. We were beholden to the Rural Development Council for our meagre office facilities and we had very little money.

Lord Antrim, who lived at Glenarm Castle on the Antrim coast, had first joined the Committee in 1938. He was extremely energetic and his personality and capacity for hard work were to help make his chairmanship a particularly important and stimulating period. He always regarded working for the Trust as great fun and he made it fun too for those who worked with him. Committee meetings in his time were often as entertaining as they were effective – and there was a great deal to do, for it was in the years after he became Chairman that the Trust was to acquire many of its finest properties in Northern Ireland.

Some members were anxious about the state of Tollymore Park in Co. Down and in 1947 we made representations to the Ministry of Agriculture, who had acquired it from the Roden family. The property had deteriorated after occupation by the military during the war and we felt that commercial afforestation was likely to diminish the beauty of the Shimna Valley. We therefore put before the Ministry the idea which some years later germinated and blossomed into the very beautiful Tollymore Forest Park. In the meantime we obtained for our members permission to use the amenities of the estate.

We badly needed a social occasion and so it was decided to have a lunch for all members. A visit by Lord Macmillan, chairman of the Pilgrim Trust – which had contributed generously to both the White Park Bay and Collin Glen funds – was a suitable occasion and in May 1947 a lunch in his honour was held in the Grand Central Hotel, Belfast. Lord Antrim presided and the speakers were Lord Macmillan, Sir Basil Brooke, Prime Minister of Northern Ireland, and the vice chancellor of Queen's University, Sir David Lindsay-Keir. About 120 members and friends attended.

In 1946 the Trust nationally had made its Jubilee Appeal – to celebrate, a year late, the fiftieth anniversary of its foundation in 1895 – and while we extended the fund-raising to Northern Ireland, the principal appeal here was in respect of Collin Glen. In England the Government gave one pound for every pound subscribed to the Jubilee Appeal. In Northern Ireland the Minister of Finance not only gave a similar grant in respect of local subscriptions to the Jubilee Appeal, but also counted public subscriptions to the Collin Glen fund as ranking for grant.

Under the 1946 National Trust Act local authorities could now make contributions to the Trust, and Fermanagh County Council was the first to subscribe, with £20 in January 1948; Antrim, Armagh, Down and Londonderry followed.

Early in 1948 we advertised the job of Organising Secretary – our first paid post – and Lt. Comm. Harry White, of the Royal Naval Volunteer Reserve, was appointed in a part-time capacity. He was secretary of the King George's Fund for Sailors of which Lord Antrim was chairman; it suited Lord Antrim to have him working for both organisations and it suited the Trust, as half a salary was all we could afford. He was appointed on 1 April 1948 and continued part-time until 1952. I carried on until

October 1951 as Secretary, responsible for publicity, minutes and annual reports. In 1951 Harry White was able to devote more time to the Trust, and Austin Brown and I resigned our voluntary duties in the autumn of 1951. Brown's work as Treasurer and Estates Secretary had been invaluable. Jack Kingan, who had joined the Committee in June 1951, took on the job of Treasurer in October 1951 and Trevor Montgomery of the Committee's accountants, John McCullough & Sons, attended meetings and later was appointed as a member of Committee.

The Committee gradually became renewed, vacancies caused by death or resignation being filled by headquarters on the Committee's recommendations. On the resignation of John Mogey and Dorothy Robertson, Irene Calvert, Independent MP for Queen's University, and George Paterson, curator of the Armagh County Museum, were appointed in 1948. The Deputy Chairman, Gregg Wilson, died in April 1951. New members in 1952 were Fred Storey, the Trust's benefactor for Coney Island; Viola Grosvenor of Ely Lodge, County Fermanagh, and Jack Sayers, editor of the *Belfast Telegraph*. After the death of Charles McKisack in 1954, the Hon. Jean O'Neill, of Ahoghill, Co. Antrim, and Captain Peter Montgomery, of Blessingbourne, Co. Tyrone, joined the Committee in 1955. Charles E.B. Brett was appointed in 1956, following the death of his grandfather, Alfred Brett, and after the death of Alex Davison – a member since 1943 – Captain Michael Armstrong, of Armagh, joined the Committee in 1957.

In January 1953 it was decided to form a finance and general purposes committee. The first members were the Chairman, Austin Brown, John Perceval-Maxwell and Jack Sayers.

John Mogey, who unfortunately only served on the Committee for a year, had produced an attractive illustrated bulletin in May 1947. We got good press reports when a new property was acquired, but these, with the annual reports, were our only means of publicity. The appointment of Charles E.B. Brett, however, made a difference. He attended a meeting of the finance and general purposes committee in October 1957 and put forward proposals for a booklet about the properties, with drawings and maps; it would cost about £350 to print. The Committee granted up to £500, and Brett went ahead and produced a booklet which was the best thing the Trust had issued in Northern Ireland. It gave particulars of all the properties and details of access and opening times. The cover design, drawings and maps were by the local artist James MacIntyre. In May 1958 an exhibition of MacIntyre's drawings and of Trust photographs was held in the foyer of the Whitla Hall at Queen's University; Tyrone Guthrie opened the exhibition with a brilliant speech.

Charles Brett continued to develop publicity. In February 1959 the very energetic James Stormonth Darling, secretary of the Scottish National Trust, and his assistant, John Kerr, gave advice to the Committee on successful methods of publicity pursued in Scotland, and addressed a meeting of members and others in Bryson House, Belfast.

On 25 March 1959 John Betjeman, an enthusiastic supporter of the Trust, addressed a crowded Whitla Hall on the need to preserve the architectural heritage. His lecture, which was illustrated by a film, was witty, stimulating and provocative and led seventy-five members of his audience to join the Trust on the spot. It was not Betjeman's first visit to Belfast and he loved the city, particularly St Anne's Cathedral. In his talk he surprised and delighted many people by his appreciation of the City Hall, the Great Northern Railway station, the gas works building and St Mark's Church, Dundela.

Brett went on to produce for publication a three-page appeal folder, and arranged

Lt. Comm. Harry White, Secretary of the Committee, with John Betjeman in 1959. The poet addressed a public meeting in Belfast in support of the Trust's work.

for the Ulster Office in London to display photographs in Regent Street. Exhibitions in Bangor and Limavady were arranged in 1959.

In his UK budget statement in 1946, Hugh Dalton, the Labour Chancellor of the Exchequer, announced that he was setting aside a sum of £50 million as a National Land Fund, to be used for the creation of national parks and the acquisition for the public of stretches of coast and tracts of open country. In the Northern Ireland budget debate in Stormont in June 1947, Irene Calvert – not then a member of our Committee – asked whether a comparable fund could be established in the Province, since the Planning Advisory Board had recommended the setting-up of national parks here. The Finance Minister, Major Maynard Sinclair, said that if he were convinced it would be of advantage to have a fund here he would consider the matter, but at the moment he could see no point. He made it clear that we got no benefit from the Great Britain fund of £50 million. This matter was discussed at our next meeting and Lord Antrim wrote to Sir Basil Brooke asking for a similar fund here. The Prime Minister replied that no case had ever arisen in Northern Ireland in which land had been offered in payment of death duties: if a case did arise, special action could be taken to preserve the property if the Government thought it desirable to do so.

Nevertheless, Maynard Sinclair became attracted to the idea and in the Finance Act (Northern Ireland), 1948, the Ulster Land Fund was established for the purpose of the satisfaction of death duties by accepting property. This was quickly followed by a promise from the Minister to introduce a Bill, which became in 1949 the very enlightened Ulster Land Fund Act. This extended the purposes of the fund to the acquisition of land and buildings 'for the purposes of preserving or improving the natural beauty or amenities of any area, and of preserving the flora, fauna, or geological or physiographical features or features of ethnological, archaeological, architectural, historical, scientific or other special interest'; for the repair and maintenance of buildings and their contents; and for making grants or loans towards the acquisition of land or the maintenance of buildings. This Act was, in fact, ahead of Westminster which only caught up with it with the passing of the Historic Buildings and Ancient Monuments Act of 1953.

As early as November 1945 Lord Antrim suggested that the clifftop Mussenden Temple on Sir Hervey Bruce's estate at **Downhill**, Co. Londonderry – which had been acquired by Frederick W. Smyth – would make an admirable acquisition for the Trust, and the Committee asked him to approach the new owner. By 1949 Smyth was prepared to give the building to the Trust through his solicitors, L'Estrange & Brett, who were also the Trust's solicitors. Charles A. Brett suggested that Smyth make a gift of the temple, plus agreement to the 'sterilisation' from building of a 200-foot strip along the whole length of the cliff face, with no land other than a reasonable path to the temple from the Bishop's Gate. The Committee and the executive committee in London accepted the offer in December 1949.

A Cork architect, Henry H. Hill, with experience of eighteenth-century buildings was appointed, and started on the work of repair. Unfortunately he died in February 1951, and after discussion with the Earl of Rosse, chairman of headquarters' historic buildings committee, it was decided to give the contract to a London architect, David E. Nye. He employed the Dublin firm Dockrells for the restoration. The work had stopped for the Christmas holiday when, on the last day of 1952, Lord Antrim wrote to Nye that a fierce northerly gale had stripped much of the new copper off the roof and more was likely to be blown away. Dockrells was prepared to send men straight away, but it was almost impossible to work on the very exposed building at that time of year. In 1950 a press and radio appeal had been made for funds, but only £92 had been subscribed. Lord Antrim therefore went to the Minister of Finance, Maynard Sinclair, and by June 1953 £4,637 had been paid from the Ulster Land Fund towards the restoration of the temple, including the repair of the damage caused by the gale.

In September 1947 Lady Dorothy Lowry-Corry, sister of the Earl of Belmore, wrote to us about the possibility of **Castle Coole**, outside Enniskillen, being handed over to the Trust for preservation. The Committee appointed a sub-committee (the Chairman, Alfred Chart and myself) to look into the matter. With Charles A. Brett, Alfred Chart and I met Lady Lowry-Corry and explained the position under the impending Ulster Land Fund Bill. Following the death of the 6th Earl of Belmore in March 1949 she wrote again. On 8 November 1949 the Ulster Land Fund Act became law, and when the new Lord Belmore took up residence he got in touch with us. He wished to sell the house, together with ornamental parts of the demesne, and to loan the furniture and other contents of the house of which he was life tenant, provided his heir consented to this arrangement. In October 1950 Maynard Sinclair agreed to pay £50,000 (£20,000 for purchase and restoration, and £30,000 as endowment). In August 1951 the Ministry of Finance paid £50,000, including £12,500 purchase money, plus an endowment. On 28 June 1952 Castle Coole was officially opened by Sinclair, with a happy speech to about 300 people. In thanking the Minister, Jack Rathbone, secretary of the Trust as a whole, said that the house was probably the finest eighteenth-century neo-classical house in the Trust's care.

In June 1949 John S.W. Richardson offered **Derrymore House**, Co. Armagh, to the Trust. Committee member and architect John Seeds estimated that the cost of repairs would be about £2,750 and the annual upkeep about £50. The Committee asked Richardson for an endowment or grant of surrounding land, and in the meantime prospects under the Ulster Land Fund Bill were awaited. David Nye's opinion was sought and in September 1950 he estimated that £5,000–6,000 would be needed to put the house in order. John Seeds was now strongly opposed to the proposal, as he did not think the building important. Two further meetings were held at the second of which Seeds was still against the proposal, and it was again decided to ask Richardson for more land. Richardson agreed to this and also offered £700 towards the restoration of the property, and it was decided to submit the proposal to headquarters' historic buildings committee before going to the Ministry of Finance. (It took the Committee some time to get used to the discipline of going to the

144

Members of Castle Coole Cricket Club's first eleven in 1895: back row, from left, Revd A. Harris, M.J. Keenan, J. Cranston and C.J. Puxted; seated centre, from left, the Hon. C.L. Corry, Revd C.M. Stack, team captain Lord Corry, Capt A.P.T. Collum and Lt. Col. J.H. Eden; front, from left, H. Brady and W.J. Howard

headquarters committees before going to the Ministry of Finance.)

In August 1951 the Minister agreed a sum not exceeding £14,000 towards restoration and maintenance, including £1,000 to establish and fit out in the 'Treaty Room' a museum of memorabilia connected with Lord Castlereagh and the Act of Union. Committee member George Paterson, who had urged both the owner to give and the Committee to accept Derrymore, was asked to create the Castlereagh Museum by collecting and selecting furniture and pictures.

Nye, supported by Lord Antrim and Paterson, recommended demolition of the early-nineteenth-century addition made by the then owner Sir William Young – an entrance hall added on the north side of the U-shaped courtyard and entirely enclosing it. However, the historic buildings committee did not agree, and further discussions involving Lord Rosse, took place. Finally in June 1952 Lord Antrim, Lord Rosse and Robin Fedden, headquarters historic buildings secretary, visited Derrymore and agreed that the Young addition should come down: the demolition was carried out successfully. In October 1952 Perceval-Maxwell gave a talk on BBC radio about Derrymore which had now been legally transferred with parkland of forty-three acres.

In 1953 there was a lot of trouble over thatching Derrymore, a job which was being done with Norfolk reeds by the English firm Keebles. Lord Esher, by then chairman of the historic buildings committee, wrote to Lord Antrim on 24 March 1955: 'I think that we the administrators are not free from blame for the troubles that have arisen. For many years and with no success I have endeavoured to impress upon the staff that geographical propinquity is an essential factor in the selection of their architect . . . Northern Ireland is just the last straw which has exposed how pernicious this method is, and how easily it can lead to disaster. In this case not only the architect but the builder selected are supposed to operate from London in Northern Ireland . . . No genuine supervision, no real watch over conditions or over accidents can be expected under such circumstances.'

Despite the problems, Derrymore was officially opened by Lady Margaret Wakehurst, wife of the Governor of Northern Ireland, on 8 June 1957, when 300 people were present.

In January 1952 Committee member Jack Kingan offered a gift of **Ballymacormick Point**, Co. Down, consisting of thirty-five acres of land with his lease of the Crown foreshore. The Committee gladly accepted. The safeguarding of this point, so near to the expanding town of Bangor, was seen as an important step in the protection of the coastline of north Down.

If there was anywhere in Northern Ireland which would have suffered badly from postwar development, especially tourist development, it was **Cushendun**, a quiet coastal village in the Glens of Antrim, much loved by local people and by discriminating visitors. Committee member Austin Brown had a house a mile from the shore, and in October 1951 he was approached by Esther McNeill Moss (daughter of Ronald McNeill, Lord Cushendun, the law lord who had largely been responsible for the sensitive development of the village). She was considering selling her property – Cushendun House, the village, Rockport Lodge – over 100 acres in all. Austin Brown suggested that she should hand it over to the Trust, so she then got in touch with Lord Antrim and had a talk with him. A valuation was agreed and in January 1953 Lord Antrim went to Maynard Sinclair, who said he was willing to give £9,000 from the Ulster Land Fund, but suggested that the Trust should also acquire Glenmona House with its grounds of nineteen acres facing the middle of the bay. He pointed out that if this property were to be sold for speculative building, the object of the Trust would be defeated. The Committee agreed, subject to finance, and when Esther McNeill Moss agreed a valuation for the property, including Glenmona, the Ministry promised in all £20,000 from the Land Fund (the purchase price of £17,000; repairs, legal charges, etc. of £1,000; and an endowment of £2,000). The negotiations for the transfer of the property to the Trust were exceptionally quick and harmonious, though tragically Maynard Sinclair, a key figure in this and other acquisitions, and indeed the virtual creator of the Ulster Land Fund, died in the *Princess Victoria* ferry disaster in February 1953.

The Trust was concerned about the removal of sand from Cushendun beach, so warning notices were put up and the police were asked to help. In 1954 John McBride was employed as warden. He was succeeded in 1955 by William Robert McIlreavey who kept a note of permitted annual removals of sand, at Austin Brown's direction. This helped a little, but each year the problem continued; the police were unable to help. In the summer of 1957 John McNeill, known locally as 'John of the Rocks', succeeded McIlreavey as warden. The National Trust bylaws had been made as from 1 December 1955, but were not confirmed by the Northern Ireland Government until November 1957 when they became enforceable. It seemed probable that sand was being taken by or for builders for use outside the parish of Cushendun, so in the summer of 1958 notices were put up at Cushendun to the effect that unauthorised people found taking sand or gravel from the beach would be prosecuted. Charles E. B. Brett was spending a holiday at Cushendun and observed the frequency of the removal of sand. The warden took the names of Daniel McQuillan and Thomas McGreer, of Knocknacarry, who continued to take sand even though they had been warned not to, and the Committee's acting Secretary, Christopher Wall – a young ex-Guards officer from Trust headquarters covering for White who was ill – had summonses issued against them.

The case was to be heard in the Petty Sessions court in Cushendall on 4 September.

The Inspector General of the Royal Ulster Constabulary had warned Lord Antrim of the strong feeling locally against the National Trust for proceeding against local residents, and Lord Antrim undertook to discuss the matter with Glensman James McSparran QC. In the meantime Christopher Wall was instructed to ask for an adjournment of the court proceedings. Lord Antrim talked to McSparran and his brother Archie, who were regarded as leaders of the community in Glendun. They explained that the problem was linked with personality conflicts. Thomas McGreer was about to be prosecuted for removing sand that was needed for a repair job he was doing for James McSparran's own house. 'John of the Rocks', who had named McGreer and McQuillan, had not increased his popularity while doing a difficult job. The McSparrans explained that in 1920 Lord Cushendun had called a public meeting at the school at Knocknacarry, when he had said that he would allow residents in the parish to take whatever sand they needed for their own use from either end of the beach, provided they kept away from the 'warren', and that nobody abused the privilege by selling the sand to contractors.

In November 1958 Lord Antrim reported on his discussions with the McSparrans. It seemed to him that through the years Lord Cushendun's concession had been abused and by the time the National Trust acquired the property there was in fact no control over the exploitation of the sand. The Committee decided that the proceedings should be discontinued, but that a statement on the Trust's position should be made in court and published; that a meeting should be called to explain the Trust's views to local residents; and that notices be erected detailing the restrictions on the removal of sand and gravel. Nicholas Stevens of the Geography Department of Queen's University was asked to report on methods of maintaining the foreshore.

In December 1950 Perceval-Maxwell reported to the Committee that Lord Bangor (the writer and broadcaster Edward Ward), who had recently succeeded to the title on the death of his father, wished to hand over to the Trust, with certain reservations, the whole estate of **Castle Ward** in Co. Down. The proposal was warmly welcomed by the Committee. As usual there were trustees to be consulted and other doubts and delays. Lord Antrim was cautious about Castle Ward, but the Committee was enthusiastic. Colonel Charles Brocklehurst, a Trust agent, visited it and reported favourably on its position and the outstanding beauty of its lands. Rathbone also came over and loved Castle Ward, particularly the lands. The historic buildings committee was very favourably disposed and in March 1952 the Ministry of Finance said it would give £30,000 out of the Ulster Land Fund. We decided to ask the Ministry for a further £5,000, and in May 1952 Lord Antrim had an interview with the Minister, Brian Maginnis, who agreed to give a total of £35,000. The Dowager Lady Bangor was to continue to reside in the house. In April 1953 legal formalities were completed: the grounds were opened to visitors in 1953 and the house in 1955. Furniture in the public rooms was lent by Lord Bangor.

In August 1952 Lord Antrim visited **Florence Court** in Co. Fermanagh at the invitation of Lord Enniskillen (the 5th Earl). He had made over the house to his son, Lord Cole, but it was the father who was keen for the house to be taken over by the Trust. An offer followed from Lord Cole; the Committee welcomed it and it was accepted by the historic buildings committee in October, subject to finance. In April 1953 the Ministry of Finance agreed to give £45,000 for repairs and maintenance: £35,000 on completion of the legal formalities and £10,000 for payment of accounts. In May 1954 300 people attended an official opening by the Northern Ireland Governor, Lord Wakehurst.

The big fire at Florence Court on 22 March 1955 was a disaster, but Professor Sir Albert Richardson, President of the Royal Academy, was invited by Lord Antrim to come over, which he immediately did, and under his guidance the Belfast architect T.T. Houston arranged for the erection of a temporary roof which was put on by Robert Pierce of Enniskillen. Pierce did excellent work on the morning of the fire with encouragement and guidance from Committee member Viola Grosvenor: much of the furniture was saved and, in particular, damage to the dining-room ceiling was prevented. In April 1955 Richardson estimated that repairs would cost £25,000. There was much trouble from dry rot, but by January 1957, thanks to Pierce's work, it had been arrested. A Handel concert was held in Florence Court at the beginning of June 1959 and on 24 June a reopening ceremony was performed by Lord Rosse, with 250 members and guests present.

In October 1951 the Dowager Marchioness of Londonderry offered the gardens of **Mount Stewart**, on the east shore of Strangford Lough, to the Trust for a nominal sum; she would also covenant to pay £2,000 per annum during her lifetime towards the cost of upkeep. The Minister of Finance was consulted, as upkeep would eventually fall on the Trust, and for this the help of the Land Fund would be needed. In May 1952 the transfer of additional land was agreed with Lady Londonderry to provide a carpark and access to the gardens. The Ministry of Finance agreed to provide £2,600 for the purchase of the extra land, legal charges and the provision of a carpark and access. The transfer from Lady Londonderry and her daughter Lady Mairi Bury was completed in March 1955. Lady Londonderry continued to manage the gardens (eighty acres in all) which were opened to the public from 1 May 1956. In that year Lady Londonderry compiled and produced at her own expense an illustrated guide to the gardens for sale to the public, the proceeds going to the Trust. After the death of Lady Londonderry, Lady Bury took over the supervision of the gardens.

Lord Antrim and the Committee were not impressed with the importance of Mount Stewart House and Lord Antrim actually discussed with Lady Londonderry the possibility of taking over the house 'alienably', so that it could be used by the Trust for whatever purpose seemed best to it – Lady Londonderry had at one time suggested that it might be used in connection with the gardens, as a horticultural school or something similar. In July 1952 Rathbone had been to the Mount Stewart gardens and saw over them with Lady Bury. He wrote to Lord Antrim: 'I thought the whole place rather pretentious, cluttered up with gnomes and statues and that ugly topiary . . . Lord Bury wants us to take the house and I think Lady Londonderry would like us to do so too' . . . but 'Lady Londonderry does not, I think, at all like the idea of giving us a covenant over the house.' Rathbone was not keen to take on the house.

In negotiation with the Trust Lady Londonderry was always generous, but often elusive. On one such occasion, which involved headquarters, Lord Antrim wrote to Lord Esher: 'Lady Londonderry seems to have cast something of a spell over the office. Will it be any good your recalling to them the fact that Ramsay MacDonald was inveigled out of the Labour Party by her?'

In the first half of 1955 Lady Londonderry made strenuous efforts to get the Trust to take over the house; she wrote to Lord Antrim, to Rathbone, to Lord Esher and to Lord Brookeborough, the Northern Ireland Prime Minister. The reply given to her by all four was that the house was not considered to be architecturally up to the high standards set by the Trust, standards which had been raised in recent times, particularly when houses were taken over out of the Ulster Land Fund or other public funds. Eventually, however, in 1976, the Trust did acquire the house (see Chapter 5).

Maynard Sinclair had been keen to ensure the preservation of **Rowallane** Gardens, Co. Down, for the nation, but had failed in early negotiations with Hugh Armytage Moore, their owner and creator. Later Perceval-Maxwell approached Armytage Moore tentatively on behalf of the Trust, but reported that 'he was quite determined to hold on to his garden to his last breath without interference from anyone'. In May 1954 Lord Antrim asked Perceval-Maxwell's advice, as the Trust committees in London were anxious about the future of these great gardens. Lord Antrim, in a letter to Lord Esher, suggested an approach by David Bowes-Lyon of the Royal Horticultural Society, stressing the value that that society put upon the work Armytage Moore had done at Rowallane. This approach was successful and Armytage Moore wrote to Bowes-Lyon on 2 July 1954: 'As I approach the end of my Rowallane road . . . you suggest a procedure which may well dispose of certain personal anxiety as to the days to come . . .' He indicated that he would like to discuss with Lord Antrim the whole subject of the Trust and Rowallane. In a letter dated 20 July 1954 Rathbone wrote that the Trust's executive committee and gardens committee had agreed that the Rowallane Gardens were of top importance and should be preserved by the Trust, if possible. Authority was given to go ahead, subject to satisfactory financial arrangements.

Armytage Moore died in December 1954, leaving the property to his nephew K.M. Goodbody, subject to a life tenancy reserved to his widow, Jane. From a wasteland of whin and outcrops of rock Armytage Moore had created, over a period of more than fifty years, the attractive undulating gardens that have since been enjoyed by so many people. The property consisted of 207 acres of land, fifty-eight of them gardens and 149 arable or wild land. To enable the Trust to buy the property the Ministry of Finance gave £52,000 from the Ulster Land Fund. Committee member Jean O'Neill agreed to supervise the gardens for the Trust, and in May 1956 they were opened by Lady Cynthia Brookeborough, wife of the Northern Ireland Prime Minister. The opening was broadcast by the BBC and the gardens were the subject of a television programme. Jane Armytage Moore died in 1960 and her husband's extensive gardening library was presented to the Trust by K.M. Goodbody.

In January 1956 Captain William Lenox-Conyngham wrote to Lord Antrim offering **Springhill** House and grounds in Co. Londonderry and asking him to go and see them. Lord Antrim did so and was charmed. Charles Brocklehurst came over in March to see them and recommended acceptance. In March 1957 Lenox-Conyngham made a formal offer of the whole property and this was accepted. The house dates from the seventeenth century and had been continuously occupied by members of the Conyngham family. William Lenox-Conyngham made a gift of the house and sold to the Trust, for a sum representing only a fraction of their value, the contents, including much interesting furniture and many valuable pictures. The great house, the beech avenue leading to a ruined tower whose foundations dated from earlier times, and the garden were included in the gift. Considerable repairs had to be undertaken and the Government made a grant of £60,000 for repairs and an endowment. Unhappily Lenox-Conyngham died on 5 June 1957, but the transfer was signed before his death and the Trust came into possession on 1 July 1957. The property was officially opened on a fine spring day in April 1960 by the then Northern Ireland Minister of Finance, Captain Terence O'Neill.

After the civil defence authorities finally vacated **Lisnabreeny** on 1 August 1949 the YHA declined a tenancy offer, owing to the cost of the repairs and adaptations which would have been necessary. In February 1950 architect Denis O'D. Hanna reported that repairs and decorative work would cost at least £1,000. In May 1950

Harry White and a builder inspected the roof and found it generally satisfactory, with some minor repairs to be attended to. In September 1950 repairs had been completed and the house was advertised to let. In February 1951 a private tenant, A.D. Turner, was accepted on a twenty-one-year repairing lease.

A Committee meeting was held at **Killynether** in June 1947, followed by a discussion with representatives of the youth organisations using the house. Subsequently laurels were cut and about ninety trees were cleared away from in front of the house and sold. The house was found by White and chartered surveyor Hugh Frazer to be generally in good order and repairs were carried out. The remainder of the lands were derequisitioned. In August 1949 the Committee again held the monthly meeting at Killynether and inspected the building. It was estimated that the removal of the Nissen hut bases would cost £1,600, but the War Department offered only £400. After negotiations the Committee accepted £600. The joint committee of youth organisations and the YHA continued as tenants. Their caretaker, employed by the Trust, was prosecuted for illegally disposing of timber from the estate and was fined £5. In 1952 the joint committee gave up the tenancy, but the YHA continued as tenants until November 1953. There was now considerable dry rot and repairs were carried out. Private tenants were sought, but during gaps in occupation vandalism occurred. A tenant was installed in September 1955.

In October 1956 **Ballymoyer** was leased to the Ministry of Agriculture subject to public rights of way over various paths and to the planting of a good proportion of hardwoods. In May 1959 John Workman, the Trust's headquarters adviser on woodlands, reported favourably on what the Ministry was doing.

The only thing that ruffled the quiet beauty of **White Park Bay** during this period was the occasional presence of a bull on the strand. In September 1950 there was a letter from headquarters saying that an English member of the Trust, on holiday at the nearby village of Ballintoy, had complained about the bull being at large on the property. In September 1944 Mrs Bowyer, a member, when remitting her annual subscription, had written: 'Do you think anything could be done next year to make a visit to White Park Bay less of an ordeal to people like myself who are rather timorous of full grown bulls?'

Dan Logan, from whom the bay had been bought, was the life tenant, with the grazing rights, and he regarded the bull not only as a quiet beast but as having an inalienable right to graze upon the bay. We asked him nevertheless to restrain the bull during the summer period. Minutes record that the bull appeared again in 1946 and 1948. In the latter year local landowner and jurist Sir Malcolm Macnaghten was asked to bring his authority to bear on the matter. Logan said that the animal was quiet and that he had had no complaints. Inquiries by White in the district indicated that no-one had been attacked, and the matter was quietly let drop.

The period covered by this chapter was one of great expansion in the Trust's holdings in Northern Ireland, due largely to the indefatigable work of Lord Antrim and to the very ready help of successive Ministers of Finance. In promoting the Ulster Land Fund Act, Maynard Sinclair showed great imagination, and Lord Antrim's relationship with him and his successors was one of mutual trust. Lord Antrim regarded it as of the utmost importance that the Trust should aim for the highest standards and should ask the Government for assistance only in relation to properties that reached those standards, and then only for money that was absolutely necessary. The achievement of this period was to acquire, in addition to Ballymacormick Point, nine great properties, all of them with substantial help from the Ulster Land Fund.

In 1958 the Organising Secretary, Harry White, became ill and went into hospital. He came back to work in September 1958 and said that he was fit again. He was a most faithful servant to the Trust and, under Lord Antrim's constant direction, must have been working beyond his physical capacity. Lord Antrim and Robin Fedden did all the work of furnishing Castle Coole, Florence Court, Castle Ward, Derrymore, and Springhill, with some help from James Lees-Milne (headquarters adviser on historic buildings) but White was in constant attendance. For example, on Thursday 2 July 1959 Fedden, apropos of curtains for Florence Court, sent a memorandum marked 'Urgent' to White: 'Can you possibly arrange to send me, as a matter of urgency, two threads from the Aubusson carpet in the Drawing Room to give me the shade of the darker plum colour and the predominant green? If you could get these to me by Wednesday it would be the greatest help.' It is not recorded whether the deadline was met.

As late as 6 January 1960 White wrote to Lord Antrim about a collection of vehicles that the Ulster Museum wished to be housed in a Trust property. Only two days later he died.

4

1960–64

John Lewis-Crosby was appointed as Secretary in March 1960. Educated at Harrow and Trinity College, Dublin, he had wartime service in the Irish Guards. Before taking up the Trust post he was secretary general of the Council for the Encouragement of Music and the Arts in Northern Ireland.

In 1960 Alfred Chart, a founder member of the Committee, died and Trevor Montgomery retired. William Blease, Northern Ireland officer of the Irish Congress of Trade Unions, was appointed. George Loxton retired in 1961, and following Viola Grosvenor's retirement in 1962, Gerard Newe, secretary of the Northern Ireland Council of Social Services, was appointed. In 1963 John Perceval-Maxwell, a founder member and former Chairman, died; he had been a most active member, associated with the acquisition of a number of properties, notably Castle Ward. In May 1963 William Blease retired, and Lord Dunleath, of Ballywalter Park, Co. Down, joined the Committee in 1964.

In October 1962 Lord Antrim had treatment for heart trouble and he wished to have a Deputy Chairman appointed. He invited Lord Clanwilliam, of Montalto, Ballynahinch, Her Majesty's Lieutenant for Co. Down, to join the Committee and proposed that he be appointed as Deputy Chairman with power to transact the Trust's business in the Chairman's absence. Lord Clanwilliam attended his first Committee meeting in November 1962: at Lord Antrim's request, he agreed to supervise the management of properties in Counties Armagh, Down and Fermanagh, acting in consultation with Lord Antrim who continued to be responsible for properties in Counties Antrim, Londonderry and Tyrone. But Lord Antrim's period of relaxation was short and he again started to work in high gear in general control of the Committee's work.

In 1961 we moved our offices to 82 Dublin Road, Belfast. In 1962 Ian Sidgwick, a land agent, was appointed Assistant Secretary and Jeanne Cooper Foster to the post of Publicity Secretary, both paid posts. In September 1960 changes were made in the Committee's structure. The full Northern Ireland Committee was in future to deal only with matters of policy, and the executive committee (formerly the finance and general purposes committee) was to take all routine decisions in connection with finance. In turn, the executive committee handed over to three sub-committees detailed work on publicity, entertainments and a new 'Gardens Scheme'. The routine management of properties was undertaken by John Lewis-Crosby in consultation with the Chairman, expenditure being controlled through detailed annual estimates.

However, the separation of finance from policy is difficult and it became the Chairman's custom to report the decisions of the executive committee to the main Committee, an awkward procedure which often involved a rediscussion of matters decided. There was, too, a feeling amongst those members who were not on the executive committee that they were wasting their time, and this led to a decline in attendance. So it was decided in January 1964 that the Northern Ireland Committee should meet every month and that, meanwhile, the executive committee should be suspended. This arrangement continued until 1966 when a finance committee was formed (see Chapter 5).

In January 1962 Patrick Robinson, publicity officer of BBC Northern Ireland, joined the publicity committee, and in March 1962 the gardens committee was enlarged by the addition of eleven people.

John Lewis-Crosby,
Northern Ireland Regional
Secretary from 1960 to 1979

The publicity committee set to work in 1960 to increase the participation of members in Trust-related activities: visits to Government House at Hillsborough and to Baronscourt, Co. Tyrone, a reception at Springhill, a Georgian cricket match at Castle Ward against the Irish Georgian Society, and a visit to the Boyne Valley. Ten public lectures were given, in addition to lectures on the Trust's work; exhibitions were held at five centres in Northern Ireland as well as in London, and there was a series of six programmes on Ulster Television. The purpose of these activities was to increase membership as well as to stimulate the interest of members.

In 1961 Rathbone addressed a lively annual members' meeting and there were twenty-five events for members and others, including a ball at Castle Ward, a lecture by art historian Sir Anthony Blunt on country houses in the seventeenth and eighteenth centuries and a lecture by Nesca Robb on 'King William III, Lord of the Manor and Patron of the Arts'. In 1962 the Committee's twenty-fifth anniversary dinner was held at Parliament Buildings, Stormont (a year late); there was a wine party in the Belfast Harbour Office and there were twelve other members' events including a conference on landscape architecture and a gardens tour of south-west Scotland and Northern Ireland. A highlight of 1963 was a large public meeting in Derry, addressed by Mary McNeill on 'The Earl of Bristol, Bishop of Derry', and there were fourteen other events for members. The Committee organised three tours in Ireland. In 1964 there were twenty-one members' events, three tours were organised in Ireland and a Tours Assistant was appointed in May 1964.

In September 1961 the Chairman and Secretary attended as a deputation before Belfast Corporation in an appeal for funds, and, with encouragement from Sir Robin Kinahan, the Corporation undertook to give the Trust £200 a year. The Ulster Coastline Appeal was launched by the Committee in March 1962, the Pilgrim Trust starting it off with £500. In March 1963 an attractive leaflet on the appeal, prepared by the publicity committee (with drawings by James MacIntyre), was circulated to the Ministers concerned, Members of Parliament, Senators and planning officials. This appeal was a precursor of 'Enterprise Neptune' which was launched by the Trust as a whole in May 1965, and with which it was then merged. The Ulster Coastline Appeal had by June 1964 brought in sufficient funds for the North Antrim Cliff Path to be completed.

An entertainments committee, chaired by Lady Coralie Kinahan, was established in 1960 and worked hard for two years; it organised a number of events which, in addition to bringing in useful funds, provided entertainment for members and helped to generate publicity for the Trust.

Another innovation in 1960 which was to be of lasting benefit was the Gardens Scheme, through which the owners of private gardens opened them in aid of the Trust and other charities. The first gardens were opened on 16 April – Shane's Castle at Antrim (owned by Lord O'Neill) and Craigdun, Cullybackey (owned by Commander R.P. Martin) – and these were followed by twenty-five others. Under this scheme 60 per cent of the admission fees came to the Trust and the remainder to other charities. In 1961 thirty-nine gardens were opened; in 1962 twenty-four; in 1963 twenty-four; and in 1964 twenty-three. Jean O'Neill was chairman of the gardens committee and there was an organiser for each county. These garden openings were an immense success: they gave much pleasure to the public, they were a great advertisement for the Trust, and they brought in valuable funds. In 1964 ten thousand people visited the gardens and the net profit to the Trust was £530.

Membership grew substantially between 1959 and 1964 – from 834 to no fewer than 3,700 ordinary members. The number of life members grew from 49 to 120 and the number of corporate members from 27 to 39.

At the suggestion of George Paterson, the Committee commissioned Max Lock, the London architect/planner, to make a list of buildings of architectural merit in the city of Armagh. The funds for this came from local firms and organisations. The main idea was to draw the attention of Government to the need for listing in Northern Ireland. By August 1964 the list was completed, the first of its kind in Ireland, and in December 1964 Lewis-Crosby wrote to the Ministry of Finance suggesting that a listing of buildings throughout Northern Ireland should be undertaken.

George Paterson had drawn the Committee's attention to **Ardress**, a seventeenth-century house in Co. Armagh, with a main front added in the second half of the eighteenth century and with fine plasterwork. The house and 100 acres were available for purchase, and were acquired by the Committee in 1960 by means of a grant from the Ulster Land Fund. The work of renovation, decoration and furnishing was put in the hands of Belfast architect Robert McKinstry and James Lees-Milne. Some of the furniture belonged to the house, some came by legacy and gift and some was purchased. Michael Stapleton's original designs for plasterwork, on view during the first three months the house was open to the public, provided a guide for Lees-Milne in his scheme of decoration. During this period the garden was replanted under the direction of the Hon. Kathleen Armstrong, of Armagh. On 30 March 1962 the house was opened to the public by MP Sir Norman Stronge, of Tynan Abbey.

In 1960 the Trust obtained an option to buy the Bishop's Gate at **Downhill** and in 1961 the Ministry of Finance granted £3,000 from the Ulster Land Fund to buy, renovate and endow the gate and the gate lodge. Seventeen acres of land behind the gate also became available and the whole transaction was completed in 1962. In November 1962 Janet Eccles became resident caretaker and started her remarkable work of making a delightful woodland and water garden, and finding and restoring many of the Earl Bishop's classical trophies.

Also in 1960 the Committee secured an option to purchase the assets of the company which leased the **Giant's Causeway**, on the north Antrim coast, together with the freehold interest of the ground landlord, Captain Hugh Lecky. In the following year these options were exercised by means of a grant of £75,000 from the Ulster Land Fund. This secured all the Causeway land, with its famous rock formations, below the clifftop. Sir Anthony Macnaghten gave the land between the Causeway and the two hotels (the Royal and the Causeway) for a token sum and sold the headland between

Runkerry and Causeway Head for £100 an acre.

On 24 June 1963 the Giant's Causeway was declared open by Captain Terence O'Neill, by then Prime Minister of Northern Ireland, in the presence of over 1,000 people and in the teeth of a gale. By the end of 1963 negotiations carried out by Lewis-Crosby with farmers along the route of the **North Antrim Cliff Path** had reached a satisfactory point. Ninety-three acres had been purchased outright; there were restrictive covenants over forty-three acres; and right-of-way agreements over three and a half miles. The cliff path was completed in 1964 and on 20 June, in a ceremony at Dunseverick, it was opened by Lord Kilmaine, secretary of the Pilgrim Trust. A public right-of-way had been established and clearly tramped out on the ground over ten miles of one of the most attractive coastlines in the British Isles.

The rocky peninsula of one acre, on which the ruined **Dunseverick Castle** stands, was given to the Trust in 1962 by farmer Jack McCurdy. The site, halfway between the Causeway and White Park Bay, was of great importance in forming a link between these two properties.

Planning legislation at this period was weak and the Committee was concerned at the possibility of building along the Lagan Valley outside Belfast. The Government appointed Professor Robert Matthew to prepare a plan for the Greater Belfast area, and pending his report the Committee was pleased to hear the announcement in December 1961 that Government would provide 100-per-cent grant in respect of compensation paid by the local authorities for refusal of development permission in the area of Shaw's Bridge and the Minnow Burn. The Trust's small **Minnowburn Beeches** property, being so near Belfast, was vulnerable to the menace of dumping and at the beginning of 1961 the Committee had welcomed an anonymous gift of £500 for fencing. New fences were put up and the South Belfast Troop of Rover Scouts did much clearance work. In 1962 a field of seventeen acres became available adjoining the Minnowburn Beeches and the Committee acquired it by means of an Ulster Land Fund grant.

At this time the owner of Terrace Hill, a property prominent in the landscape of the Shaw's Bridge area, applied for planning permission for a large number of villas. The Committee feared that such development would spoil the area and, with the help of a further Land Fund grant, acquired 100 acres and opened up new footpaths. The Trust had now a holding of 128 acres and this Trust presence, together with other amenity developments in the area, was a significant factor in the establishment in 1974 of the Lagan Valley Regional Park.

In 1962 Lady Mairi Bury generously handed over to the Trust the elegant Temple of the Winds on land of five acres in the grounds of **Mount Stewart**. It is a replica of the Temple of the Winds in Athens and is attributed to the architect James 'Athenian' Stuart. In 1966, after repairs and restoration, the temple was opened to the public by the Governor of Northern Ireland, Lord Erskine.

Two new small properties acquired at this period were Derryscollop Grove, in Co. Armagh and the **Templetown Mausoleum**, in Co. Antrim. The hilltop beech trees known as Derryscollop Grove, near **Ardress**, had been given to the trustees for the people in the neighbourhood by Mrs Townley Balfour at the beginning of this century. S.J. Elliot, son of the last surviving trustee, gave the property to the Trust in 1963.

In November 1962 W. Henderson Smith, owner of Castle Upton, a Robert Adam house at Templepatrick, agreed to offer to the Trust the Templetown Mausoleum, also by Adam, in the graveyard which lies in the grounds of the house. Lord Templetown, head of the family for whom the mausoleum was built, approved the proposal. In

155

Lord Antrim, Chairman of the Northern Ireland Committee from 1947 to 1964, and of the Trust as a whole from 1965 to 1977

1963 Sir Robin Kinahan bought Castle Upton and he and Henderson Smith jointly gave the mausoleum to the Trust. The Ministry of Finance gave a grant of £2,400 as an endowment out of the Ulster Land Fund. The mausoleum was opened to the public by Lady Coralie Kinahan in 1966.

The task of furnishing Trust properties was made easier in 1962 when Lord Rossmore offered a loan of indefinite length of a large number of pictures and items of furniture from Rossmore Castle, Co. Monaghan. The Committee gratefully accepted this offer, and pictures and furniture were arranged at Castle Coole, Florence Court, Castle Ward and Ardress.

Important improvements were also made to several properties during this period. In 1960, following Lady Londonderry's death a year earlier, the Committee negotiated with the Ministry of Finance for an endowment for the gardens at Mount Stewart. The Ministry proposed to make an annual grant, but the Trust preferred a capital sum. Lord Antrim talked to Terence O'Neill about this and wrote to Rathbone on 19 January 1961: 'Times have changed over the Ulster Land Fund and we are going to have much more difficulty in getting money in the future, and that is chiefly because the Land Fund is going to be seriously reduced in order to finance an extension of the Museum and Art Gallery in Belfast and the creation of a Folk Museum.' In March 1961 the Committee agreed to accept an annual grant of £4,000 to date from Lady Londonderry's death in 1959. In 1960 Lady Mairi Bury took over the supervision of the gardens and put in hand a major scheme of renovation. In 1964 the garden ornaments were completely renovated by John Beattie, son of the original maker. He was in turn assisted by his son, Thomas, a student at the Belfast College of Art. The ornaments are made from materials mixed to the original sculptor's secret formula.

In 1963 an international work party organised by the Quakers demolished the wartime hut sites at **Derrymore House**. The thatching of the house with Norfolk reeds had not been a success, and in 1963 the Trust rethatched it with hand-threshed Irish wheat straw, suitably treated with bluestone. The house once more took on a completely native appearance, the English-style ridge having disappeared.

156

An unemployment relief scheme – the first of its kind in a National Trust property in Northern Ireland – was carried out at **Cushendun** in 1962, when marram grass was planted to combat the erosion of the beach and the warren. The scheme was only partly successful, but with another similar scheme in 1964 the beach's erosion defences were more securely rebuilt.

During the battle with the fire at **Florence Court** in 1955 a section of the house had become saturated with water. As a result, dry rot developed, and efforts were made to contain this throughout 1960. The infected rooms were then left for restoration until the following year. In 1964 the Minister of Finance authorised a grant of up to £20,000 for urgent repairs to the pavilions and to essential outbuildings and a further grant of £10,000 for the endowment of the property.

When the Trust took over the gardens at **Rowallane** a considerable part of them, and notably the rock garden, had returned almost to nature on account of the difficulty of employing adequate labour during and immediately after the war. Jean O'Neill and John Hanvey, who had been head gardener at Rowallane for forty years, planned and worked throughout the late 1950s and early 1960s to restore Armytage Moore's achievements; and in May 1964 the seal was set on their success when the rock garden was opened by Lord Wakehurst. In 1965 Hanvey was elected an Associate of Honour of the Royal Horticultural Society.

The great achievements of the period were the acquisition of the Giant's Causeway and the creation of the North Antrim Cliff Path, both very dear to Lord Antrim's heart. He was made chairman of Enterprise Neptune in 1964 and chairman of the general purposes committee at Trust headquarters in July 1964, a very onerous post requiring much travel in England and Wales and, having established Lord Clanwilliam as his successor, he resigned from the chairmanship of the Northern Ireland Committee with effect from 24 October 1964. He remained a nominal member of the Committee until September 1965 and he continued, from his key positions in London – he became chairman of the executive committee and of the Trust as a whole in 1965 – to exercise a benevolent interest in our affairs. From Glenarm he constantly visited properties in Antrim and Londonderry and kept up a stream of stimulating comment and advice.

In his seventeen and a half years as Chairman of the Northern Ireland Committee Lord Antrim's leadership lifted the Trust into a position where it could protect many of the best Ulster houses and gardens and much of our heritage of fine landscape. His commitment to the work was tremendous; before the present motorways were made he took long tiresome journeys to Fermanagh, Londonderry and Armagh to talk to wishful but apprehensive donors, to check colour schemes and to place furniture and pictures.

5

1964–78

With the appointment of Lord Clanwilliam as Chairman, the Committee took a new look at its financial arrangements with headquarters, and proposals for a form of greater integration with headquarters were approved. As a local committee, the Northern Ireland Committee had had to balance its books; as a regional committee, it could draw on the finances of the Trust as a whole. In taking on this new status we had to sacrifice a degree of independence, but in practice headquarters continued to treat us sympathetically.

Fred Storey died in May 1965, Michael Armstrong resigned in November 1965 and Irene Calvert, who had helped the Trust in Parliament and in getting support from industry and commerce, resigned in January 1966. Desmond McKee, Professor Alick Potter and naturalist Denis Leroux joined the Committee in May 1966 and in that month a finance sub-committee was formed, consisting of the honorary Treasurer, Jack Kingan, Brett and McKee. This committee met quarterly, and whenever possible Lord Clanwilliam took the chair; otherwise meetings were chaired by Kingan.

John Seeds died in December 1966, Jack Sayers in May 1969, and George Paterson in May 1971. Sayers had brought a fresh, independent and critical mind to bear on the Trust's work and he was of great help in the field of publicity. In March 1970 Austin Brown said that he would not allow his name to go forward for reappointment, a decision which the Committee accepted with regret for he had served them well for twenty-seven years, particularly in the lean 1940s, and later when he kept an eye on Cushendun. In July 1970 chartered surveyor John Williams-Ellis and Brian Rankin, a solicitor and chairman of the Northern Ireland Housing Trust, joined the Committee. In 1971 a new system of selecting Committee members was approved. The annual meeting of Northern Ireland members could elect two people – provided vacancies existed – and the names would be submitted to headquarters for approval. In May 1971 the first two members were appointed under this system: Margaret Garner and C. Douglas Deane.

Lord Clanwilliam,
Committee Chairman from
1964 to 1978

In July 1971 Anne Davey Orr, a designer/director in BBC Northern Ireland, and Patrick Robinson – who had been co-opted to the publicity committee and had served for about four years – resigned, and soon afterwards that committee was dissolved, but Brett was asked to continue to take a special interest in publicity.

In February 1972 Nesca Robb resigned when she went to live in England. Her resignation was received with great regret because of her long service and her generous gift of Lisnabreeny. She died in May 1976 and under her will the Trust in Northern Ireland was named as a residuary legatee. In June 1972 the annual members' meeting nominated for appointment to the Committee Major Gerald Reside and Jeanne Cooper Foster. In March 1973 Denis Leroux retired owing to ill health. The death in September 1976 of Brian Rankin was a great loss to the Committee.

The Northern Ireland 'troubles' broke out in the summer of 1969: the number of visitors to properties fell, and the times were not propitious for fund-raising. The Trust was involved in an early effort to improve community relations when a 'Pop for Peace' concert for young people was held at Minnowburn with the permission of the Trust's tenant. The violence was to continue, however, and Trust properties were the targets of bomb attacks several times in the 1970s.

As tenants of Belfast Corporation, the Trust had occupied Malone House, in lovely surroundings overlooking the Lagan Valley, since September 1971 when they had moved from Dublin Road. At 11 a.m. on 11 November 1976 members of the Ulster Tourist Development Association were arriving for their monthly meeting at Malone House. Three terrorists – two men and a woman – gained access with them, held the staff at gunpoint and planted two bombs, one on the ground floor and one upstairs. Within a very short time the bombs exploded and the house was on fire. It was a depressing sight, made worse by the spectacle of a fire engine sitting at the end of the drive as the house burned. Some divisions of the Fire Service were involved in a dispute and refused to fight fires unless life was at stake. Eventually part of the building was salvaged, and firemen, policemen and Trust staff carried out some important contents, including the portrait of Trigo, Sir William Barnett's Derby winner, but the Ulster Museum's costume collection, including its internationally important linen, was lost. As staff and friends of the Trust stood on the lawn surrounded by a few relics and sodden items salvaged from the shop – knowing that all the records, files, photographs and maps were lost – it was hard to know where to turn. The next day, however, the entire office staff descended on Rowallane House, at the invitation of John and Sheila Lewis-Crosby, whose home it was. They generously gave over the whole of the house, retreating into two rooms; and typewriters, desks, photocopiers and piles of stationery were squashed in among beds, sofas and tables, much to the bewilderment of the Lewis-Crosbys' four dogs.

Bombs were also planted by republican terrorists at Derrymore House on six occasions between 1972 and 1979. Some of them caused damage, but fortunately the caretaker, Edmund Baillie, and his two sisters, who live in part of the house, were unhurt. The damage would, however, have been catastrophic if it had not been for the great courage of Edmund Baillie in carrying out some of the bombs to the garden. After the first bomb attack the Committee presented him with a small token in appreciation of his devoted service, and he attended the Queen's garden party at Buckingham Palace on 17 July 1980.

Despite the troubles, recruitment to the Trust remained healthy and the years 1965–72 saw an increase in the number of full members in Northern Ireland from 3,935 to 5,937. The numbers of life, corporate and junior members also showed small

The Baillie family at Derrymore House. Caretaker Edmund Baillie more than once saved the house from severe bomb damage in the 1970s.

increases. From 1965 to 1969 there was an average each year of sixteen events for members, with no fewer than twenty-four in 1970. Although the number of events fell to nine in 1971, October of that year saw the formation of the first National Trust Members' Centre – in Belfast – to help recruitment and to involve members more personally in Trust work by participation in lectures, visits and functions. In future members' activities would be organised largely by the centre rather than by the Committee's staff. The centre's first chairwoman was Jeanne Cooper Foster; Peter Rankin became chairman in 1973. Funds raised by the centre in 1974 purchased a grand piano for Malone House and a wheelchair for disabled visitors to the gardens at Mount Stewart. In the years 1975, 1976 and 1977 the centre's chief interest was the creation of a theatre at Castle Ward and a gift of £500 for birdwatching display boards at Strangford Lough.

Throughout the period 1965–75 the Committee organised tours at home and abroad. They were both educational and social, covering gardens, architecture and landscape, and ranging from Ireland to the Middle East, India, the United States, Australia and the USSR. The average number of tours was three a year and the average net annual profit was £870. However, the policy from headquarters tended not to favour tours as a fund-raising activity, and after 1975 they were discontinued.

The Gardens Scheme continued to be a valuable source of funds, and many generous people opened their gardens in this period, bringing much pleasure to the public. The annual net profit rose from £568 in 1965 to £3,491 in 1977. The gardens committee was chaired by Jean O'Neill (or Lady O'Neill of the Maine, as she became) until 1975, when Margaret Reside took over.

The period of Lord Clanwilliam's chairmanship saw a change in the pattern of property acquisitions, with a shift away from 'big houses' and towards areas of unspoilt coast and countryside. The acquisition of coastal properties was largely made possible

160

through a major new nationwide National Trust campaign – Enterprise Neptune. The aim of the campaign, launched in 1965, was to raise enough money to buy some 900 miles of undeveloped coast around England, Wales and Northern Ireland. In June 1965 Commodore Rives Shillington was appointed local part-time director of Enterprise Neptune and in September 1965 the campaign was launched by the Lord Mayor of Belfast in the City Hall. The Mayor of Londonderry launched the campaign there early in 1966. At the end of 1965, £9,506 had been contributed and by the end of 1966 the figure was £35,714. The amount raised in Northern Ireland rose steadily to £96,968 by 1974; by that time the £2 million mark had been reached by Neptune in the Trust as a whole, so the local figure, just less than a twentieth of the overall total, was very creditable.

In 1965 the Trust acquired the virtually deserted village of **Kearney** on the outer shore of the Ards Peninsula – thirty-one acres of foreshore and four acres of village land with thirteen houses and covenants over a further 284 acres. This was the first local purchase with Enterprise Neptune funds. In the following year the adjoining **Knockinelder** beach was bought with Neptune funds – eight acres of beach and adjoining land, with covenants over thirty-nine acres. Together the two properties cover two miles of coastline.

Two more Co. Down acquisitions through Enterprise Neptune were the **Mourne Coastal Path** and **Blockhouse Island and Green Island**. The Mourne path came into being after some fifty-eight acres were bought in 1968, and the Trust took the opportunity of an unemployment relief scheme to open up walks from Bloody Bridge, both for access to Slieve Donard and southwards along the coast. In June 1976 one acre to the south of the Trust's property was acquired from Stanley and Rosemary Reid in exchange for life membership for themselves and their children. In September 1977 the Four Winds Trust gave £1,000 for the path. Blockhouse Island and Green Island, comprising together two acres at the mouth of Carlingford Lough, were accepted in 1968 as a gift from the Kilmorey estate as a result of the Neptune appeal. They are nesting sites for common, arctic and roseate terns and are managed without expense to the Trust by the Royal Society for the Protection of Birds.

The first Neptune acquisition in Co. Antrim was a two-acre field overlooking the north end of the beach at Cushendun, and purchased in 1965. Between then and 1978 the Trust gained five more Antrim coast properties, including some of the North's most spectacular scenery.

Buying a salmon fishery is not an everyday event, but when **Carrick-a-Rede**, east of Ballintoy, came up for sale in 1967, the Trust seized the opportunity to buy it by tender, using £14,000 from Neptune funds. The property included two fisheries, Carrick-a-Rede and Larrybane, thirty acres of land, a number of islands and a mile of cliff land. The Carrick-a-Rede fishery was let for the 1967 season, the tenants agreeing to erect the traditional rope-bridge to Carrick-a-Rede Island for that year. This satisfactory arrangement has continued and the use of the rope-bridge has been a great delight to thousands of people ever since. The bridge is taken down from mid-September to early May. One of the islands acquired was Sheep Island, a perpendicular stack with a flat grassy top, a great breeding ground for puffins, razorbills and guillemots. The other islands were those at Ballintoy Harbour and north east of White Park Bay. Carrick-a-Rede was declared open to the public by Northern Ireland Senator Millar Cameron in 1970.

Larrybane itself was not acquired until eleven years after Carrick-a-Rede. The limestone headland had been virtually destroyed by quarrying, but it is still a beautiful stretch of coast and in 1978 the Trust was able to acquire fifty-eight acres of coastline, including the disused limeworks and basalt quarry. This was achieved with Neptune funds and a grant from the Four Winds Trust.

I think it was the geographer Estyn Evans who first suggested that **Murlough Bay** should be preserved by the Trust and I spent a weekend just after the war discussing with the local landowners, the Stewart family of Benvan, how this might be done – but with no result because the Committee then had no money. In March 1967 John Lewis-Crosby completed negotiations for the purchase of 337 acres from Patrick McCarry for £4,755 and of 185 acres of the Stewart land from Mary McCloy (née Stewart) for £2,770. Lewis-Crosby also successfully negotiated with Neptune funds for long leases on land at **Fair Head**, bringing the total acreage taken under Trust management in this year to 764. In 1969 the Trust bought two cottages, together with land for a small carpark, at Coolan Lough, a clachan on Fair Head. Benvan House, in its fine setting on the cliff overlooking Murlough Bay, was bought in 1978 with Northern Ireland Committee funds.

In 1968 four acres of land at Dunseverick, including the little harbour, were purchased with Neptune funds and added to the **North Antrim Cliff Path**, and in 1973 another Neptune purchase was a small area of land at **Layde**, outside Cushendall, where a path was made leading from the carpark to a small beach, passing by the ruins of Layde Church.

Of the many projects which John Lewis-Crosby promoted as Secretary, the **Strangford Lough** Wildlife Scheme was the most his own and also the most successful. In September 1964 he reported that a preliminary meeting of interested groups had taken place and that various proposals had been considered for the conservation of wildlife, particularly birdlife, in the area of the lough. He put a detailed scheme before the Committee in October 1964 and a steering committee was appointed, representing naturalists, wildfowlers and landowners with three members from the Trust –Wilfrid Capper, Lord Dunleath and myself. I was asked to chair the steering committee, a position which I undertook because, being neither a shooter nor a very good naturalist, I was comparatively neutral on the vital question of the control of wildfowling.

In January 1965 we held a press conference and Lewis-Crosby consulted landowners and farmers around the lough by letter for their views on the proposals. In May 1965 we reported to the Northern Ireland Committee and it was decided that a house at Ringhaddy should be rented for a warden, whom it was proposed to appoint. We advertised the post and, on a happy day for the Trust, selected keen ornithologist Arthur Irvine. The steering committee's blueprint, drafted by Lewis-Crosby, was approved by the Northern Ireland Committee and the steering committee was wound up on 2 February 1966. Major Hugh Montgomery, of Rosemount, Greyabbey, was appointed chairman of the new Strangford Lough committee, a sub-committee of the Northern Ireland Committee. The new committee had observers from the Stormont Ministries of Home Affairs and Development and had consultants from the Wildfowlers' Association of Great Britain and Ireland, the Nature Conservancy and the Wildfowl Trust.

The scheme was inaugurated in May 1966 by the Minister of Home Affairs, Brian McConnell, and was supported by an annual deficiency grant given by his Ministry and later by the Ministry of Development. The project has been a great success in conserving the bird population, in protecting wildlife habitat, and in terms of its acceptance by the public and by local and central government.

An important strategy employed by Lewis-Crosby and the committee was the acquisition of foreshore which became the basis of the scheme. Leases over areas of foreshore were granted to the Trust by the Crown Estate Commissioners, Lady Mairi Bury, William Montgomery, Lady Cynthia Nugent, Georgina Stone and Jacqueline Day. Land to provide hides and carparks was donated in 1975 by Lady Mairi Bury, William and Clare McCully, Tony McCleery, Annie Lemon and Thomas McCann, and foreshore was given by the trustees of the Harrison estate. Informal arrangements were made with the Baroness de Ros and James Mackie about other areas of foreshore.

In the first year the committee established refuge areas at Castleward Bay, Ringdufferin, Quoile Pondage, Mahee Bay, the north-east of the lough – at the points known as the Sluice-gates, the Maltings and the Butterlump Stone – and on the Montgomery islands off Greyabbey. The Trust also acquired from Margery Glendinning woodlands bordering on Mahee Bay, and a small carpark and a hide were built there in 1968 and opened to the public by the Minister of Development, William Fitzsimons. On the same day the Duke of Edinburgh explored by boat and on foot many parts of the whole scheme. In 1968 the Trust took a lease on Shoan Island, off the mouth of the Quoile river.

In November 1969 Hugh Montgomery died and in December Dr Patrick Boaden, director of Queen's University Marine Biology Station at Portaferry, was appointed chairman of the committee. In 1970 a viewpoint, with a display panel provided by Shell and ICI, was established at Ballyreagh (the Maltings), and a picnic site was provided at Greyabbey, on land already given by Hugh Montgomery. A hide over-looking the Audley's Bay refuge, and named in memory of the naturalist Robert Eagleson, was opened at Castle Ward.

In 1972 a sponsored litter collection around the lough was a great success; sixty-eight acres of foreshore were cleared in a single day by some 500 volunteers who gathered 2,000 sackfuls – or twenty tons – of litter. A sum of £500 was raised for the wildlife scheme.

A certificate of merit was awarded to Patrick Mackie in June 1976 in recognition of his contributions to the breeding of wildfowl (mainly mallard, greylag and barnacle geese); to research into the ringing of wildfowl at Mahee Island; and to the co-ordination of a bird-count data bank for Strangford Lough. At Mahee Island 6,000 duck were ringed, and returns from this operation confirmed the summer breeding grounds of our winter-visiting wildfowl to be mainly centred on northern Scandinavia and Soviet Siberia. The data bank has enabled the Trust to defend its policies relating to the size and siting of refuge areas. In October 1977 Anne Montgomery opened a hide in her husband's memory at Castle Espie on land given by Tony McCleery.

Not far from the lough, the Glastry Ponds, between Kircubbin and Ballyhalbert on the Ards Peninsula, were given in 1976 by the Coalisland Brick and Pipe Company. The site consists of forty acres of disused claypits and adjoining land, and in April 1977 the Carnegie Trust gave £750 which enabled an outdoor educational display to be made there.

Another major conservation scheme undertaken during Lord Clanwilliam's chairmanship was the establishment of the **Murlough Nature Reserve** at Dundrum, Co. Down. As early as 1963 Lord Downshire had offered the Trust 200 acres of sandhills at Murlough Bay, together with restrictive covenants over the rest of his property there. Unfortunately, however, the sandhills had been leased to the Ministry of Agriculture for forestry, and the trustees for the Downshire estate were unable to carry out Lord Downshire's wish. The value of the sand-dunes for scientific purposes was appreciated by a number of people, notably in the Archaeology and Natural

History Departments at Queen's University, and the Trust persevered in negotiations for four years until in 1967 the Ministry of Agriculture relinquished its interest and the Trust was granted a lease in perpetuity for 475 acres of beach and dunes. The rent was fixed at £197 per annum, the Trust undertaking to hold the land inalienably, only to admit the public along established rights of way and to employ a warden. The Ministry of Finance gave an endowment of £20,000 and Queen's University Botany Department co-operated in the employment of a warden. In 1967 Reginald Parker became chairman of the reserve management committee and Jo Whatmough was made warden of both the reserve and a new 'field centre'. The access arrangement then made has continued, the public being admitted freely to the shore and the dunes immediately facing the sea, while the inland area is conserved. The reserve was recognised as a National Nature Reserve in 1979.

In the early 1970s Murlough House was no longer required by Lord Downshire as a summer residence and his trustees offered to sell the house to the Trust. The Trust wished to control but not to own the house, and an arrangement was made with the trustees and Queen's University whereby the university acquired the house, subject to protective covenants with the Trust which retained the stable block, including accommodation for an assistant warden. In all, 928½ acres were bought in 1967 and 1974 by means of the Ulster Land Fund. A further half-acre was acquired in 1975 with Neptune funds. Nine acres, including a cottage, for a carpark and information centre, were bought in 1977 with Neptune funds and from a bequest from naturalist Grace Drennan.

Alongside these important developments in nature conservation work, the Trust was also acquiring other 'different' types of historical property, including a mill and a printing press.

In 1966 J.S. Henderson offered **Wellbrook Beetling Mill** in Co. Tyrone to the Trust; the mill had stopped working only a year previously, and the Committee recommended acceptance, subject to finance for renovation and for endowment. By 1968 the mill and one acre had been acquired, and by 1969 the machinery was in working order; the wheel could once again operate the beetles to deafening effect. This achievement was due to a public appeal and generous support from the Landmark Trust. In 1970 a further three acres were added and the restored mill was formally opened to the public by John Gray, chairman of the Linen Industry Council.

In 1965 **Gray's Printing Press**, with its attractive bow-shaped front in Main Street, Strabane – and the nineteenth-century press itself – was purchased by means of a grant from the Ulster Land Fund. It was in this shop that John Dunlap, printer of the American Declaration of Independence, learned his trade. It was opened to the public in June 1966 by Dean Francis B. Sayre, of Washington, grandson of President Woodrow Wilson. In 1971 the shop suffered bomb damage, with other buildings in Main Street, and in September 1973 it was damaged yet again, in a bomb attack on the bank opposite the building.

In 1972 the Ulster Architectural Heritage Society offered to appeal for funds to acquire **Hezlett House**, Co. Londonderry, a thatched cottage important because of the unusual construction of its roof. The society made the appeal and in 1976 the Trust bought the house with the funds obtained, assisted by a grant of £33,500 from the Ulster Land Fund.

In 1965 the Committee agreed to act as managing agent for the traditional homesteads of the forebears of President Woodrow Wilson and President Chester Arthur, at Strabane, Co. Tyrone, and Cullybackey, Co. Antrim. Both houses had been acquired by the Government of Northern Ireland, and Terence O'Neill, when he was still Minister of Finance in 1963, had been keen that the Trust should take them over, but the headquarters executive committee turned them down on the grounds of lack of actual proof that these were the ancestral homes. Headquarters had had an unfortunate experience in acquiring the reputed ancestral home of President Abraham Lincoln, only to have this later disproved, and was determined not to be caught out again. So the Committee agreed to act simply as agents for the Government. Eventually in October 1979 the Department of Finance agreed to take back the management of both houses.

The Mellon family house at Camphill, Omagh, ancestral home of the American bankers of that name, was acquired and managed by the Committee in the same way on behalf of the Mellon family, who funded it through the Scotch-Irish Trust of Ulster. Later the Scotch-Irish Trust developed the Ulster-American Folk Park round the Mellon home, and in 1976 took over the homestead from the Committee, to make it the nucleus of the park.

Several other interesting properties were given or purchased during this period. In 1965 the Trust acquired two gate lodges at **Castle Coole**: the Weir's Bridge lodge at the main entrance, and the attractive but dilapidated Heather Cottage. The former was acquired with local funds; the latter was a gift from the trustees of the Earl of Belmore, and the cost of renovation was provided by the Ladies Dorothy, Margaret and Violet Lowry-Corry.

Clough Castle, Co. Down, a Norman motte and bailey, with its castle ruins and one acre, was bequeathed to the Trust in 1967 by Robert Cromie Jordan. The Trust leased it to the Ministry of Finance for preservation by the Historic Monuments and Buildings Branch. In the same year Captain Dick Ker presented the forty-three-acre **Lighthouse Island**, one of the Copeland Islands, lying to the south of the entrance to Belfast Lough. The Copeland Bird Observatory was already established there and the island continues to be managed, on the Trust's behalf, by the observatory. In 1968 **Glenoe**, a glen of four acres with a waterfall, adjacent to the village of Glenoe in Co. Antrim, was given by Thomas Shaw and Lord Trevor. The Trust constructed steps, a bridge and a small carpark.

Acquisitions in the mid-1970s included Cockle Island, about half an acre off the Co. Down coast near **Ballymacormick Point**, given by Gavin Perceval-Maxwell; and **Bar Mouth**, at the mouth of the Bann river – nineteen acres and shooting rights over a further twenty-two acres – purchased with funds raised by a special appeal. Craigagh Wood, a mile from **Cushendun**, a mixed deciduous wood with some Scots pine, which is beautiful in all seasons, came under the Trust's protection in 1976 when Patricia English gave covenants over its seventy-four acres. The Trust's influence at Cushendun itself had been extended in 1969 when Margaret Brooke gave covenants over a cottage and half an acre, and in 1971 when Gilbert McNeill Moss gave a covenant over a further five acres.

As well as gaining new properties, the Trust in this period increased its holdings at two of the great estates, **Mount Stewart** and **Castle Ward** – most importantly at Mount Stewart where the house itself was eventually acquired. In 1968 340 acres of woodland on that estate, important for the shelter and enjoyment of the gardens, were acquired from Lady Mairi Bury. These woodlands were in turn leased to the Forest Service of the Ministry of Agriculture on terms which provide for replanting in areas adjoining the gardens and the lough shore. Also in 1968 the Ballycastle cottages, formerly the homes of workers, were purchased from the Mount Stewart estate. The Temple of the Winds was somewhat removed from the gardens, and so in 1971 Lady

Bury gave rights of way to enable woodland paths to be made leading out from the carpark at the temple.

Lady Bury was anxious to add to her other benefactions to the Trust by giving Mount Stewart House itself, and on 31 March 1976 she donated it to the Trust, together with its contents and an endowment of £100,000. The Ministry of Finance granted an endowment of £340,377 from the Ulster Land Fund. The house was opened to the public on 1 July 1977, twenty-one years after the opening of the gardens. The house at that time had not been considered to be up to the high National Trust standards, and yet now it was accepted without difficulty. It was a very practical decision: the gardens had been a great success and the Trust had the courage to change its mind, for it had always been conscious that a division of ownership between the house and the gardens might eventually lead to the house getting into unsympathetic hands. There was, too, a long-felt need for a major property, with a house suitable for functions, within easy reach of Belfast. Thanks to the continued generosity of Lady Bury, the preservation of the house in its beautiful setting of gardens and parkland was ensured. The gardens, however, needed further support, and in 1977 the Committee obtained an additional endowment of £95,000 from the Department of Finance.

Parts of the Castle Ward estate had not been transferred to the Trust in the settlement of 1953, but in 1968 the Trust purchased these from Lord Bangor by means of a grant from the Ulster Land Fund. The new acquisitions consisted of fifty-five acres of land on the shore at Audleystown; the dower house (Terenichol) with twenty acres of scrubland; the gamekeeper's cottage; and a reversionary interest in the woodlands leased to the Ministry of Agriculture, 204 acres in all. This brought the holding to a total of 792 acres. In the mid-1970s, a valuable amenity was secured separately, just on the edge of the Castle Ward estate. Strangford Bay is a quiet stretch of water almost surrounded by trees and lying between Castle Ward and the de Ros estate. In 1977 Baroness de Ros gave the Trust a right of way and sufficient access land to construct the Strangford Bay Path from the Black Causeway at Castle Ward along the east shore of the bay to Strangford village.

Alongside considerable physical expansion, the 1960s and 1970s saw a significant extension of the Trust's operations in terms of educating and involving the public. In 1967 and 1968 the publicity committee designed and prepared guidebooks and proposed the production of a film about Trust properties in Northern Ireland. Entitled *Beauty to Last*, the film was made in 1968 and received its première in February 1969. By the end of that year it had been shown in twelve countries and translated into eight languages, and twenty-six copies had been sold. It was directed by Derek Bailey and the script by Jeanne Cooper Foster was read by Denis Hawthorne. The film cost £1,209, and was paid for by contributions from the Gardens Scheme, the Northern Ireland Tourist Board and the tobacco company Carreras. Also in 1969 a new folder guide was written by Noel Mitchell and there were twenty programmes on television featuring the Trust in Northern Ireland.

Declan Leyden was appointed as Northern Ireland Field Education Officer on 1 April 1968 and started a new phase in Trust activity, visiting schools, organising field trips and work parties at Trust properties. In 1969 he visited thirty-five schools and organised as many field trips and work parties. Five nature trails were opened, 'Acorn camps' were set up at Castle Ward and Murlough Bay and Acorn groups – parties of young volunteers – did useful work at several other properties. These activities were increased in 1970, 1971 and 1972. In July 1972 Leyden resigned and, as his post was not filled, the momentum of educational activity was diminished, but schools

166

continued to use the properties, and after the appointment of Lyn Gallagher as Regional Information Officer in 1975 a notable innovation was the preparation of school information packs for Castle Ward, Murlough Nature Reserve and Mount Stewart.

The Committee under Lord Clanwilliam endeavoured to maintain properties to a higher standard than had been possible in the past, and at the same time to make them more attractive to the public. The staff at those houses open to the public also began actively to recruit new members.

At **Springhill** the dovecote in the lower yard was renovated in 1965, and opened to the public in 1966, and the costume museum was expanded under the care of Marie Adams. At Castle Ward the laundry was furnished and opened to the public in 1968; under the supervision of Margaret Garner this became one of the estate's outstanding attractions. A carpark and lavatories were provided in the lower farmyard, and elsewhere on the property the Temple was renovated and the Temple Water cleared with the help of a grant from the Ulster Land Fund. A scheme of replanting around the Temple Water was planned by landscape architect Lanning Roper to recreate the original landscape. A wildfowl collection was established as part of the Strangford Lough Wildlife Scheme, with the help of generous donations from the Mackie family and the Gallaher Mitchell Trust.

Lady Bangor left Castle Ward in 1968, and it was decided to appoint a custodian. A scheme of redecoration was undertaken, directed by interior designer John Fowler, and a flat for the custodian was provided on the top floor and a lift installed with the help of a grant from the Ulster Land Fund. In June 1972 the Civic Trust made an award for the Temple and the Temple Water, and in September 1973 the Calouste Gulbenkian Foundation made a grant of £2,500 for the theatre. In 1974 Lord and Lady Enniskillen left Florence Court and Lord Anthony Hamilton was appointed administrator there.

On account of the long history of dry rot at **Killynether**, it had not been possible to find satisfactory tenants who were prepared to stay in the house, and so with great regret the Trust had it demolished in 1966. The Countryside and Wildlife Branch of the Department of the Environment acquired Scrabo Hill and its tower and proposed to develop the hill as a country park. The Committee therefore decided to lease the Killynether woods to the DoE so that the two properties could be managed together, and an agreement to that effect was made in 1978. The Scrabo Country Park has now been successfully established.

At Cushendun a carefully screened park for touring caravans was laid out on Trust property in 1968 by Antrim County Council. By 1977 nearly all the cottages in the village itself had been modernised internally, and the harbour and the mouth of the river had been improved. A breakwater was constructed to reduce sand erosion on the beach and to improve the anchorage.

At **Downhill** the Earl Bishop's fish ponds were restored in 1968, to constitute a three-acre lake.

In 1967 John McConaghy was appointed as North Coast Warden and in March 1968 an information centre was opened at Causeway Head. In 1972 Antrim County Council widened the road down to the **Giant's Causeway** sufficiently to permit a small bus to be used on it. The Ulster Tourist Development Association provided a bus which was handed over at a ceremony at the Causeway by John Swan, chairman of the UTDA.

Throughout this period successive government schemes for the relief of unemployment were used by the Trust to get work done. All such schemes were beneficial to the Trust, particularly as the men who were employed from the countryside always had useful rural skills. From 1968 to 1975 there were about sixteen schemes in almost continuous operation, employing about 100 men. The well funded Enterprise Ulster took over in 1976 and under it the Trust benefited even more, recouping all expenditure from Government on a monthly basis; for the financial years 1976–7 and 1977–8 allocations of £100,000 and £190,000 respectively were made to the Trust.

In the period of Lord Clanwilliam's chairmanship the Trust achieved much in acquiring new property, in developing and conserving existing property and in recruiting and holding the interest of the public. Some twenty-two properties were acquired, apart from the two presidents' houses and additional lands at Cushendun, Castle Coole and Castle Ward. In the field of nature conservation outstanding work was done in creating the Murlough Nature Reserve and in developing the unique Strangford Lough Wildlife Scheme.

When he took over from Lord Antrim, Lord Clanwilliam had already had a period as Deputy Chairman in which he was responsible for properties in the southern half of the province, and this experience stood him in good stead. The Committee set him the formidable task of supervising the management of properties on its behalf, and he took his role seriously, spending a great deal of time on the many varied problems that the Trust's growth had created. He made a point of 'walking' the properties at least once a year and he was particularly expert on the management of land and on the furnishing and decoration of the historic houses in the Trust's care.

On his inspection tours Lord Clanwilliam had developed a particular detestation for a silo at the limestone quarry on Larrybane Head, which he saw as a blot on this beautiful landscape, and he had asked, a little tentatively, if he might be allowed to press the plunger which would dynamite the tower into oblivion. This was seen as an opportunity for a farewell party to the Chairman on his retirement in 1978, and the Trust's staff asked Graham Harron, the goldsmith, to make a silver model of the plunger decorated with representations of Trust work to present to Lord Clanwilliam. The idea was behind the times, of course, for it turned out that plungers were no longer used, and that modern-day dynamiting was done by the press of a button. The next complication was that Lord Clanwilliam himself could not press the button, as he might be personally liable for any damage inadvertently caused, so it was arranged he would fire a rocket flare, giving the signal for the blasting to start. To add to the complication, it was felt by the detachment of troops who were helping the Trust to dynamite the tower, that it would be better to evacuate the whole village of Ballintoy in case of accident. An explanatory letter was hand-delivered to every household, inviting the people of Ballintoy to come to Carrick-a-Rede where they would get a cup of tea and where they could watch the spectacle.

A small group of staff gathered on the headland itself on a bright, clear afternoon, and after a brief presentation to Lord Clanwilliam all was ready. He fired the rocket. The watchers saw a huge cloud of dust rising at the headland, heard the resounding explosion and stared as the cloud settled . . . to reveal the tower absolutely intact. Two days later, it succumbed to bombardment and it now lies in great chunks on the floor of the bay.

6
1978–81

Dr Alan Burges, an Australian by birth and education, joined the Committee in 1977 and was appointed Chairman from February 1978. As first vice chancellor of the New University of Ulster at Coleraine, he had successfully launched and developed that institution, and amongst his voluntary activities had chaired the committee which established the Ulster-American Folk Park in Co. Tyrone.

John Lewis-Crosby attended his last meeting in June 1979 and then retired, having served for almost twenty years. Those of us who saw him in action were always impressed by his immense industry and his dedication to the Trust's work. There were some objectives which he did not attain, like the conservation of the north Londonderry coast from Downhill to the mouth of the Foyle, but in spite of setbacks, not least the political and security crises which made administration and finance very difficult, he had done much in the acquisition of new properties and the development of coastal paths. His greatest achievements were, in my view, the development of the North Antrim Cliff Path, the acquisition of Fair Head and Murlough Bay, the creation of the Murlough Nature Reserve at Dundrum and the Strangford Lough Wildlife Scheme. John Lewis-Crosby's successor, Anthony Lord, attended his first meeting as Regional Director on 1 May 1979. He had come from the Lake District Region of the Trust, where he had been Assistant Land Agent from 1958 and Regional Director from 1973.

In February 1979 Lt. Col. John Hamilton-Stubber joined the Committee and in 1980 David Good, who had earlier been on the staff as Assistant Secretary to the Committee, was appointed to it. In 1978 the Committee received a legacy of £6,550 from Irene V. Emerson and a further £5,000 from the residue of the estate of Nesca Robb.

The Trust continued to raise its public profile in these years and it attracted more and more new members. The media took an increasing interest in our work, and in 1979 Lyn Gallagher took part in a regular weekly radio programme on Trust gardens. She and a number of wardens and other staff also took part in various radio and television programmes. In 1978 1,065 new members joined, compared with 600 in 1977 and 343 in 1976. The work of recruitment at Trust houses increased, particularly at Florence Court and Springhill. From the static figure of 5,500 for the mid-1970s, overall membership in Northern Ireland rose to 7,500 by the end of 1980.

The Trust received much help from teachers' groups, education authority advisers, Department of Education inspectors and teaching colleges, and in-service courses for teachers were held at Mount Stewart, Castle Ward, Rowallane, Springhill and Wellbrook. The theatre at Castle Ward was well used in this period, both by the Trust and its Belfast Members' Centre and by outside bodies who hired the facilities; and a visit by the Young National Trust Theatre was a great success. In 1980 Castle Ward was given the Sandford Award by the Council for Environmental Education.

Although fewer new properties were acquired in these years, there was significant expansion and development of many existing holdings. One important and unusual new acquisition, however, was that of a well known Belfast public house. The **Crown Liquor Saloon** in Great Victoria Street was acquired in 1978 with local funds and with the co-operation of Bass Ireland who agreed to manage the pub. It is high-Victorian, rich in decorative woodwork, mirrors, ceramics, tiles and glass. After renovation, it was declared open by TV newsreader Angela Rippon who arrived in a brewer's dray, driving two shire horses.

Australian-born Dr Alan
Burges, Committee
Chairman from 1978
to 1981

In 1979 Nevill MacGeough Bond made a gift of his family home, **the Argory**, a Greek Revival house, together with its demesne of 293 acres and sufficient of the contents to enable the house to be shown to the public. Overlooking the Blackwater river in Co. Armagh, it was built in 1820 by the architects A.&J. Williamson, associates of Francis Johnston. It is lit by gas, and the stableyard houses the last surviving example in Northern Ireland of a working acetylene gas plant. Another curiosity is an organ made by Bishop of London, built into the house in 1824. The Department of Finance provided an endowment for the property and funded initial repairs to a total of £1,084,650. The house was opened to the public by Lord Clanwilliam on 1 July 1981. The estate includes a bog known as the Argory Mosses which has rich fauna and flora. The Ulster Trust for Nature Conservation has agreed to manage this area.

At **Springhill** five and a half acres of woodland were added in 1978, and in 1980 an additional ten acres of agricultural land, adjacent to the beech walk and garden – an important element in the view from the rear of the house – was acquired with local funds. To celebrate the 300th anniversary of Springhill a birthday party was held there in May 1980, an informal occasion involving the local community, with classical, traditional Irish and bagpipe music, children's shows and candlelit tours of the house. This event was enjoyed by over 2,000 people.

The holding at **Murlough Bay** was extended when Benvan farmhouse and a quarter-acre of land was bought in 1978 with local funds. A further 181 acres of coastline and woodland to the east of Murlough Bay were added in 1980, acquired with funds raised by an appeal in memory of Lord Antrim, who died in September 1977. The day chosen for the dedication of this new property was 19 August 1980. The simple stone cottage at Benvan, without water or electricity, was to host a lunch party for friends of the Trust including lords and ladies and leading figures from headquarters; with Lord Antrim's family and friends they were ferried by minibus down one of the most precipitous tracks in Ireland to this superb unspoilt corner of Co. Antrim. The television cameras were there too, having been promised beautiful views, but the guests were greeted by one of those north Antrim days damp and heavy with a thick mist, and nothing to be seen. Just as Lady Antrim and Lord Gibson, the national chairman, drew back the National Trust flag to reveal the simple stone plaque in the low wall, to the accompaniment of swirling bagpipes, the mist lifted, the clouds parted and Fair Head rose into view in sunshine. Taking in the landscape, Lord Gibson said that he could think of no prospect in the whole of the Trust's keeping which bettered it. The farmhouse and outbuildings at Benvan are now being converted for use as a base camp for volunteers helping with conservation work along the coast.

The **North Antrim Cliff Path** was lengthened in 1979 when the Committee used Enterprise Neptune funds to buy the rights to take sea-wrack and sand between Ballintoy Harbour and the east end of White Park Bay, and with these came the right of access along the shore. The public way was thereby extended to Ballintoy Harbour.

The **Strangford Lough** Wildlife Scheme continued to develop in 1979 and 1980 as the Committee acquired a number of properties which added greatly to the Trust's presence in this area. Gibb's Island, in the outer estuary of the Quoile river, consisting of thirteen acres partly on the island and partly on the mainland, was bought with a grant from the Countryside and Wildlife Branch of the Department of the Environment. Covenants over a cottage and one acre were given by Dr P. Ferguson. Horse Island, an area of forty-six acres of mainland and island south of Kircubbin, was also bought with a grant from the Conservation Branch. Jane's Shore, a beautiful wooded area of almost six acres on the banks of the Quoile near Downpatrick, was given by Lord Dunleath. Two islands in the outer estuary of the Quoile were bought with local funds and a grant from the Countryside and Wildlife Branch: Salt Island (fifty-two acres) for its ornithological interest and Green Island (eighteen acres) for amenity use. Ballyhenry Island, a five-acre rocky island north of Portaferry, which may be approached on foot at low tide, was acquired in 1980 with money donated in memory of Lord Antrim. The following year Darragh Island, twenty-one acres north of Ringhaddy Sound, was acquired for conservation and recreation, with money from a bequest by sculptor Rosamond Praeger.

At **Mount Stewart** in 1979 Lady Mairi Bury gave the Trust some land edging Strangford Lough, and in 1980 she agreed to allow the chapel in the house to be shown to visitors. She also allowed some more bedrooms to be open to the public.

Other properties extended during 1980 included **Castle Ward**, where two acres of pond and bog were bought; the **Mourne Coastal Path** where one and a half acres at Glasdrumman were acquired with Neptune funds; and **Coney Island**, Lough Neagh. The original acquisition of this island had not included the burial ground of the Charlemont family, but this land was now transferred to the Trust by the Representative Church Body of the Church of Ireland. In the same year Lord Antrim's son, Viscount Dunluce (the 14th Earl of Antrim), gave the Trust covenants over 685 acres of woodland in the upper glen of **Glenarm**, above his ancestral home.

As early as 1967 a Portstewart Strand Committee had been set up by the Trust in conjunction with the Portstewart Urban District Council and the Northern Ireland Tourist Board; its purpose was to make the best use of this splendid, but at that time frequently and dangerously overcrowded, beach. The committee first met under the chairmanship of Alan Burges, then vice chancellor of the New University of Ulster. However, in spite of constant efforts to acquire the land and the consideration of various joint schemes, nothing had come of it. When Dr Burges became Chairman of the Trust he was therefore delighted to be able to preside over efforts to bring the scheme to a successful conclusion. In 1981 the strand and dunes, comprising 185 acres, were acquired for £130,000. The money was provided by a loan from headquarters, a grant of £27,500 from the Countryside and Wildlife Branch, Neptune and local funds. On 7 July 1981 the Committee, before holding its monthly meeting (at nearby

Hezlett House), walked the strand and the dunes, and plans for management were approved. Charges for admission of cars were made from the following weekend; portable buildings for warden's accommodation, a small shop and refreshments were provided. Motorbikes were prohibited after alternative cross-country facilities were found for them.

The appointments of Peter Marlow as Historic Buildings Representative, Desmond Norris as Buildings Manager and Sam McConnell as Area Forester enabled the Trust in this period to attend to the care of buildings, their contents and woodland in a way which had not hitherto been possible. Various government training schemes and unemployment relief schemes also helped in the maintenance of outbuildings and in other aspects of estate management. Notable improvements were the introduction of basic housekeeping measures in all the Trust houses, with proper cleaning equipment being purchased, underfelts and window-blinds being fitted, and windows in the historic houses being treated with ultraviolet retardant varnish. Fire precautions and security were tightened up.

The roofs of almost all the estate buildings in Castle Ward were repaired or replaced, and a base camp was opened there, helped by a £500 grant from the Clement Wilson Trust. At **Castle Coole** serious defects were discovered in the stonework: the wrought-iron cramps, fastening each block of the exterior Portland stone to the next and to the interior, were being affected by damp, expanding as the result of rust formation, and in places bursting the external stonework. The Trust decided to remove all the exterior stone in phases, replacing the wrought-iron cramps with best-quality stainless steel. The Historic Monuments and Buildings Branch of the Department of the Environment made an *ex-gratia* payment of £70,000 to enable the work to be started. In the meantime the state bedroom, dressing-room and breakfast-room were refurbished and opened to the public. At **Florence Court** the garden was much improved and enlarged with new paths made through to the forest park which was opened by the Forest Service in June 1981.

At **Murlough Nature Reserve** a carpark was completed and Enterprise Ulster workers created a new information centre/shop in the cottage. A workshop/laboratory, as well as accommodation for the assistant warden, was provided in the stable block at Murlough House.

Important conservation work was carried out at Springhill, where the extensive collection of costumes (over 1,700 items) was catalogued and better storage provided. The beech avenue was replanted in 1980, the 'official' planting being performed by Diana McClintock, a sister of the donor of Springhill.

At **Ardress** during 1980 farm animals were introduced to add atmosphere to the display of agricultural implements around the farmyard. Most of these implements had been collected by Craigavon Historical Society and restored under the supervision of George Robinson, a member of the society who was also superintendent of works in the Historic Monuments and Buildings Branch at Moira.

The Trust had adopted an age limit of seventy for chairmen and so Alan Burges retired in September 1981. His administrative experience had proved an advantage and he had been a very businesslike Chairman. His was a régime in which consultation with Committee members and staff played a big part and in which the affairs of the Trust ran smoothly. In addition to the acquisition and extension of properties, the Committee in his time instituted a more effective policy of conservation, and in this it was assisted by better staffing and more generous financial treatment from headquarters.

7

1981–6

Lord O'Neill, of Shane's Castle, Co. Antrim, became Chairman in September 1981. He had the initial management advantage of being a landowner and farmer and his experience chairing the Ulster Countryside Committee and the Northern Ireland Tourist Board was useful in dealing with central and local government. As the owner of a woodland nature reserve and a private railway at Shane's Castle, he understood how to maintain a balance between conservation and meeting the leisure needs of the public.

In January 1982 the North Coast Committee, which had looked after the Trust's interests on the north coast since 1968, was wound up and its chairman, Dan McLaughlin of Coleraine, was appointed to the regional Committee. In May 1983 Thomas McLaughlin of Cushendall joined the Committee. In April 1983 a national advisory committee, under the chairmanship of John Arkell CBE, made comprehensive recommendations on the Trust's organisation and on the relationship between the management, the members and the public. Following the adoption of the Arkell Committee's report, which limited the length of service of members, Charles Brett and Douglas Deane stood down in May 1983, Brett returning to the Committee a year later. Annesley Malley (a chartered land agent and surveyor who had joined the Committee in 1978) stood down in 1984, returning in 1985. In December 1983 Jack Kingan resigned as honorary Treasurer, a position he had held with cheerful diligence for thirty-two years; he retired from the Committee in April 1985. Thomas McLaughlin then agreed to help the accountant with financial advice and direction when required. Henry McCandless joined the Committee in April 1984, followed in October by Jack Torney, of the Ulster Bank, and in July 1985 by John Cowdy, of the Northern Bank, and Ann Davey Orr. In July 1985 Dan McLaughlin was appointed Deputy Chairman.

In April 1984 Eleanor Eyre-Maunsell agreed to chair an *ad hoc* group to advise the Committee on the regional consequences of the Arkell Report. One of the group's recommendations was to make an educational appointment for the region, and Marion Machell, who had already done good work as Education Officer at Castle Ward, was appointed Regional Education Officer in 1985.

The loss of Malone House, and the decision not to relocate the office and shop there after it was restored, left a gap which was partly filled in September 1982 by the establishment of a National Trust shop in Botanic Avenue, Belfast. It was officially opened by Lord O'Neill, with the help of local TV presenter Sean Rafferty who had succeeded Peter Rankin as chairman of the Belfast Members' Centre. A members' association for the north coast was formed in 1985, and is now developing interest in the Trust in Counties Londonderry and Antrim, with a lively series of events.

The Ulster Appeal Committee (under the chairmanship of Alan Burges) launched the 'Ulster in Trust' appeal in June 1983 when a hot-air balloon took off from Botanic Gardens, Belfast, carrying Lord O'Neill and the current Miss United Kingdom, Alison Smith. The appeal was for money to replenish the Trust's capital funds in Northern Ireland. Lesley Mackie, head of the Belfast engineering firm, succeeded Alan Burges as chairman of this committee in January 1985. Events in aid of the appeal included a gala performance of *Swan Lake* at the Grand Opera House in Belfast. The funds raised have been used in a number of the most recent purchases. The appeal had raised £80,000 by 1 July 1986.

Under the leadership of Lord O'Neill and Anthony Lord, the Committee pursued a policy of greater consultation with the members and with the public. Mindful of its responsibilities for Strangford Lough, it fought the proposed barrage scheme for the generation of electricity, submitting memoranda to the Northern Ireland Economic Council and the government departments concerned. It reluctantly opposed the de Ros marina planned for Castleward Bay and gave evidence at the planning inquiry. On the other hand, it gave its blessing to a Killyleagh marina, subject to satisfactory arrangements for the dumping of dredged material.

In connection with Trust plans to restore the eighteenth-century landscape at **Castle Ward**, a meeting was held with representatives of the Down District Council, the wildfowlers and the Strangford Lough Committee at which the Trust's plans were fully discussed. This was important because the issue of the wildfowl collection and the Temple Water at Castle Ward was a contentious one. The wildfowl collection had been started in the late 1960s as an integral part of the Strangford Lough Wildlife Scheme, and was regarded by wildfowlers and many lovers of wildlife as an important breeding base for birds, as a significant refuge and as an important outdoor classroom where visitors could get close to flightless examples of the many species of bird which use the lough.

On the other hand the Trust was sensible of a responsibility to the landscape quality of the Temple Water, one of a very few remnants of early formal landscape planting in Ireland. There was the financial consideration, too, and the extremely high cost of running the wildfowl collection had become a luxury in times of stringency. At the public meeting Committee members and staff presented their case to a packed theatre at Castle Ward. Some lively discussion and impassioned speeches ensued, and no doubt some members of the audience remained unconvinced, but the experience was an important piece of consultation with the public, and led to some modification of the Trust's plans. Subsequently the Lime Walk was planted, the predator fence was

Lord O'Neill, of Shane's Castle, Chairman of the Regional Committee from 1981 to 1991.

Anthony Lord, Regional
Director from 1979 to 1990

removed from the Temple Water area and most of the wildfowl collection moved to Robin's Pond. In 1984 it was decided that the Decoy Pond field would be managed to provide waterfowl nesting and feeding habitat, and the old walled garden would be developed as an enclosure for the wildfowl collection.

The annual members' meeting in 1984 was held at Castle Coole – very well attended in spite of IRA bombing in Enniskillen the previous day – and the Trust's proposals for restoring the stonework were fully explained to the large audience in the hall and under the scaffolding outside. Similarly, the annual members' meeting in 1985 was at Downhill where a number of alternative proposals for the treatment of the ruins were illustrated and evaluated in Castlerock church hall, before the ruins were explored and plans explained on site.

Private garden owners generously continued to open their properties under the Gardens Scheme and the net profits to the Trust increased steadily. The profit in 1985 was £9,955, compared with £4,143 in 1982 and £2,559 in 1978. Margaret Reside was chairwoman of the gardens committee until November 1978 when she was succeeded by Lady Mulholland. She in turn was succeeded by Dr Molly Sanderson, who chaired the scheme until August 1983 when Eleanor Cowdy took over.

Overall membership of the Trust in Northern Ireland was about 11,000 in 1986, having grown from 7,639 in less than five years, and an intensive recruitment campaign is continuing, as part of a general policy of increasing awareness of the Trust's work and encouraging public involvement.

The emphasis in the 1980s has been on increasing the professionalism of all the Trust's operations, improving housekeeping, conservation and land management. Physical expansion has taken second place but, nevertheless, some new small properties have been acquired and some larger ones extended and developed.

When the Trust acquired **Florence Court** in 1954 only fourteen acres of land came with it: this consisted of a garden to the south of the house, and the flanking yards, but did not include the two-and-a-half-acre front lawn. In 1981 the Committee acquired this lawn from the Forest Service; then in 1985 the Trust acquired from Lord Enniskillen 120 acres to the west (or rear) of the house, consisting of woodland, parkland, the gate lodge and north drive, the dower house, forge, sawmill and carpenter's shop. All this land and the buildings are intimately involved with, or significantly visible from, the big house. The dower house has been sold on a 150-year full repairing lease, subject to covenants, but the acquisition of the other buildings will enable the Trust, when funds are available, to recreate the concept of a self-contained community at Florence Court.

John Richardson, who had given **Derrymore House** to the Trust, died on 21 December 1985, and under his will left the residue of the Derrymore estate to the Trust. The gift included the Woodhouse, the main residence on the estate, built in 1840 with an addition made in 1900; six gate lodges; a farm cottage and farm buildings; twenty-five acres of agricultural land; and thirty acres of mature woodland. This generous gift not only completed the Derrymore property, but will provide much-needed additional income for the Trust.

Like Florence Court, **Castle Coole** deserved to be protected by a greater area of parkland than the Trust had originally been able to acquire. In 1983 the Committee was enabled to purchase 340 acres of rolling countryside surrounding the house for £319,000, by means of grants from the National Heritage Memorial Fund and from the Countryside and Wildlife Branch of the Department of the Environment. The repair of the stonework at Castle Coole was continued throughout this period. At first it was feasible to keep the house open to the public, but the Committee decided to close it for four years from mid-September 1983 to enable the work to be completed. At the same time a five-year programme of tree planting was started, to take full advantage of the additional land acquired from Lord Belmore, and the public were encouraged to use the grounds.

The Trust gained a new property in Co. Fermanagh in 1981 when the wooded **Tonregee Island**, of five acres – part of the Belle Isle estate in Upper Lough Erne – was acquired by means of local funds and an £8,000 grant from the Countryside and Wildlife Branch.

Three coastal paths were developed in the early 1980s: Neptune funds purchased seven and a half acres at Coolranny for the footpath south of **Torr Head**, and an additional one and a half acres for the **Mourne Coastal Path** in 1982. Between December 1981 and November 1983 about six and a half acres in five separate lots were acquired for the Dundrum Coastal Path near the **Murlough Nature Reserve**.

Orlock Point, a mile of foreshore close to **Ballymacormick Point** in north Down, was accepted as a gift in 1982 from John Aird Lowry, with an endowment of £2,000 provided by the Orlock Residents' Association. In the same year a canal lockhouse, known as Moneypenny's Lockhouse and built about 1805, was acquired as a holding operation, with a grant from the Historic Monuments and Buildings Branch. It is situated on the Newry Navigation Canal, near Portadown. The Trust held this property for three years before transferring ownership to Craigavon Borough Council. Also in 1982, 114 acres of hill land at Creevedonnell, Co. Londonderry, was bequeathed to the Trust by Grace Delap Stevenson. It is held alienably, that is, the Trust is not obliged to hold it forever.

The Trust's holdings around Strangford Lough continued to grow in the 1980s. Part of the former Nugent estate at Portaferry – twenty-nine acres of woodland and agricultural land in the grounds of Portaferry House – was acquired in 1983 with Neptune money and Lord Antrim Memorial funds. This woodland, which forms an essential part of the view from Castle Ward, is being held as part of the memorial to Lord Antrim. Another new Strangford property was Taggart Island, ninety-four acres off the west shore of the lough, a mile north of Killyleagh. It has much wildlife, amenity and educational interest and the Trust purchased it in 1984 for £76,000 with a 75-per-cent grant from the Countryside and Wildlife Branch and money from the Ulster Appeal.

In September 1982 the Trust was given by Lady Mairi Bury, as part of the Mount Stewart endowment, an area of foreshore of great ornithological interest, covering 5,040 acres in the north-east part of the lough. This is the largest area of inter-tidal shore actually owned by the Trust in Strangford Lough. The following year Lady Bury also donated Tir Nan Og, the Londonderry family burial ground within the gardens at Mount Stewart.

In January 1982 Arthur Irvine retired after twenty-one years as warden of the Strangford Lough Wildlife Scheme. The success of the scheme was due in large part to his untiring devotion to the lough and the respect which lough-users had for him. He and his wife, Olive, continue to live at Castle Ward where he works part-time for the Trust. He was succeeded by ornithologist Dr Bob Brown, and in April 1984 lawyer William Marshall was appointed as chairman of the Strangford Lough Committee in succession to Pat Boaden.

The Trust's holding at **Downhill** had increased in 1980 when the ruins of the Earl Bishop's palace, the mausoleum and two acres were acquired with local funds. In 1983 a further eighty-nine acres of cliff land surrounding the ruins of the palace were acquired by means of a 'heritage grant' of £61,000 from the Countryside and Wildlife Branch, and a loan from headquarters to be repaid from the Ulster Appeal. The Committee decided that the front elevation of the palace ruins and part of the sides should be retained and strengthened, but that the rest should be reduced in height and consolidated.

Another Co. Londonderry property was acquired in 1984 when the Hon. The Irish Society granted the Trust a licence for the shooting rights over an area of seventy-five acres, known as **Bar Mouth** at the mouth of the Bann, adjoining Portstewart Strand. The Trust undertook to maintain the area as a bird sanctuary and to warden it.

In 1985 a bothy at **Murlough Bay** was bought for £15,000. Murlough Cottage and sixteen and a half acres of woodland were also acquired for £30,000.

Towards the end of 1986 the future was secured for one of the Trust's most long-standing but problematic properties – **Lisnabreeny** House. Only one side of the glen had been included in Nesca Robb's original gift, but in 1980 an additional five acres was purchased with local funds which made the glen more manageable. However, the building was the main problem. Throughout the 1970s negotiations had been carried on in the hope of finding a suitable use for it. Interested organisations included the Glencraig Curative School, the Ministry of Home Affairs, the British Horse Society and Castlereagh Borough Council, but to no avail. In 1986 negotiations were success-fully concluded with Lagan College that would enable Lisnabreeny to become the first permanent home for an integrated post-primary school. The college would take a long lease over the house, garden and some farmland, in which new school buildings would be situated. The façade of the old house would be restored or replicated, and the house would be sympathetically converted for school purposes.

A biological survey of the Trust lands was completed in 1986. It showed that on some of the northern coastal properties there were sites of exceptional importance. Some of these have been given National Nature Reserve status by the Department of the Environment and others have been declared Sites of Special Scientific Interest. The **Giant's Causeway** was recommended to Unesco for designation by that body as a Heritage Site because of its geological importance.

The survey showed that the geese and wader wintering grounds at the northern end of Strangford Lough were internationally important and ought to be made into a National Nature Reserve and designated under the Ramsar convention. At Castle Coole and Florence Court, the survey highlighted deciduous woodland of rare conservation value.

The north coast properties – **Fair Head** and Murlough Bay, **Carrick-a-Rede** and **Larrybane**, **White Park Bay** and Giant's Causeway – appeared to need more effective conservation management. Discussions with the Countryside and Wildlife Branch took place with a view to creating a wardening structure for all these properties that would be in keeping with their conservation importance.

During this period the gardens committee raised for the Trust an average of £10,000 per annum and thus enabled a number of much needed schemes to be carried out. At **Rowallane** the bandstand was repaired, and specially designed bricks for wall ties were put in place. At **Springhill** a new tractor was purchased, and at **Ardress** a Coadestone urn was repaired. The committee provided a major part of the replanting costs of the Lime Walk at Castle Ward, as well as aiding irrigation schemes at Castle Ward, **Mount Stewart** and Rowallane. A trainee gardener for **Hezlett House** was paid for.

A survey was made of the need for information and interpretation along the north coast, and open-space notice boards and interpretation points were provided at Downhill, **Portstewart Strand**, Larrybane and **Cushendun**. A major interpretation centre was completed at the Giant's Causeway and opened in May 1986 by Dan McLaughlin, who also in that month opened a visitor centre at the Fisherman's Path between Larrybane and Carrick-a-Rede.

This period produced a number of new enterprises, particularly during 1986. There were new or upgraded restaurants or tea-rooms at the **Argory**, Cushendun, Florence Court, the Giant's Causeway and Mount Stewart. The new shop in the Giant's Causeway Visitor Centre was opened in May 1986 and a town shop was opened in Coleraine in October of that year. Despite having suffered, during 1985, the worst summer weather Northern Ireland had known for thirty years, trading sales were maintained at the 1984 level and, due in part to the new provision at the Giant's Causeway and Coleraine, were increased in 1986 by about 43 per cent.

In 1985 and 1986 efforts were made at the houses and at the Giant's Causeway to recruit new members. These were particularly successful at the Argory, Castle Ward, Florence Court, Mount Stewart, Springhill and the Giant's Causeway.

8
1986–92

In 1986 the Regional Committee under Lord O'Neill was meeting only four times a year, but these meetings were supplemented by several field trips and site meetings held at various properties, the venue usually determined by the need for the collective view on a current problem. As a result of the Arkell Report there was a quicker turnover of members and the Committee had achieved a good balance of expertise and geographical spread. In 1986 Rosemary Marshall from Co. Armagh and Patrick Forde of Seaforde, Co. Down, were appointed to the Committee and after a period of retirement David Good was reappointed. In April 1989 Professor Ronald Buchanan was appointed to the Committee. Charles Brett, knighted in 1990, who had been a member of the National Trust Council in London since the retirement of Lady O'Neill of the Maine, now retired from that body and was succeeded by Ronald Buchanan. In 1990 E. Acheson Aiken, of Co. Fermanagh, and John Bryson, of Belfast, joined the Committee.

The increasing responsibilities of the Trust in the province were such that the Committee appointed some of their members to a finance group – John Bryson, Thomas McLaughlin and Jack Torney, with John Cowdy as chairman. Its duties are to oversee the annual revenue budget; the annual accounts; the financial aspects of proposed acquisitions; enterprises, including trading and catering; and the funding of property management.

There were also changes in staff. In September 1989 Jo Whatmough, already a head warden, was made responsible for nature conservation advice throughout the region. Diane Harron resigned and was succeeded by Diane Forbes as Public Affairs Manager, and Jim Wells was appointed as Assistant Public Affairs Manager. Maire Bermingham was appointed as Regional Enterprises Manager, Charles McMurray became Regional Financial Controller and Frances Bailey, Assistant Historic Buildings Representative. Hugh Devlin and Paul Kendrick were appointed as land agents and in January 1991 the former was appointed to the new post of Regional Land Agent. Also, as from January 1991, Wesley Boyd was appointed to the new post of Regional Administration Manager. In November 1991 Una O'Neill joined as Regional Fundraising Manager. In March 1991 Bob Brown resigned as Strangford Lough Head Warden on his appointment as regional officer of the Royal Society for the Protection of Birds. In October 1991 he was succeeded by David Thompson, formerly of the North-West Region of the Trust.

In April 1987 William Marshall retired as chairman of the Strangford Lough Committee and was succeeded by Donald Browne, and in turn by Jack Torney in October 1989. The committee for the Murlough Nature Reserve was chaired by David Good from 1987 to 1992, when he was succeeded by Patrick Forde.

At the close of the Regional Committee meeting in July 1988 Norman Scott, warden for Minnow Burn for many years, was formally thanked by the Chairman and members for his outstanding help, which he had given on a voluntary basis.

The Dowager Duchess of Westminster died in a car accident in 1988. Amongst her many public services, she had, from 1952 to 1962, served on the Regional Committee. In her memory, an oil painting by Colin Middleton was presented to the Trust by Lord Belmore, chairman of the memorial fund, to be kept on loan at Florence Court, where in July 1988 Dan McLaughlin accepted it on behalf of the Committee.

A double change in leadership, long foreseen and carefully provided for, took place in 1990–1. In accordance with the retirement age limit, Anthony Lord stepped down as Regional Director in 1990, and following the Arkell Report rules of tenure, Lord O'Neill retired as Chairman in 1991.

As Director for over eleven years, Anthony Lord had an enormous capacity for work and was completely dedicated to the Trust. He introduced a new professionalism and paid much attention to staff training, financial control and estate management. He made sure that the region worked closely with headquarters, obtaining the financial assistance and expert advice it could provide. He was particularly anxious that the landscape should not be further spoiled and he devoted much time and energy to bringing before government the need for better country planning and, in particular, the need for an independent environmental protection agency. Although he was not successful in obtaining the latter, many of the other recommendations which he made to government on behalf of the Trust were accepted in principle.

Lord O'Neill's chairmanship was a happy one for the Trust. He was interested in the Big Houses and in their presentation to the public, and his personal knowledge of estate and amenity management helped him in his quiet and effective leadership. During his time, the Trust increased its influence in the province and, in spite of the Troubles, raised the membership and the visitor usage of the properties to a remarkable extent.

Ian McQuiston, an Ulsterman with experience in nature conservation and the administration of historic buildings legislation in the Department of the Environment, was an imaginative choice as Anthony Lord's successor. In April 1990 he became Regional Director Designate and completed a nine-month period working closely with Anthony Lord before attending his first meeting as Director. This generous overlap enabled him to get to know the properties in Northern Ireland and to become familiar with Trust policies and methods of administration.

In July 1991 Lord O'Neill was succeeded by Ronald Buchanan, who brought to the chairmanship not only a deep and intimate knowledge of Ulster – its archaeology, ecology, history and folklore – but also a strong desire that Northern Ireland should protect and enhance its natural environment and built heritage and that the Trust and its properties should improve the educational opportunities already provided for young and old. As a member of the Regional Committee and the Council, he had gained knowledge of Trust policies, so the changeover in both cases was completely smooth and unhurried.

The region took part in the Trust's Foundation for Art scheme, whose primary role is the commissioning of works of art from younger contemporary artists, relating to Trust properties, owners or donors and their families, staff and events. The Trust in Northern Ireland has acquired pictures for: Mount Stewart (a portrait of Lady Mairi Bury by Derek Hill and two views of the garden by Cheryl Fountain and Liam Thompson); Castle Coole (David Evans's watercolour of the stonework in progress and Sir Edmund Fairfax-Lucy's interior of the saloon); Ardress (still life by Brian Ballard); Crom (landscape by T.P. Flanagan); Castle Ward (interior by Hector McDonnell); and Strangford Lough (a Jack Crabtree coastal landscape in honour of the silver jubilee of Enterprise Neptune in 1990). In 1992 Jack Crabtree was commissioned to do a series of paintings at Patterson's Spade Mill.

The Gardens Scheme continued to flourish in this period. In 1989 Acheson Aiken, who had become chairman of the gardens committee in 1986, was succeeded by

Eppy Schierbeek, who in turn was succeeded by Shirley Taylor in 1992. The net share of profit to the Trust for 1986 was £6,140; in 1987, £11,500; in 1988, £6,000; in 1989, £6,500; in 1990, £11,260; and in 1991, £7,700, which has benefited various properties in terms of staffing and improvements.

In the period covered by this chapter, the rapid growth of membership is one of the achievements of which the region can be proud and it has been marked by the winning of the Trust's Regional Greensfelder award in 1991. In 1990, particularly, a substantial increase in new members was recorded: on 1 November 1990 the new membership total was 5,600, compared with 3,272 in 1989, an increase of almost 70 per cent, family membership being the fastest growing category. Two properties, Mount Stewart and the Giant's Causeway, recruited over 1,000 members in one season for the first time ever, while the Argory had a 730-per-cent increase in new membership (612 compared with 74 in 1989). The Argory also had the best direct debit (96 per cent) and deed of covenant (94 per cent) rates in the recruitment of new members for any property in England, Wales and Northern Ireland. Overall, the region's membership grew from 11,000 in 1986 to 27,000 in 1992 – an increase of 145 per cent. This success was achieved by a team of recruiters under the active and enthusiastic leadership of Jim Wells.

Throughout this period there has been an increasing trend in the promotion of events, especially family orientated ones, at properties, including open-air operas and concerts at Castle Ward, music recitals at Springhill, Italian and French evenings and balls at Mount Stewart, a summer country festival at the Argory, a Sotheby's valuation day at Castle Coole, guided walks at Rowallane, and many others. These events, some of which in 1990 were sponsored by Gilbeys, continue to be very popular and such properties have enjoyed an increase in visitor figures against the regional trend.

Annual members' meetings were held in Springhill in 1987; Crom, 1988; Castle Ward, 1989; Innisfree Farm, 1990; Rowallane, 1991; and Newcastle, 1992.

By 1992 the North Coast Members' Association had over 600 members. It has been fortunate in having each year a very active committee and an enthusiastic band of supporters, who have organised a wide range of activities, including visits to properties not normally open to the public, guided walks, holiday weekends, a midsummer concert, and a ball. It seeks to support the Trust by helping members to become better informed about its policies and activities, encouraging non-members to join and to help Trust appeals and projects. It has financially supported the Trust in Counties Antrim and Londonderry. In conjunction with the Royal Society for the Protection of Birds Coleraine Members' Group, it extended the Bar Mouth observation hide and made it accessible to disabled visitors. The names of all the dedicated team are too numerous to mention but, to name only a few, it must be said that the association is fortunate in having had the help of Jim Chestnutt, Ann Dark, George Hanns, Pat Hurl, Dan McLaughlin, Annesley Malley, Keith Thomas and Joy White.

The Belfast Members' Centre continued to interest its members with talks on architecture, the fine arts, furniture restoration and antiques. Visits are arranged to Trust properties and to places such as Lissan and the Wildfowl and Wetlands Trust at Castle Espie. A donation of £1,000 was made to Enterprise Neptune in 1990. There are over 100 members; the chairman is Fred Jeffrey and the honorary secretary is David Smith.

A members' association in Co. Fermanagh was formed in 1992. The chairman is Sam Blair and the honorary secretary is Kathryn Gault.

In March 1987 the Trust acquired the magnificent **Crom** estate from the 6th Earl of Erne, 1,350 acres of unspoilt land in the remote upper reaches of Lough Erne, a property of the highest conservation and landscape value, which was opened by the Dowager Duchess of Abercorn in 1988. The acquisition included the ruins of the early-seventeenth-century castle and other buildings on the estate. The cost was £810,000, with an estimated £633,000 for capital works of improvement of land and the buildings and an endowment of £567,000: over £2 million in all. An additional 185 acres of woodland from trustees were acquired somewhat later for £46,000. The property was bought and endowed with grants from the Department of the Environment and the National Heritage Memorial Fund; with money from National Trust defined purposes funds; and partly as a gift from the Earl of Erne. The possibility of the Castle being transferred was discussed and considered, but not included because of the cost of rehabilitation and maintenance required to show it to the public. Instead, a ten-year option to acquire the Castle by way of gift, together with a covenant, was kindly offered by the family and this option still stands.

In 1987 the 8th Earl of Belmore offered a gift of the grand yard at **Castle Coole** to the Trust, the stable block built in 1817. It is a fine building designed by Sir Richard Morrison and stands comparison with other good stable buildings in the United Kingdom. At first no funds were available, but with the reopening of Castle Coole by the Queen Mother in 1988, funding from headquarters, plus a 50-per-cent Historic Buildings grant, was obtained for the necessary expenditure on the rehabilitation of the building so that it might be shown to the public.

In the **Strangford Lough** area a number of important properties have been acquired in this period. In 1987 the School House at **Mount Stewart**, built in 1813 by Viscountess Castlereagh, was acquired with the help of a grant from the Department of the Environment, Historic Monuments and Buildings Branch. The conveyance of Tir Nan Og, the Londonderry family burial ground given to the Trust by Lady Mairi Bury in 1983, was not completed until 1990. A stone-walled eyrie overlooking the gardens, it has a rear high tower and two conically roofed round corner towers. This gift includes the hill garden surrounding the monuments, five and three quarter acres in all. The Clay Gate Lodge, formerly leased from Lady Bury, was purchased in 1988 and has been restored. This acquisition has enabled a new, much safer and attractive visitor entrance to be provided with the aid of a 75-per-cent grant from the Department of Economic Development. In 1991 Lady Bury gave two small areas of the back driveway leading to the domestic entrance to the house, in this way completing the Trust's right of access.

Anne's Point, overlooked from the Temple of the Winds at Mount Stewart, is an area of land in one of the largest and most successful wildfowl refuges in the lough. Some of it is spindly mixed softwoods and some is brackish marshland lying behind a tide bank. It is intersected by drainage channels used by kingfishers, and flooding in the adjacent fields attracts whooper swans, teal and goldeneye. The Trust has acquired three areas of land: 12 acres in 1988, 23 acres in 1989 and 15 acres in 1991. They were bought with Enterprise Neptune funds, grants from the Department of the Environment and the World Wide Fund for Nature, and a bequest from Dr G.A.M. Gillespie. Public access and carparking will be provided.

In 1987 Greyabbey Bay (3,608 acres) was bought from H.C. Montgomery. The area consists of lough bed and a number of small islands, including Chapel Island, and on the western side of the bay, Mid Island and South Island. The Trust has two carparks along the shore.

In 1991 seventeen acres of foreshore, saltmarsh and flooded grassland at Ballyurnanellan, Greyabbey, were acquired, adjoining land and foreshore already owned by the Trust. This is important habitat for Greenland white-fronted and greylag geese and other wildfowl. It was bought with grants from the Department of the Environment, the World Wide Fund for Nature and Northern Ireland funds.

In 1987 three and one quarter acres of land at Ballyquintin Point at the southern tip of the Ards Peninsula were gifted by M. McClelland; the area includes Green Island.

In 1990 Nugent's foreshore (426 acres) making up 12 miles of foreshore and comprising the entire eastern shore of the Narrows and southernmost shore of the Ards Peninsula was acquired. It was bought with money donated by readers of the *Daily Mail* newspaper to Enterprise Neptune funds, specifically for the purchase of this land. There is carparking near the entrance of a lane at Barr Hill Bay.

Also in Strangford Lough two small islands were acquired in 1991, Ogilby Island and Black Island, together with North Rock, South Rock and West Rock in the bed of the lough. These were given by Ellen Leslie Jacqueline Day and Georgina Mary Stone. In 1992 two small islands known as The Launches were purchased.

In July 1988 Dr David Erwin opened Strangford Lough Barn at **Castle Ward** as an interpretation centre, where the objects and activities of the Strangford Lough Wildlife Scheme could be explained. This scheme was aided by donations from the Skaggs Foundation and the Thornton bequest, and by a grant from the Department of Economic Development.

The multiplicity of interests surrounding Strangford Lough – environmental, recreational, commercial, ecological – made the work of the Strangford Lough Committee particularly important. The significance that the Trust attaches to the lough was demonstrated by the fact that in April 1990 Angus Stirling, the Director General, had a meeting with Peter Bottomley MP, Parliamentary Under-Secretary of State, Northern Ireland Office, and wrote in May 1990 regarding the Crown foreshore and bed of the lough; salmon farming; trawling and dredging; structure for the management of the lough; and thanking him for the Department of the Environment's continued advice and financial support. In July 1990 a management agreement for Castleward Bay was signed between the Trust and the Royal Society for the Protection of Birds.

A government report in April 1991 confirmed the Trust's views on the question of trawling and dredging in the lough and the Trust wrote to the Department of the Environment urging them to press the Fisheries Department to stop inappropriate fishing methods in the lough.

At Orlock Point, near Groomsport, Co. Down, twenty-seven acres of rocky outcrop had been given in 1982 by J. Aird Lowry and N. Johnston, with an endowment from the Orlock Point Residents' Association. In 1988 two acres of beach linking with this area were given by the representatives of the late Edgar McCutcheon.

In 1987 the Walled Garden of six acres, the dovecote/ice house and the Lion's Gate at **Downhill** were acquired. In the same year the Black Glen Gate Lodge at the Castlerock, or southern, end of the estate was acquired as a safeguard against development at the nearby caravan park. The Tughan Trust had given an interest-free loan for three years for this purpose. The property was acquired with the help of a grant from the Department of the Environment and a bequest from Grace Delap Stevenson.

The farm in Creevedonnell, Co. Londonderry, was sold in 1988. The proceeds were used towards the funding of the Bar Mouth Cottage and the Black Glen Gate Lodge. In 1990 the Bar Mouth hide was opened by David Bellamy, who later addressed a large audience at the Riverside Theatre, Coleraine, on 'Trusting in the Future', as part of the Neptune silver jubilee celebrations.

West of the Bann estuary the Grangemore Farm of 226 acres was acquired, including a semi-derelict house, 115 acres of ancient sand-dunes, almost one mile of inter-tidal mud shore along the Bann and a slightly larger stretch of inter-tidal mud shore on the bank of the Articlave river. Also in this area the house at 41 Castlerock Road was acquired.

At Knocksoghy on the **North Coast** an area of eighty-three acres adjacent to the Trust land at Larrybane was acquired in 1992. On the same coast, adjacent to the Causeway, Innisfree Farm came on the market. It lies between Aird's Snout, Weir's Snout and Causeway Head and the Trust bought it in 1990 largely as a protection against unsuitable development. It consists of a nineteenth-century house, farm buildings and sixty-two and a half acres of dairy land. A barn dance was held at the farm after the 1990 annual members' meeting.

In 1987 Magnus Magnusson declared the Causeway Coast to be a World Heritage Site as designated by Unesco. In 1990 the Bass Ireland Community Award for that year was presented to the Trust for its work at the Causeway.

At **Cushendun** the problem of the unauthorised extraction of sand became acute in 1989. A meeting took place between staff and residents and a local group was formed that meets three times a year and is convened and attended by members of staff and chaired by the local Regional Committee member, Thomas McLaughlin. In 1990 it was agreed with local residents, five of whom were later co-opted on to the group, that the Trust would provide washed sand to anyone who had historic entitlement to remove sand from the beach. By April 1991 the ban on sand extraction was working well. Planning consent was then sought for a sea and coastal defence scheme and a landscape plan was drawn up for the village.

In 1990 the Committee learned that a prominent part of the **Mourne Mountains** belonging to the Annesley estate was for sale. It was in fact the much-loved landscape of the Mourne Mountains as seen from the Newcastle, Dundrum and Murlough area, so the Committee acted quickly and with the approval of headquarters bought the land. A public appeal was made towards establishing an endowment fund for the long-term conservation of the area. A major task is the repair work necessary to rectify the severe erosion that has taken place on the Glen river path. Flautist James Galway, the appeal president, travelled to Newcastle to launch the appeal in September 1992.

The property consists of 1,288 acres of mountain land, being the northern part of Slieve Donard to its summit, the Glen river valley, Eagle Rock, the adjoining summit of Slieve Commedagh, part of Shan Slieve and the whole of Slievenamaddy, Thomas's Mountain and Millstone Mountain. It comprises all the land above the 600 feet contour, above Donard Forest and Donard Park.

By the 1980s the Victorian bandstand at Newcastle, Co. Down, was unused, rusted and becoming derelict. In 1985 a decision was made in the town to remove it from the promenade as it was unsafe and boarded up. There was a great deal of local discussion as to its future, as it had been much-loved by generations of holiday-makers. In 1986 the Trust decided, with the agreement of the local people, to translate it to **Rowallane**, where there was an old concrete base of similar size in the Pleasure Grounds. The Trust carefully moved the structure and restored and

Ian McQuiston, Regional
Director since 1991

re-erected it on the prepared site and in 1987 there was a celebratory concert in it to mark its official opening.

In 1988 Mary Peters opened the Dundrum Bay footpath.

At Carnanee, Templepatrick, in Co. Antrim an important piece of industrial archaeology was acquired in 1991. **Patterson's Spade Mill** was in operation up to December 1990 and so the building and machinery is intact. The National Heritage Memorial Fund supported the acquisition by a grant of £50,000, and a legacy from the late W.G. Martin of Donaghadee was also used. The mill will be permanently held, subject to satisfactory funding being obtained.

Islandmagee lies to the north of Belfast Lough and although its scenery is not as dramatic as the north coast, this peninsula has a long and pleasant coastline. When portions of this have come up for sale, they have been looked at by the Trust and three areas of coastal land have been acquired: one of 36 acres at The Gobbins, Ballykeel, consisting of grassland, cliff face and undercliff; one of $1^3/_4$ acres at Mullaghdoo, giving access to that land; and one of 113 acres at Skernaghan Point, grassland and boulder beach beside Brown's Bay at the northern tip of the peninsula. These were acquired with grants from the Department of the Environment, Enterprise Neptune and Northern Ireland funds.

To Cregagh Glen, part of the **Lisnabreeny** property, was added in 1988 an area of one and one third acres, the gift of Jacqueline M. Stevenson.

In January 1991 Ian McQuiston gave evidence to the House of Commons Select Committee on the Environment. Amongst other things, he said that the Trust recommended that an independent environmental protection agency for Northern Ireland should be established by the government. The select committee in its report put forward this recommendation. In April 1991 the government accepted almost all the select committee's recommendations, but the request for the independent agency was rejected.

In July of that year Ian McQuiston began a series of visits to district councils to explain the work of the Trust, beginning with North Down, Limavady and Moyle.

Professor Ronald Buchanan,
current Chairman of the
National Trust in Northern
Ireland. He was appointed
in 1991.

At the same time he was made a member of the reconstituted Northern Ireland Tourist Board.

We are already seeing signs that under the new leadership of Ronald Buchanan and Ian McQuiston the Trust will increasingly look towards the acquisition and protection of public open space as its main aim, while still maintaining and presenting its buildings with the greatest possible care. The educational use of its properties, both indoors and outdoors, will be given a high priority for two reasons: the preservation of cultural heritage and the pursuit of education for mutual understanding. The Trust hopes that the enjoyment of its properties by both its members and the public will increase through the voluntary activity of members' associations.

Dick Rogers

INDEX

Page numbers in italics denote illustrations

188